# CODE ICARUS

STAN LEE

# SOLDIER
# ZERO

DAN ABNETT

ANDY LANNING

JAVIER PINA

Ross Richie - Chief Executive Officer
Matt Gagnon - Editor-in-Chief
Adam Fortier - VP-New Business
Wes Harris - VP-Publishing
Lance Kreiter - VP-Licensing & Merchandising
Chip Mosher - Sales & Marketing Director
Bryce Carlson - Managing Editor

Ian Brill - Editor
Dafna Pleban - Editor
Christopher Burns - Editor
Shannon Watters - Assistant Editor
Eric Harburn - Assistant Editor
Adam Staffaroni - Assistant Editor

Brian Latimer - Lead Graphic Designer
Stephanie Gonzaga - Graphic Designer
Phil Barbaro - Operations
Ivan Salazar - Marketing Manager
Devin Funches - Sales & Marketing Assistant

SOLDIER ZERO Volume Two — September 2011. Published by BOOM! Studios, a division of Boom Entertainment, Inc. Soldier Zero is Copyright © 2011 Boom Entertainment, Inc. and POW! Entertainment. Originally published in single magazine form as SOLDIER ZERO 5-8. Copyright © 2011 Boom Entertainment, Inc. and POW! Entertainment. All rights reserved. BOOM! Studios™ and the BOOM! Studios logo are trademarks of Boom Entertainment, Inc., registered in various countries and categories. All characters, events, and institutions depicted herein are fictional. Any similarity between any of the names, characters, persons, events, and/or institutions in this publication to actual names, characters, and persons, whether living or dead, events, and/or institutions is unintended and purely coincidental. BOOM! Studios does not read or accept unsolicited submissions of ideas, stories, or artwork.

A catalog record of this book is available from OCLC and from the BOOM! Studios website, www.boom-studios.com, on the Librarians Page.

BOOM! Studios, 6310 San Vicente Boulevard, Suite 107, Los Angeles, CA 90048-5457. Printed in China. First Printing. ISBN: 978-1-60886-060-9

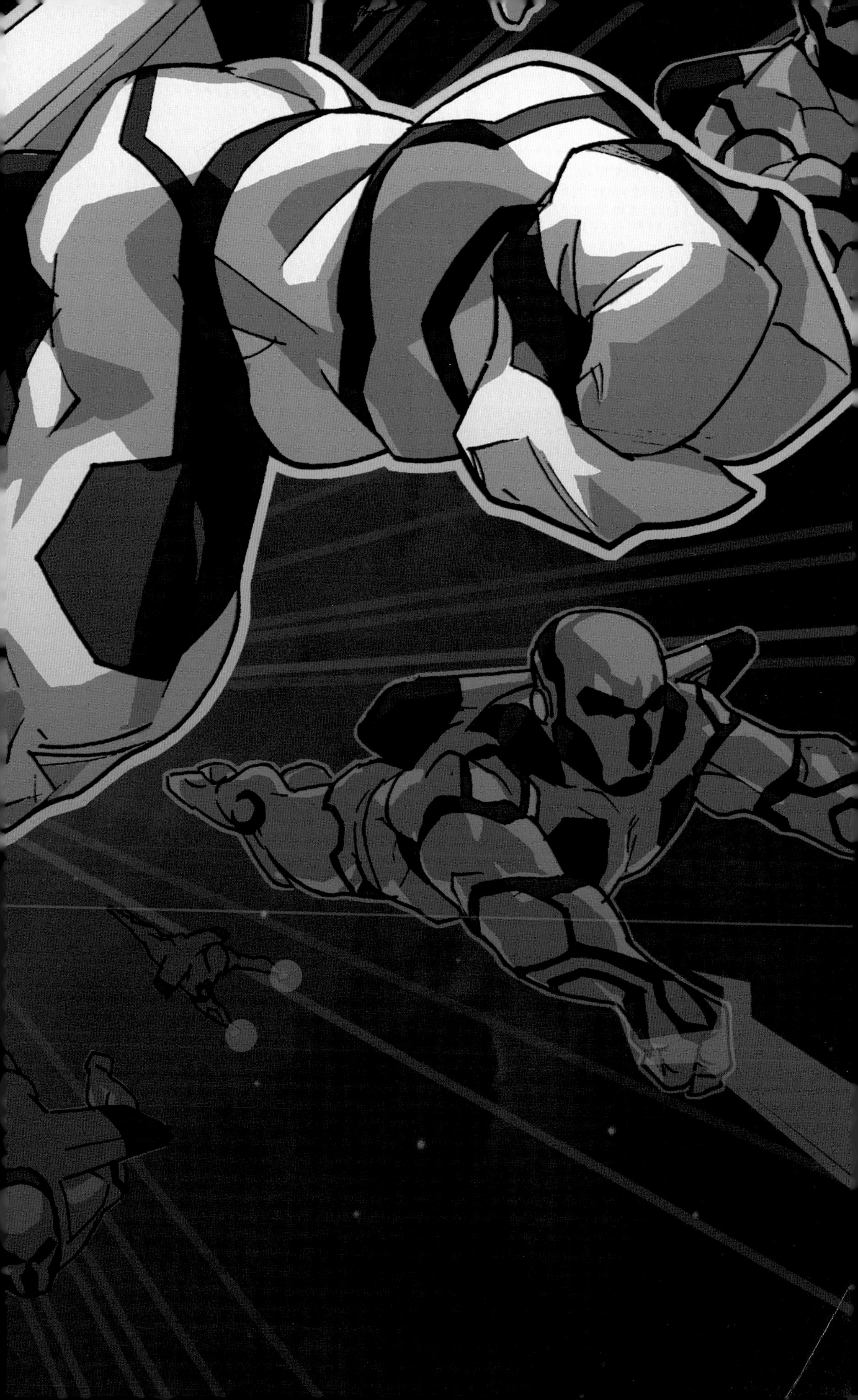

GRAND POOBAH
# STAN LEE

WRITTEN BY
# DAN ABNETT & ANDY LANNING

ART BY
# JAVIER PINA

COLORS BY
# ARCHIE VAN BUREN

LETTERS BY
# ED DUKESHIRE

SOLDIER ZERO
CHARACTER DESIGN
**DAVE JOHNSON**

COVER
**TREVOR HAIRSINE**

GRAPHIC DESIGNER
**BRIAN LATIMER**
WITH DANIELLE KELLER

EDITOR
**BRYCE CARLSON**

EDITOR-IN-CHIEF
**MATT GAGNON**

PUBLISHER
**ROSS RICHIE**

SPECIAL THANKS
**GILL CHAMPION**

BOOM!
STUDIOS

Stan Lee's
POW!
ENTERTAINMENT

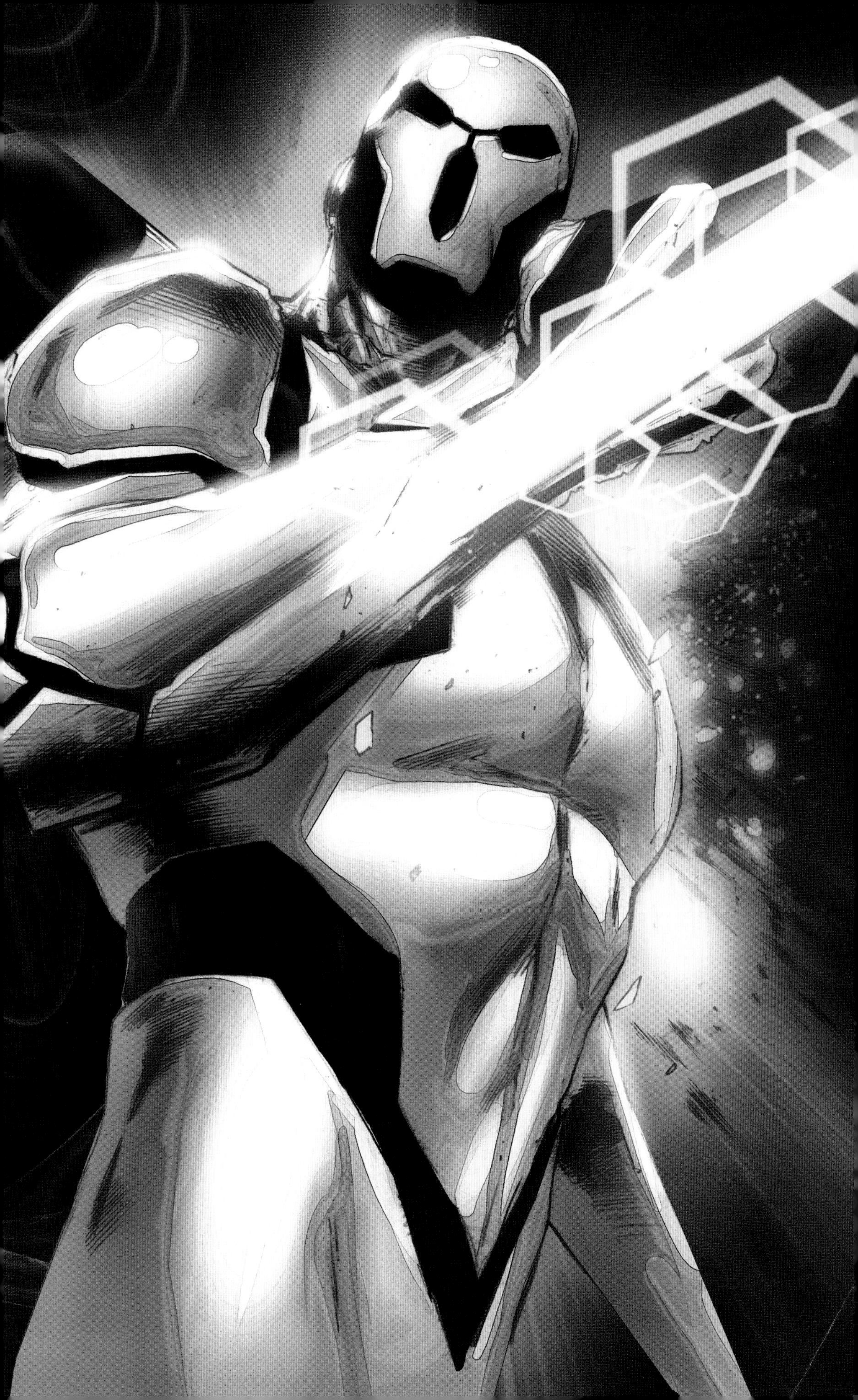

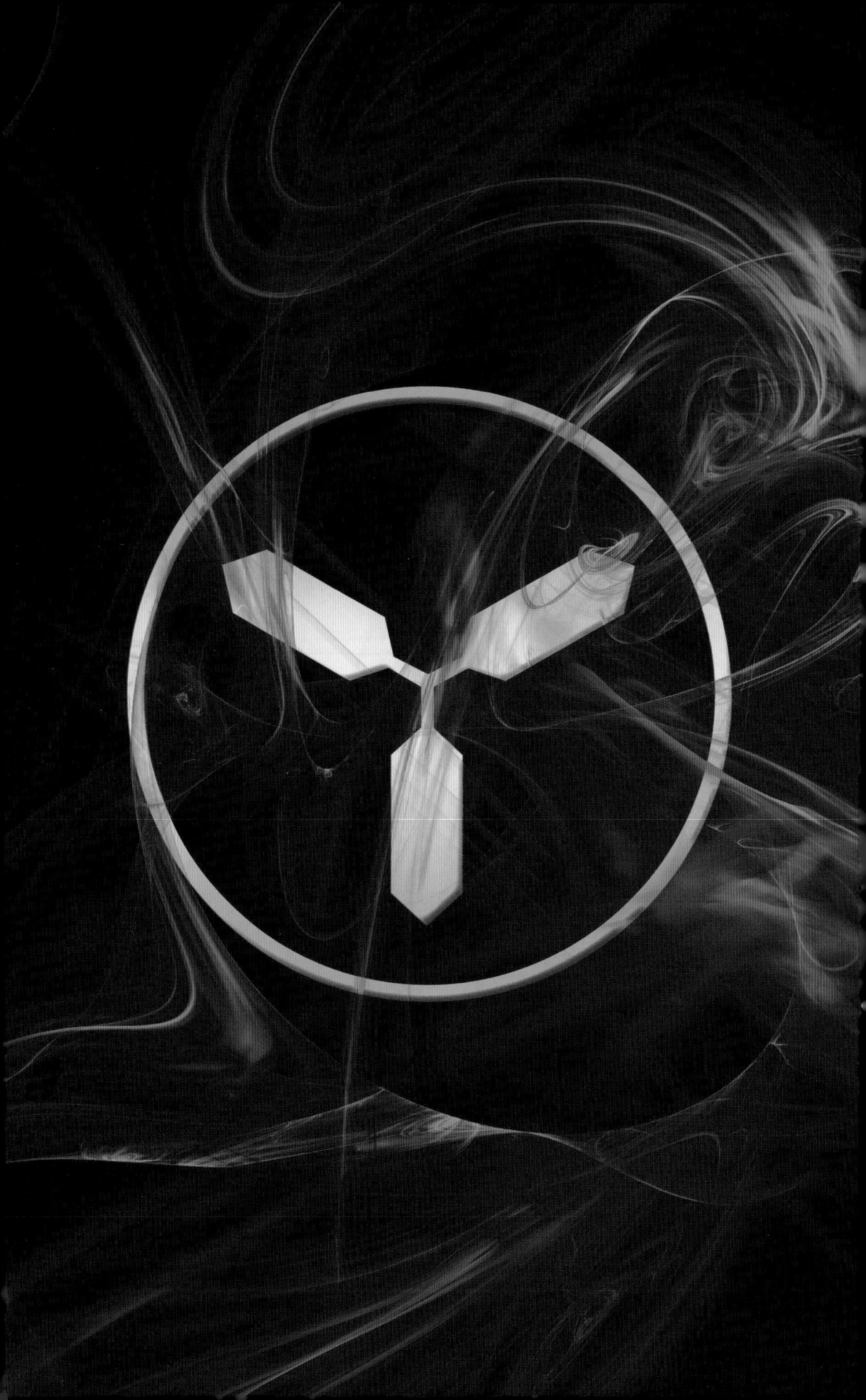

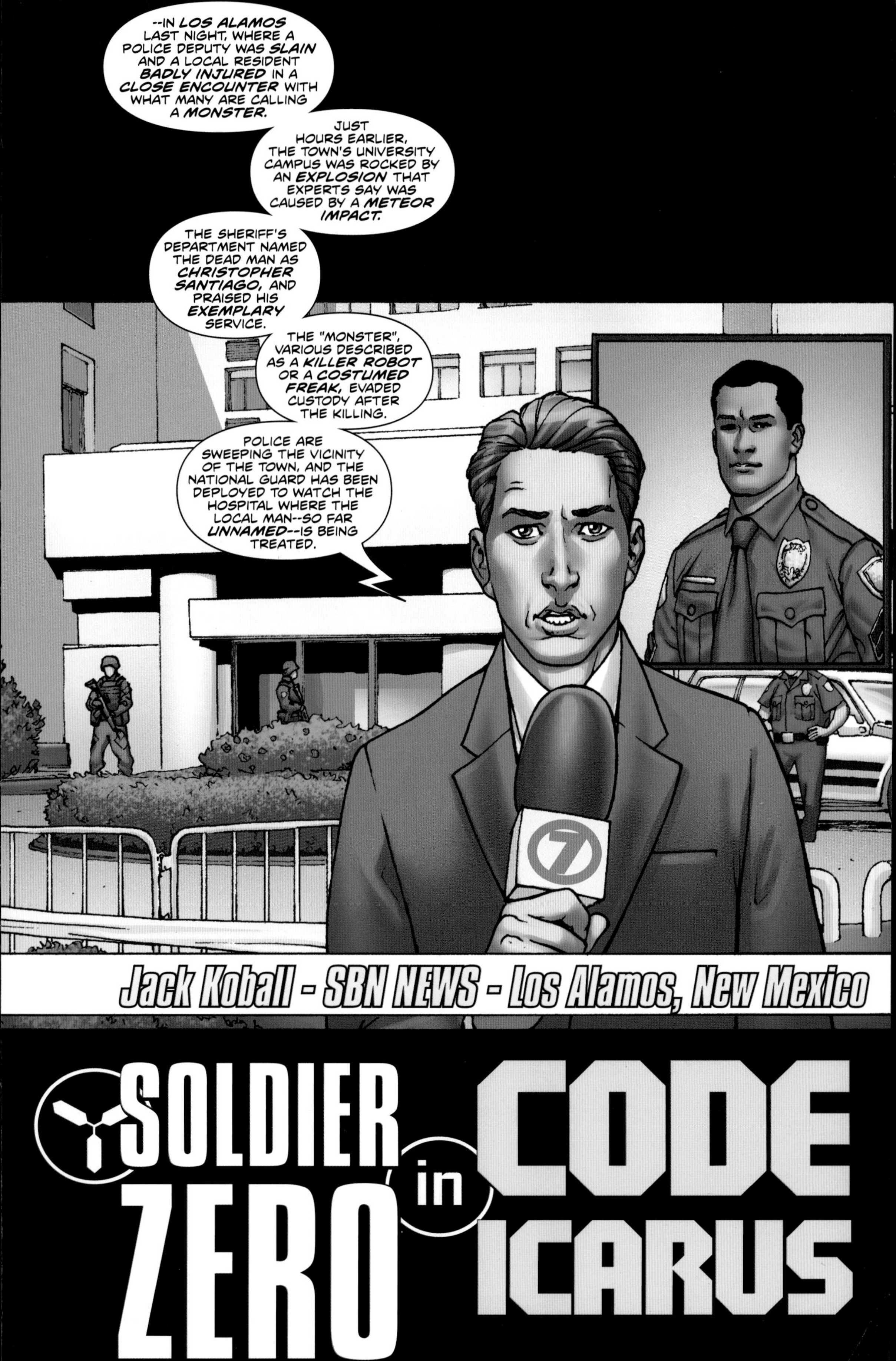
--IN LOS ALAMOS LAST NIGHT, WHERE A POLICE DEPUTY WAS SLAIN AND A LOCAL RESIDENT BADLY INJURED IN A CLOSE ENCOUNTER WITH WHAT MANY ARE CALLING A MONSTER.
JUST HOURS EARLIER, THE TOWN'S UNIVERSITY CAMPUS WAS ROCKED BY AN EXPLOSION THAT EXPERTS SAY WAS CAUSED BY A METEOR IMPACT.
THE SHERIFF'S DEPARTMENT NAMED THE DEAD MAN AS CHRISTOPHER SANTIAGO, AND PRAISED HIS EXEMPLARY SERVICE.
THE "MONSTER", VARIOUS DESCRIBED AS A KILLER ROBOT OR A COSTUMED FREAK, EVADED CUSTODY AFTER THE KILLING.
POLICE ARE SWEEPING THE VICINITY OF THE TOWN, AND THE NATIONAL GUARD HAS BEEN DEPLOYED TO WATCH THE HOSPITAL WHERE THE LOCAL MAN--SO FAR UNNAMED--IS BEING TREATED.
Jack Koball - SBN NEWS - Los Alamos, New Mexico
SOLDIER ZERO in CODE ICARUS

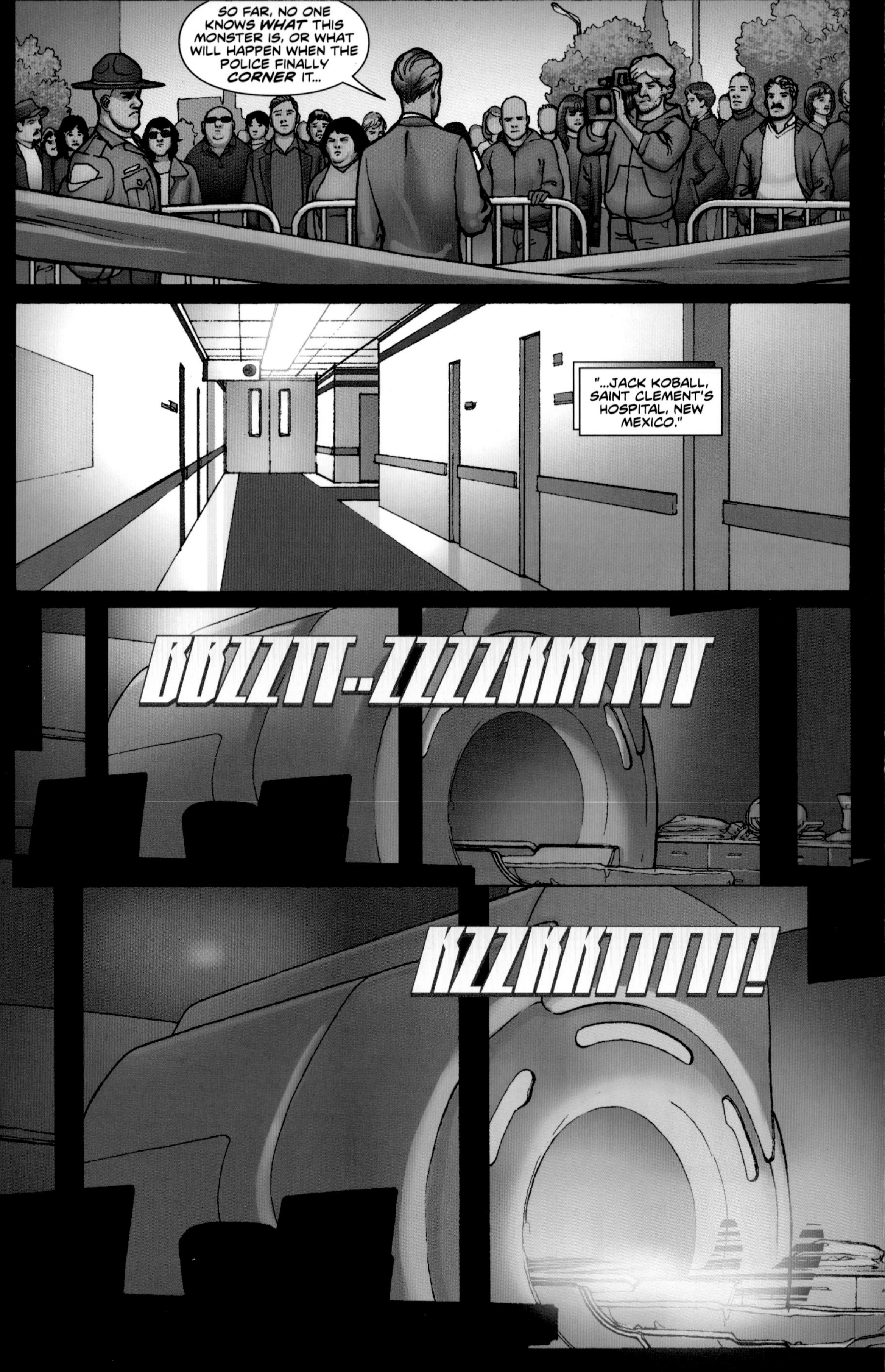
SO FAR, NO ONE KNOWS WHAT THIS MONSTER IS, OR WHAT WILL HAPPEN WHEN THE POLICE FINALLY CORNER IT...
"...JACK KOBALL, SAINT CLEMENT'S HOSPITAL, NEW MEXICO."
BBZZTT--ZZZZKKTTTT
KZZKKTTTTT!

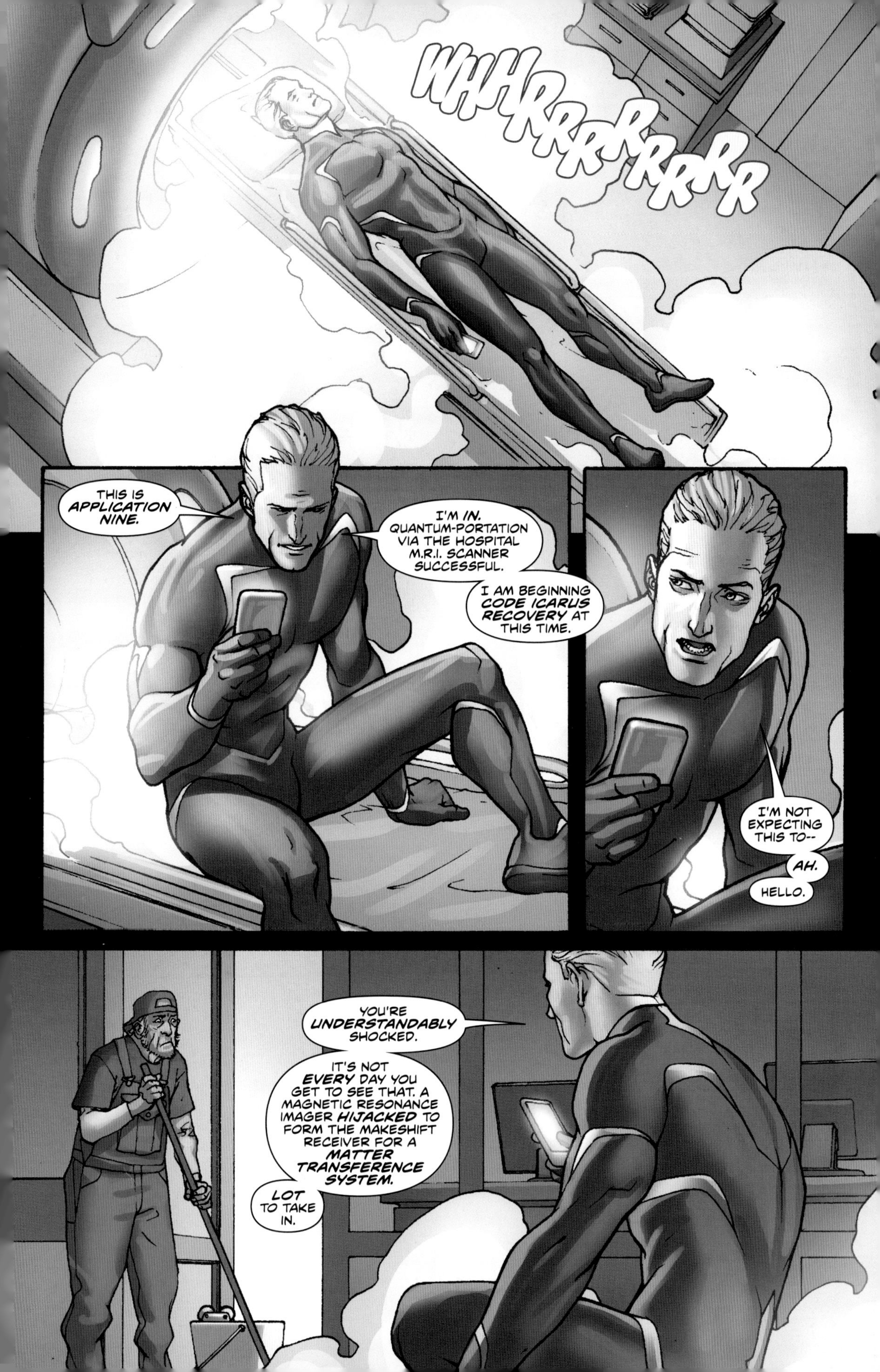
WHHRRRRRRRRR
THIS IS APPLICATION NINE.
I'M IN. QUANTUM-PORTATION VIA THE HOSPITAL M.R.I. SCANNER SUCCESSFUL.
I AM BEGINNING CODE ICARUS RECOVERY AT THIS TIME.
I'M NOT EXPECTING THIS TO--
AH.
HELLO.
YOU'RE UNDERSTANDABLY SHOCKED.
IT'S NOT EVERY DAY YOU GET TO SEE THAT. A MAGNETIC RESONANCE IMAGER HIJACKED TO FORM THE MAKESHIFT RECEIVER FOR A MATTER TRANSFERENCE SYSTEM.
LOT TO TAKE IN.

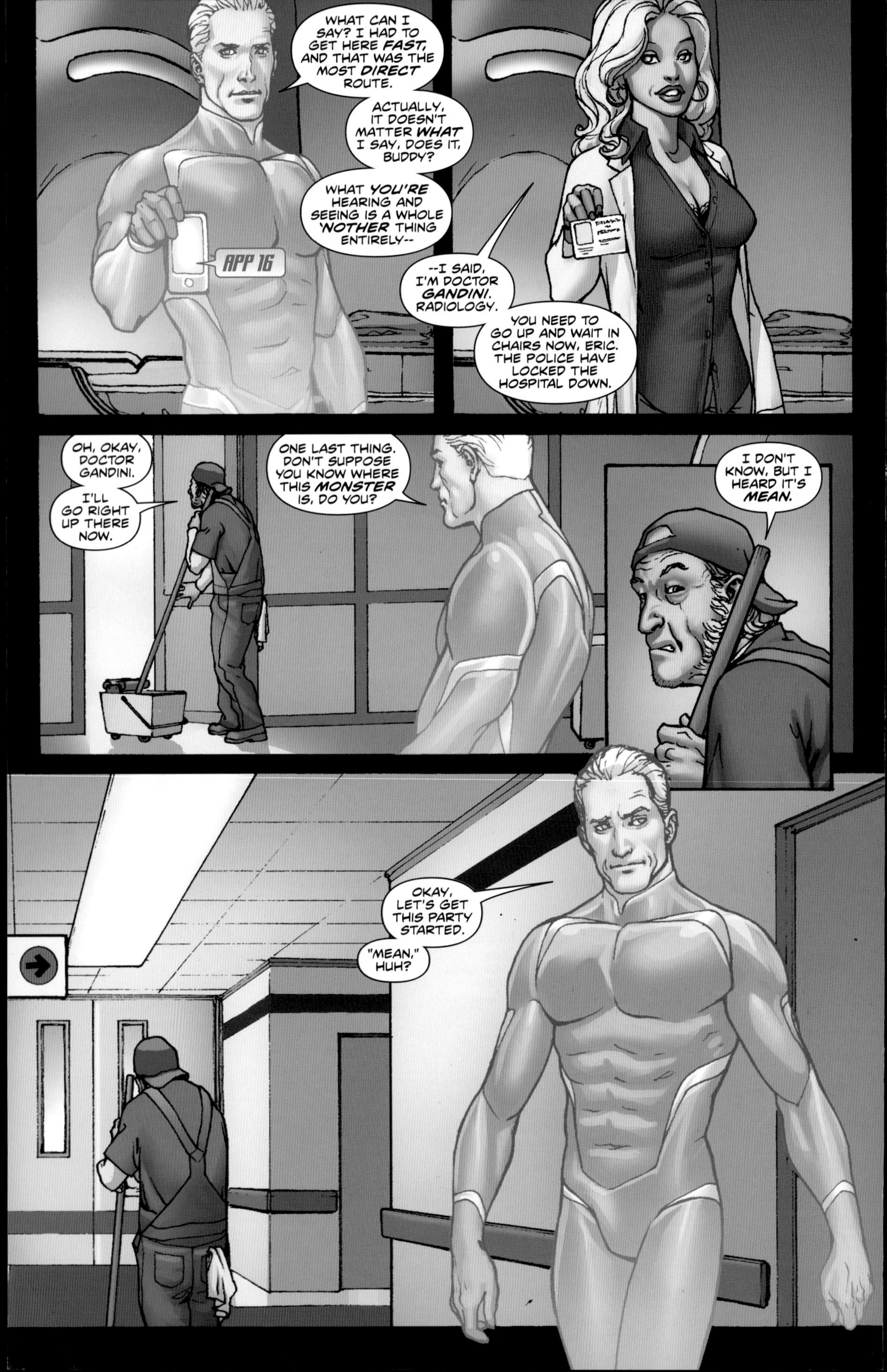
WHAT CAN I SAY? I HAD TO GET HERE FAST, AND THAT WAS THE MOST DIRECT ROUTE.
ACTUALLY, IT DOESN'T MATTER WHAT I SAY, DOES IT, BUDDY?
WHAT YOU'RE HEARING AND SEEING IS A WHOLE 'NOTHER THING ENTIRELY--
APP 16
--I SAID, I'M DOCTOR GANDINI. RADIOLOGY.
YOU NEED TO GO UP AND WAIT IN CHAIRS NOW, ERIC. THE POLICE HAVE LOCKED THE HOSPITAL DOWN.
OH, OKAY, DOCTOR GANDINI.
I'LL GO RIGHT UP THERE NOW.
ONE LAST THING. DON'T SUPPOSE YOU KNOW WHERE THIS MONSTER IS, DO YOU?
I DON'T KNOW, BUT I HEARD IT'S MEAN.
OKAY, LET'S GET THIS PARTY STARTED.
"MEAN," HUH?

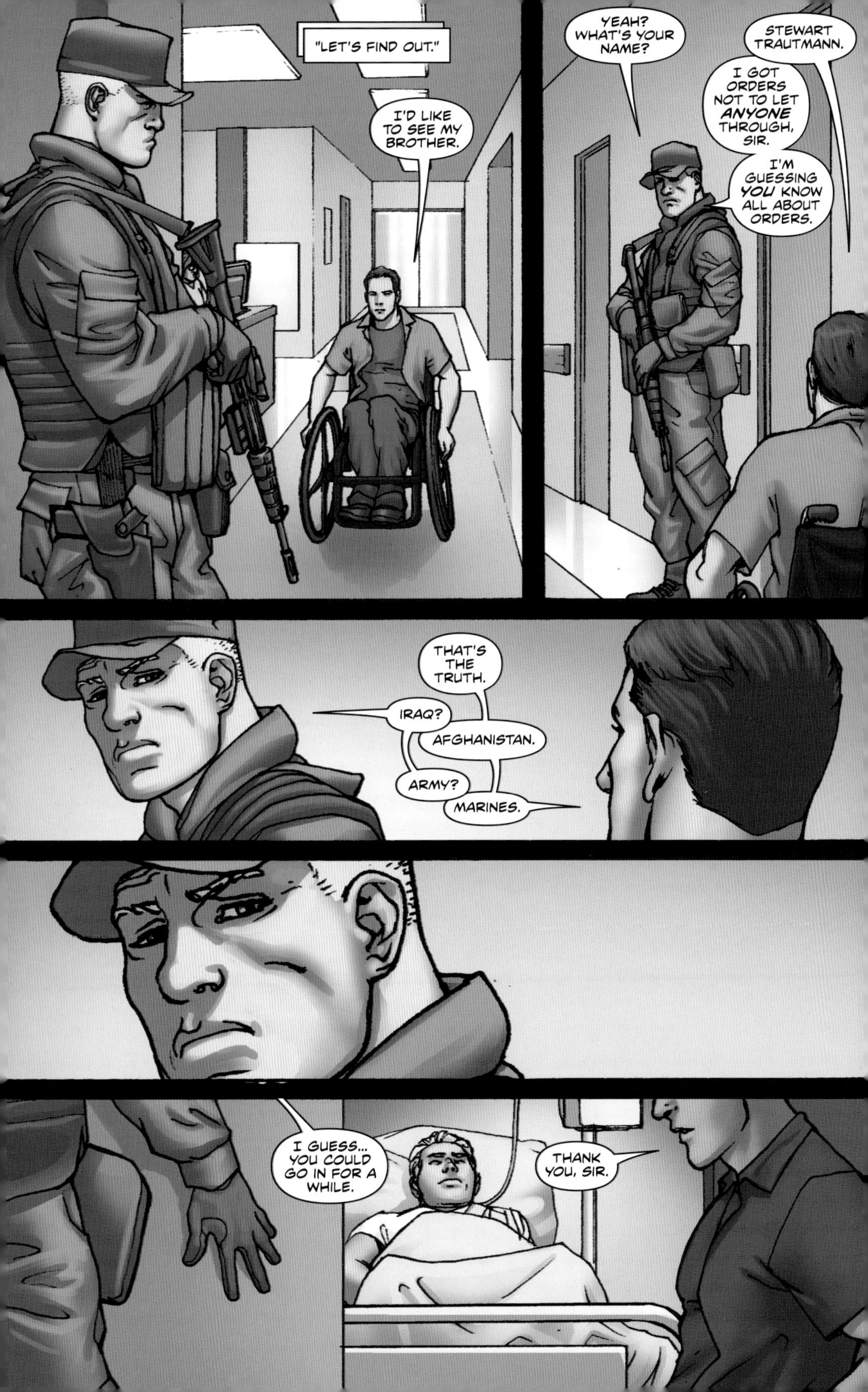
"LET'S FIND OUT."
I'D LIKE TO SEE MY BROTHER.
YEAH? WHAT'S YOUR NAME?
STEWART TRAUTMANN.
I GOT ORDERS NOT TO LET ANYONE THROUGH, SIR.
I'M GUESSING YOU KNOW ALL ABOUT ORDERS.
THAT'S THE TRUTH.
IRAQ?
AFGHANISTAN.
ARMY?
MARINES.
I GUESS... YOU COULD GO IN FOR A WHILE.
THANK YOU, SIR.

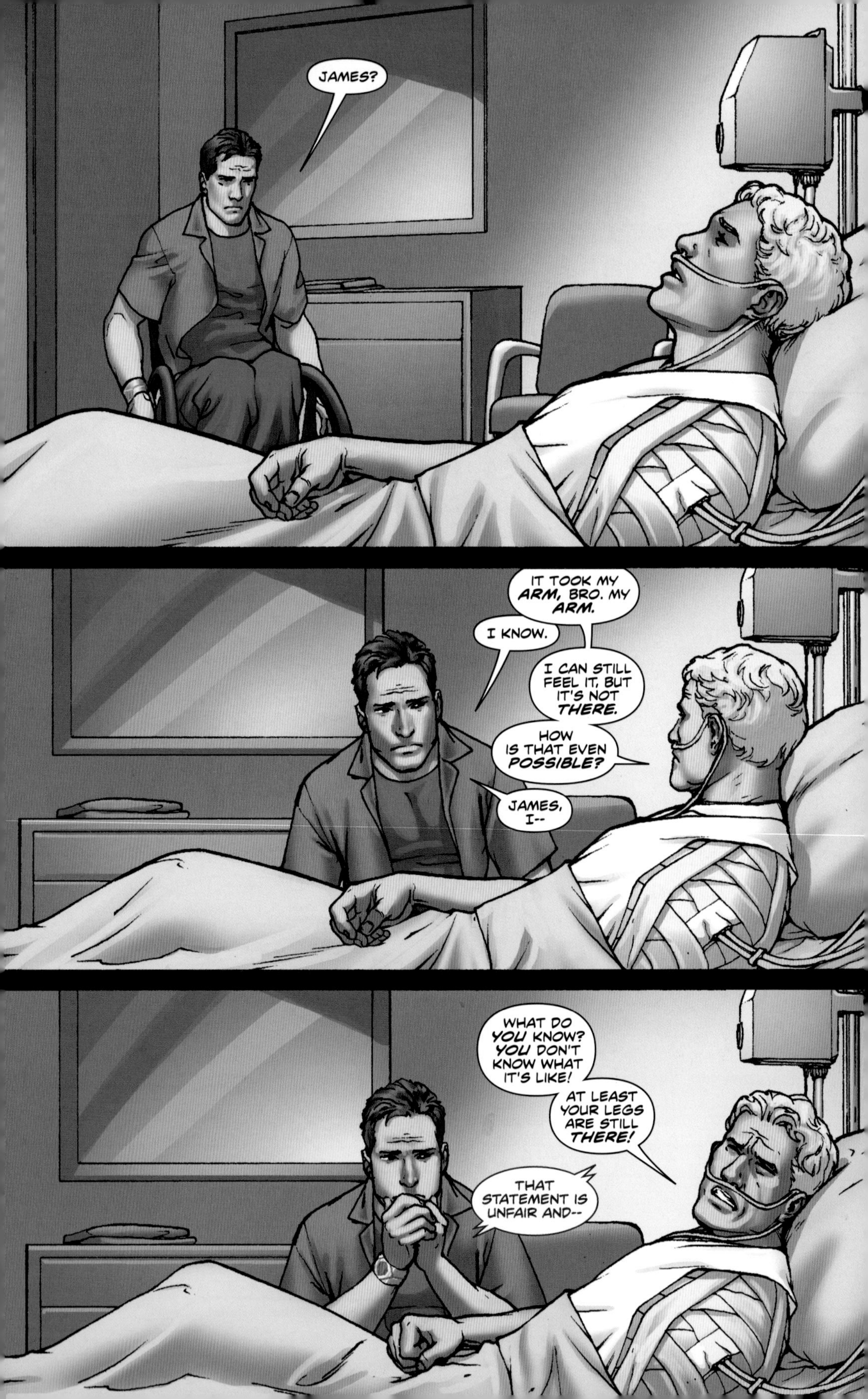
JAMES?
IT TOOK MY ARM, BRO. MY ARM.
I KNOW.
I CAN STILL FEEL IT, BUT IT'S NOT THERE.
HOW IS THAT EVEN POSSIBLE?
JAMES, I--
WHAT DO YOU KNOW? YOU DON'T KNOW WHAT IT'S LIKE!
AT LEAST YOUR LEGS ARE STILL THERE!
THAT STATEMENT IS UNFAIR AND--

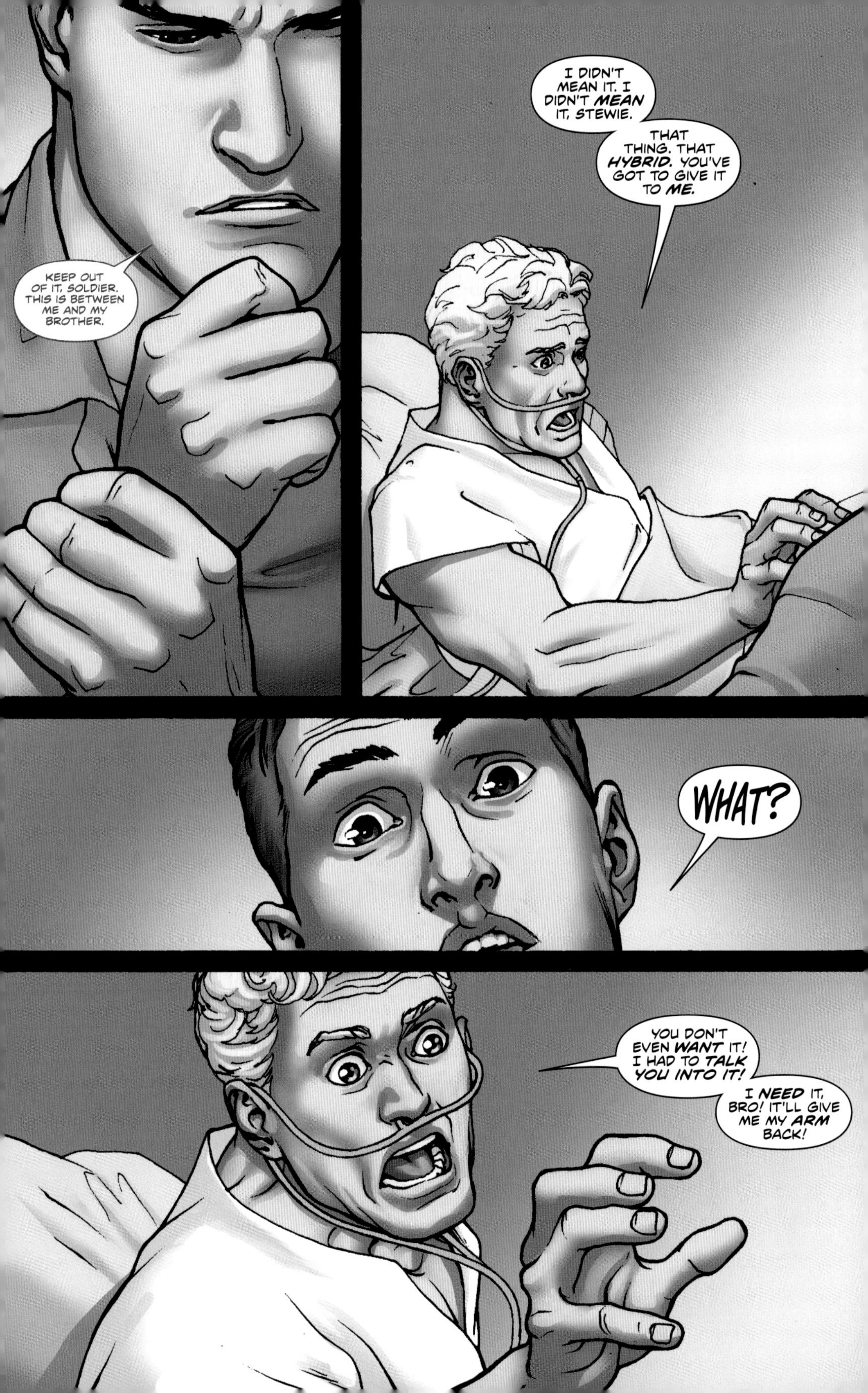
KEEP OUT OF IT, SOLDIER. THIS IS BETWEEN ME AND MY BROTHER.
I DIDN'T MEAN IT. I DIDN'T **MEAN** IT, STEWIE.
THAT THING. THAT **HYBRID.** YOU'VE GOT TO GIVE IT TO **ME.**
WHAT?
YOU DON'T EVEN **WANT** IT! I HAD TO **TALK YOU INTO IT!**
I **NEED** IT, BRO! IT'LL GIVE ME MY **ARM** BACK!

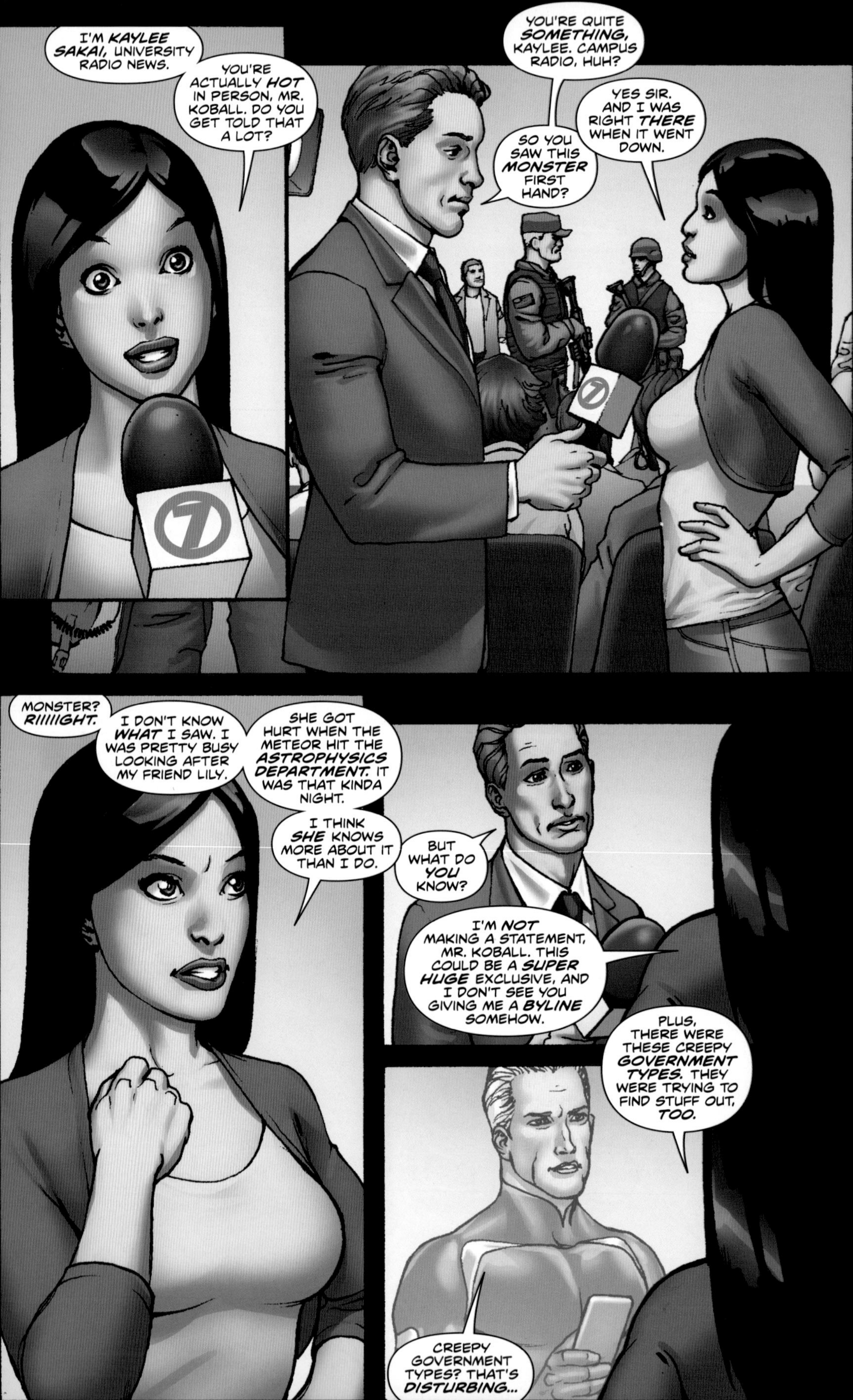
I'M KAYLEE SAKAI, UNIVERSITY RADIO NEWS.
YOU'RE ACTUALLY HOT IN PERSON, MR. KOBALL. DO YOU GET TOLD THAT A LOT?
YOU'RE QUITE SOMETHING, KAYLEE. CAMPUS RADIO, HUH?
SO YOU SAW THIS MONSTER FIRST HAND?
YES SIR. AND I WAS RIGHT THERE WHEN IT WENT DOWN.
MONSTER? RIIIIGHT.
I DON'T KNOW WHAT I SAW. I WAS PRETTY BUSY LOOKING AFTER MY FRIEND LILY.
SHE GOT HURT WHEN THE METEOR HIT THE ASTROPHYSICS DEPARTMENT. IT WAS THAT KINDA NIGHT.
I THINK SHE KNOWS MORE ABOUT IT THAN I DO.
BUT WHAT DO YOU KNOW?
I'M NOT MAKING A STATEMENT, MR. KOBALL. THIS COULD BE A SUPER HUGE EXCLUSIVE, AND I DON'T SEE YOU GIVING ME A BYLINE SOMEHOW.
PLUS, THERE WERE THESE CREEPY GOVERNMENT TYPES. THEY WERE TRYING TO FIND STUFF OUT, TOO.
CREEPY GOVERNMENT TYPES? THAT'S DISTURBING...

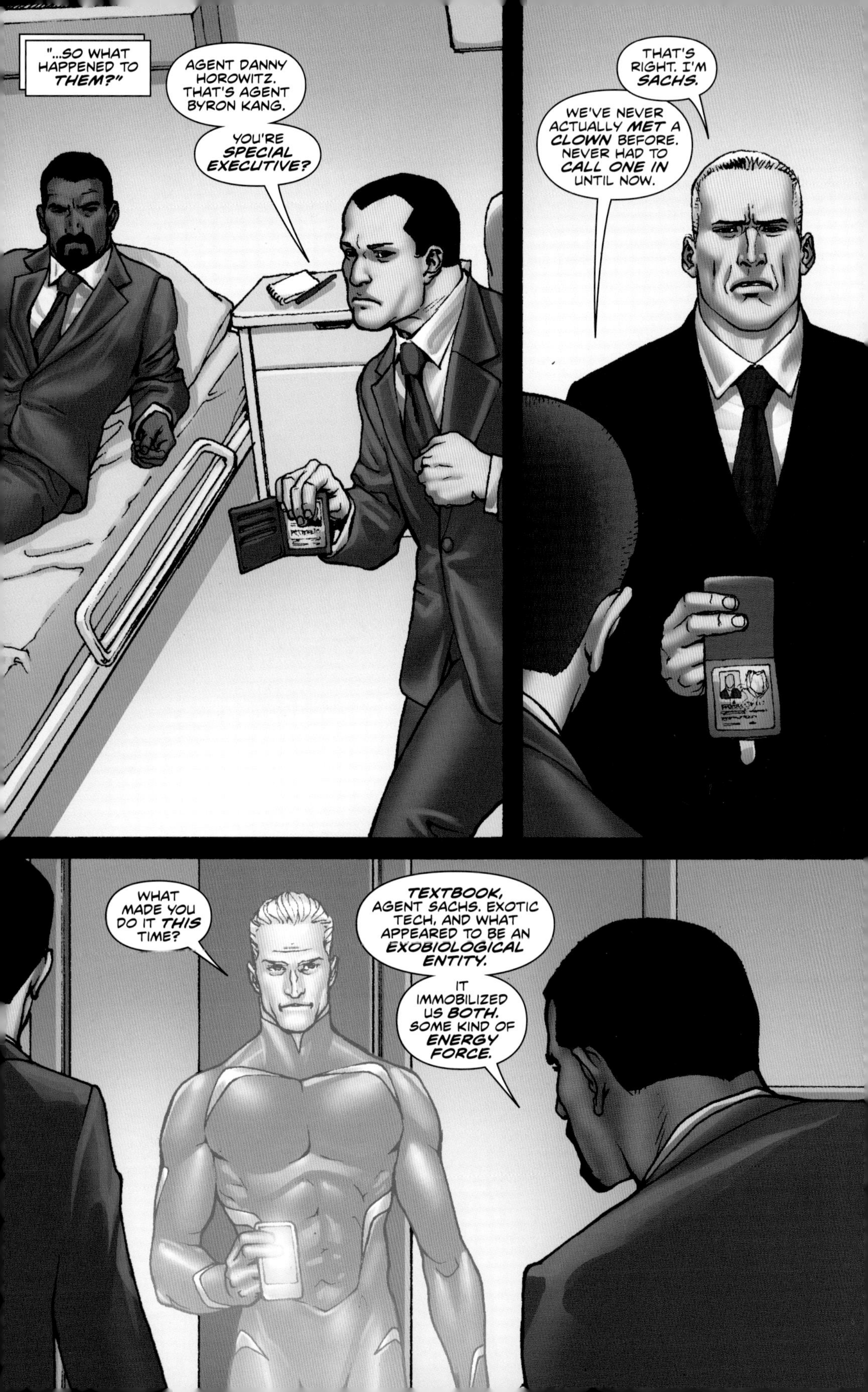
"...SO WHAT HAPPENED TO *THEM?*"
AGENT DANNY HOROWITZ. THAT'S AGENT BYRON KANG.
YOU'RE *SPECIAL EXECUTIVE?*
THAT'S RIGHT. I'M *SACHS.*
WE'VE NEVER ACTUALLY *MET* A *CLOWN* BEFORE. NEVER HAD TO *CALL ONE IN* UNTIL NOW.
WHAT MADE YOU DO IT *THIS* TIME?
*TEXTBOOK,* AGENT SACHS. EXOTIC TECH, AND WHAT APPEARED TO BE AN *EXOBIOLOGICAL ENTITY.*
IT IMMOBILIZED US *BOTH.* SOME KIND OF *ENERGY FORCE.*

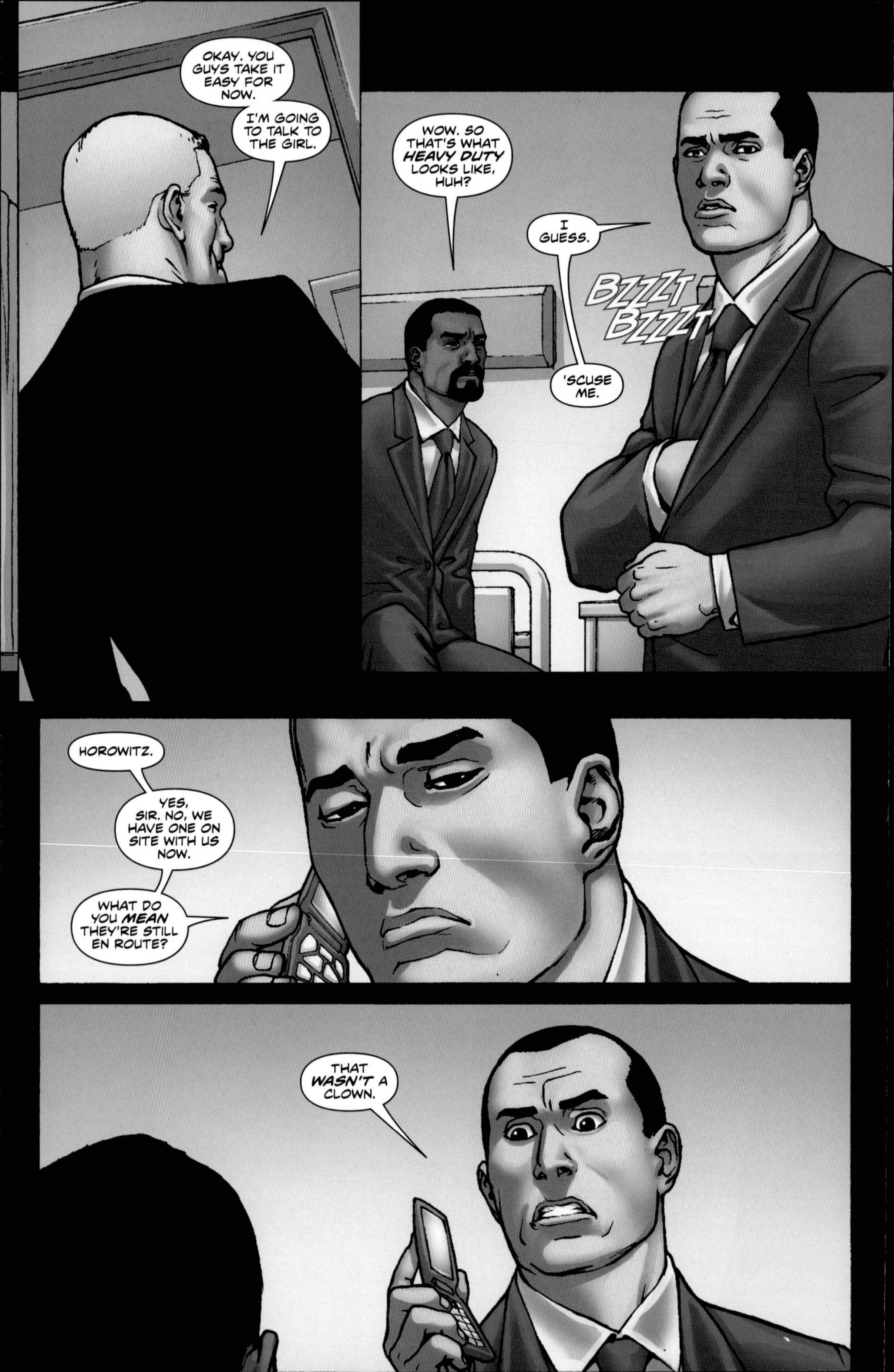

OKAY. YOU GUYS TAKE IT EASY FOR NOW.
I'M GOING TO TALK TO THE GIRL.
WOW. SO THAT'S WHAT HEAVY DUTY LOOKS LIKE, HUH?
I GUESS.
BZZZZT BZZZZT
'SCUSE ME.
HOROWITZ.
YES, SIR. NO, WE HAVE ONE ON SITE WITH US NOW.
WHAT DO YOU MEAN THEY'RE STILL EN ROUTE?
THAT WASN'T A CLOWN.

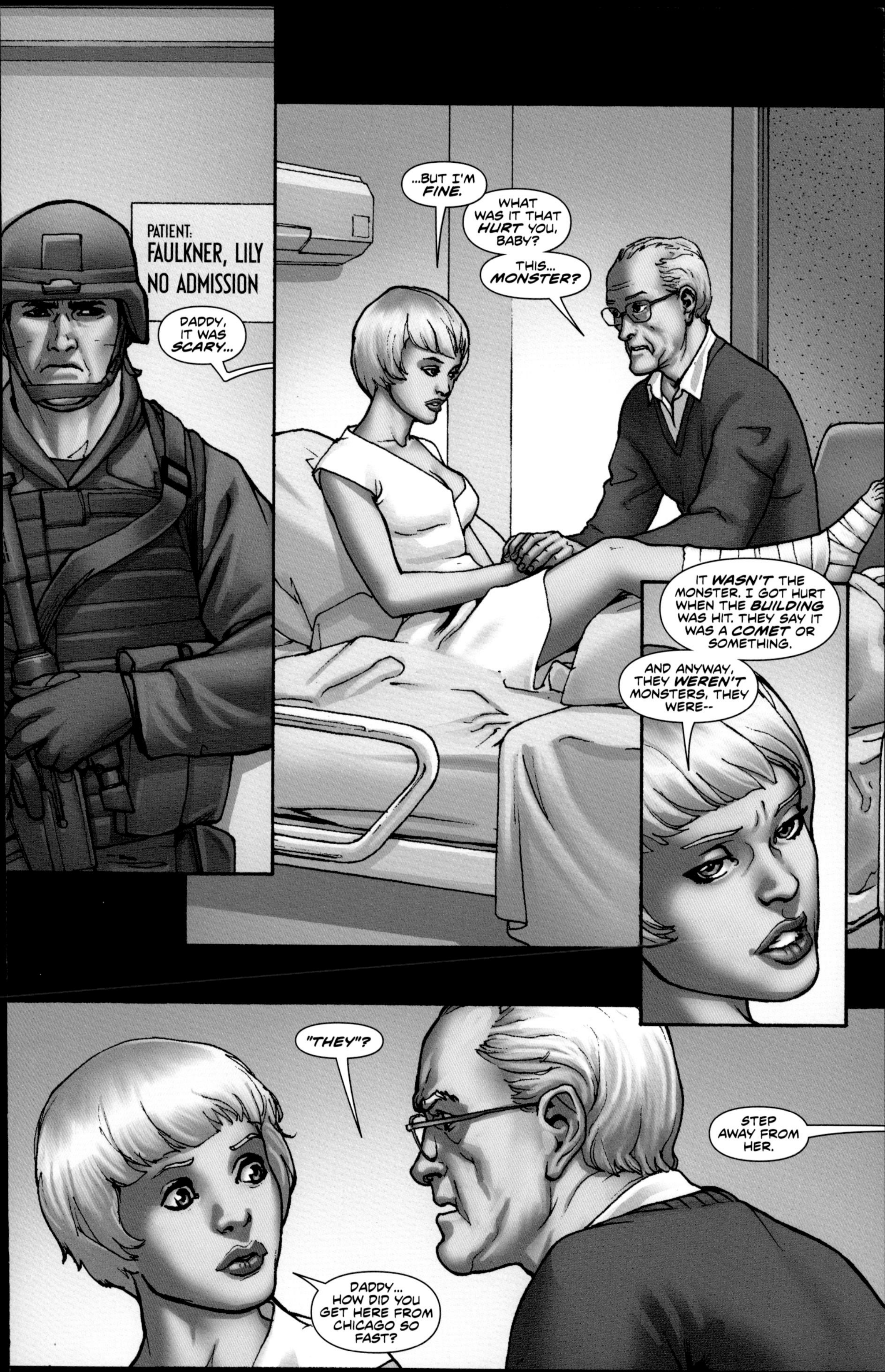
PATIENT:
FAULKNER, LILY
NO ADMISSION
DADDY, IT WAS SCARY...
...BUT I'M FINE.
WHAT WAS IT THAT HURT YOU, BABY?
THIS... MONSTER?
IT WASN'T THE MONSTER. I GOT HURT WHEN THE BUILDING WAS HIT. THEY SAY IT WAS A COMET OR SOMETHING.
AND ANYWAY, THEY WEREN'T MONSTERS, THEY WERE--
"THEY"?
STEP AWAY FROM HER.
DADDY... HOW DID YOU GET HERE FROM CHICAGO SO FAST?

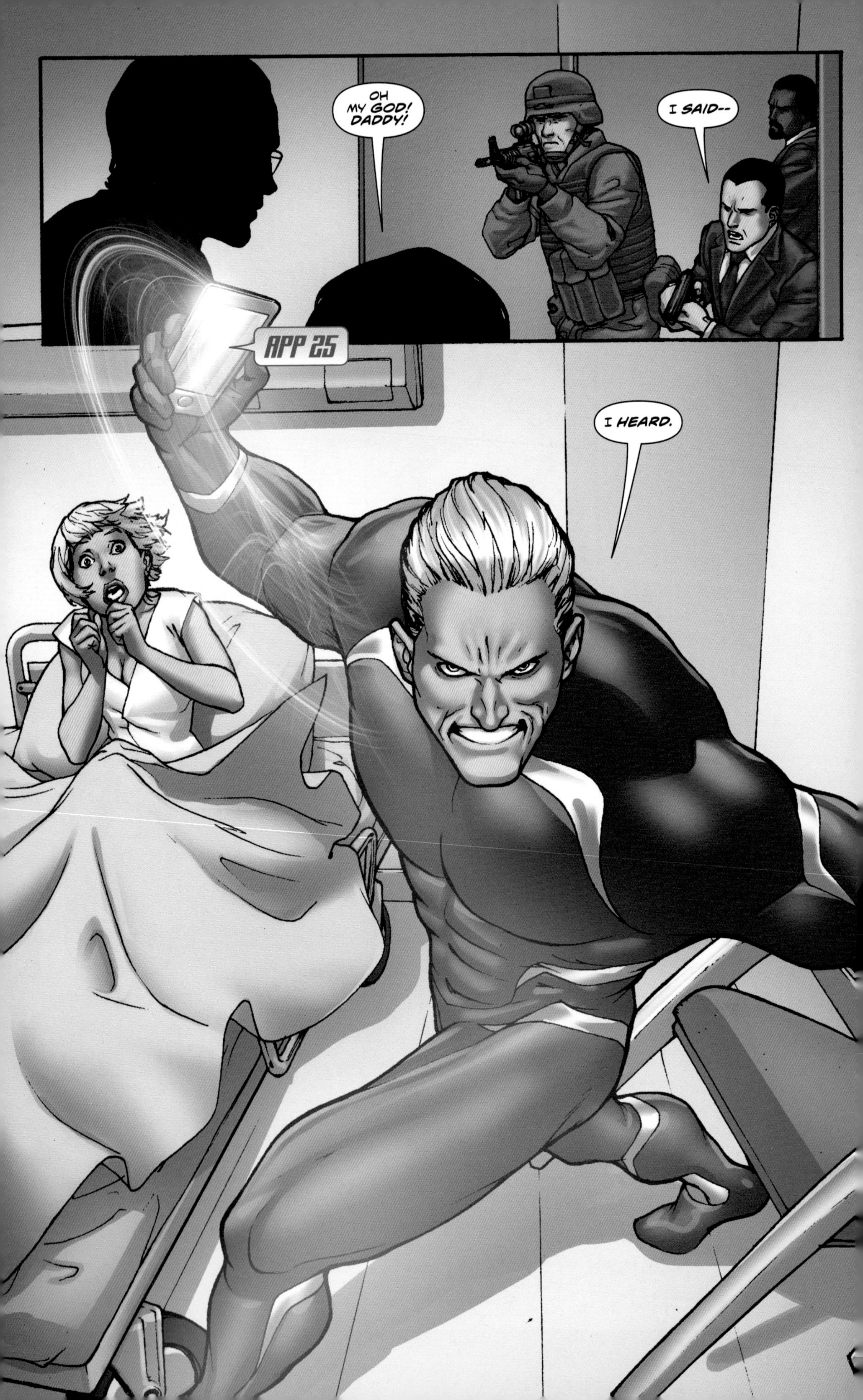
OH MY GOD! DADDY!
I SAID--
APP 25
I HEARD.

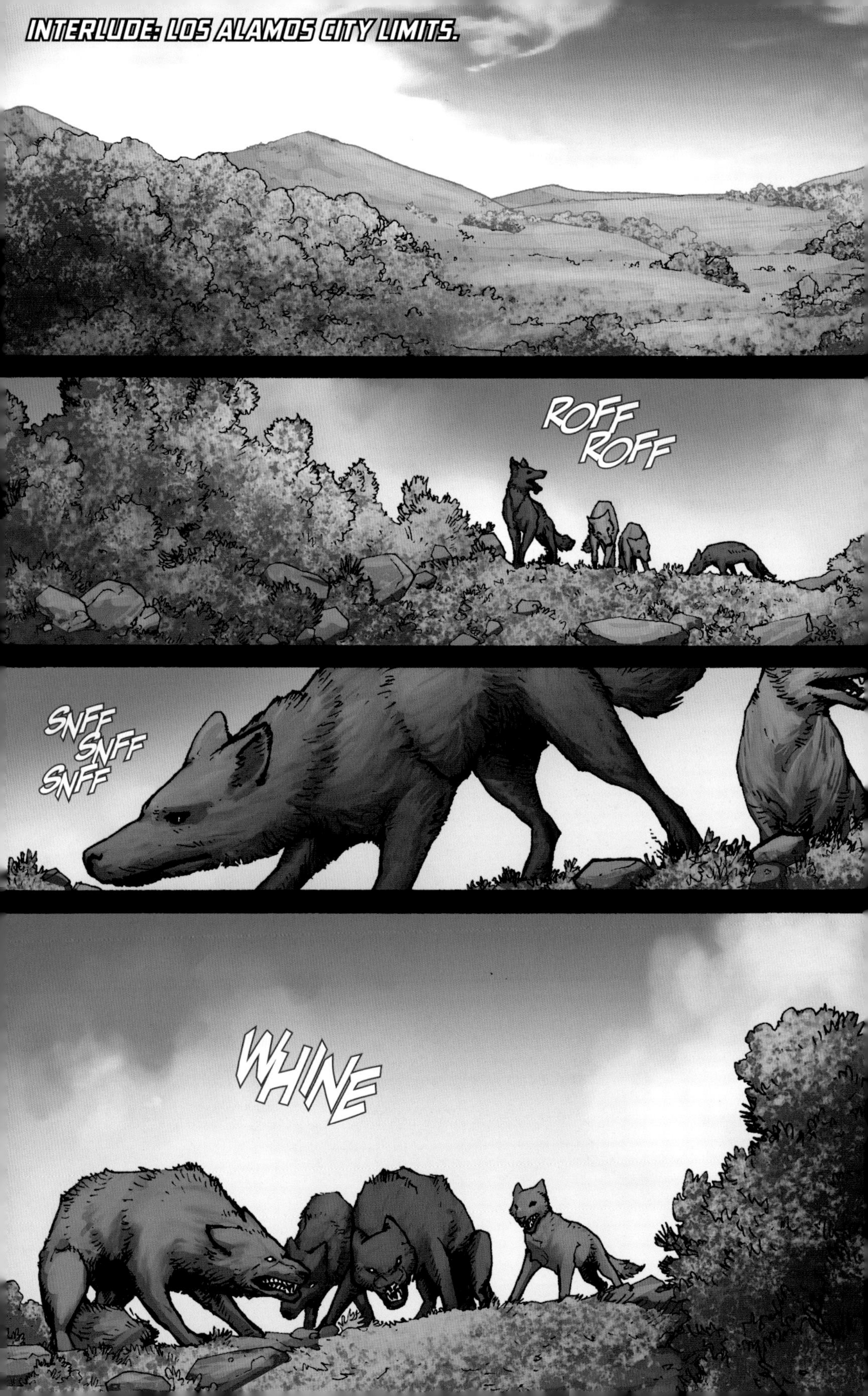
INTERLUDE: LOS ALAMOS CITY LIMITS.
ROFF ROFF
SNFF SNFF SNFF
WHINE

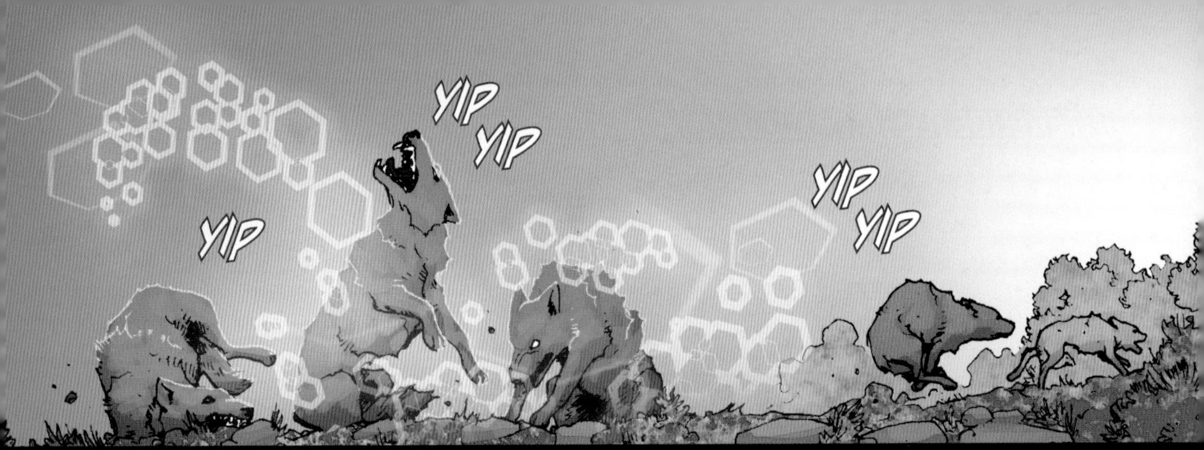
YIP
YIP
YIP
YIP
YIP

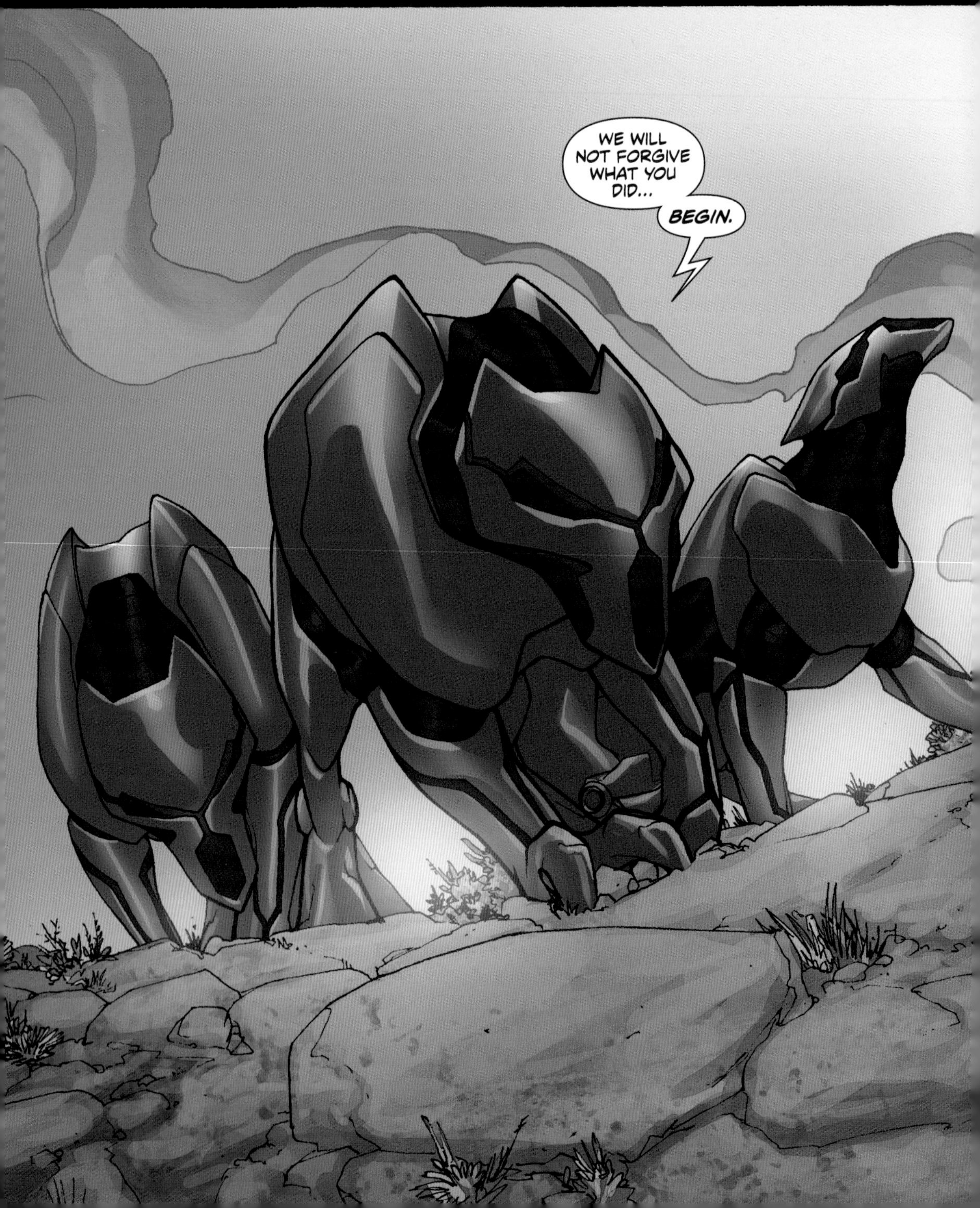
WE WILL NOT FORGIVE WHAT YOU DID...
BEGIN.

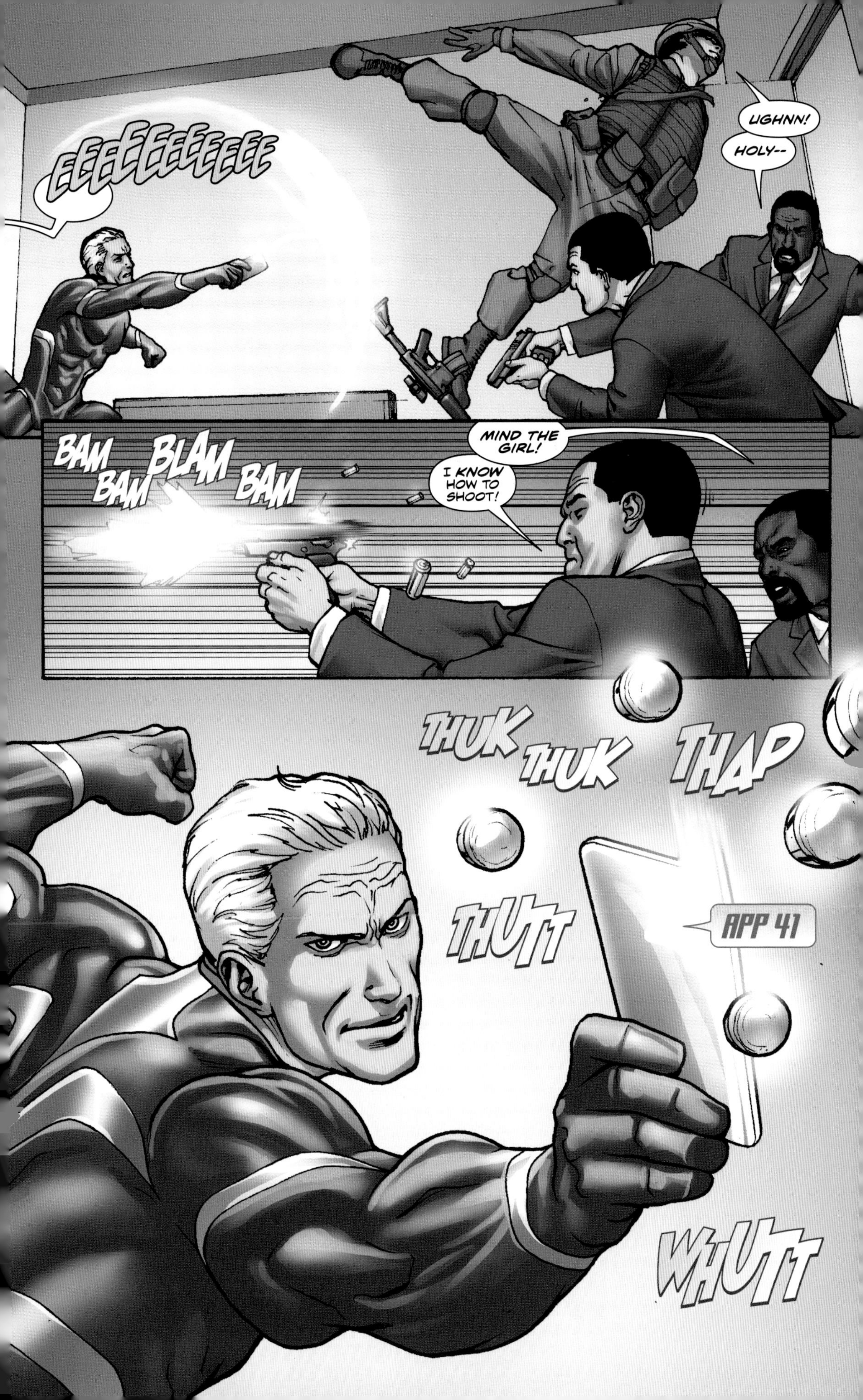
EEEEEEEEEEEE
UGHNN!
HOLY--
BAM
BAM
BLAM
BAM
MIND THE GIRL!
I KNOW HOW TO SHOOT!
THUK
THUK
THAP
THUTT
APP 41
WHUTT

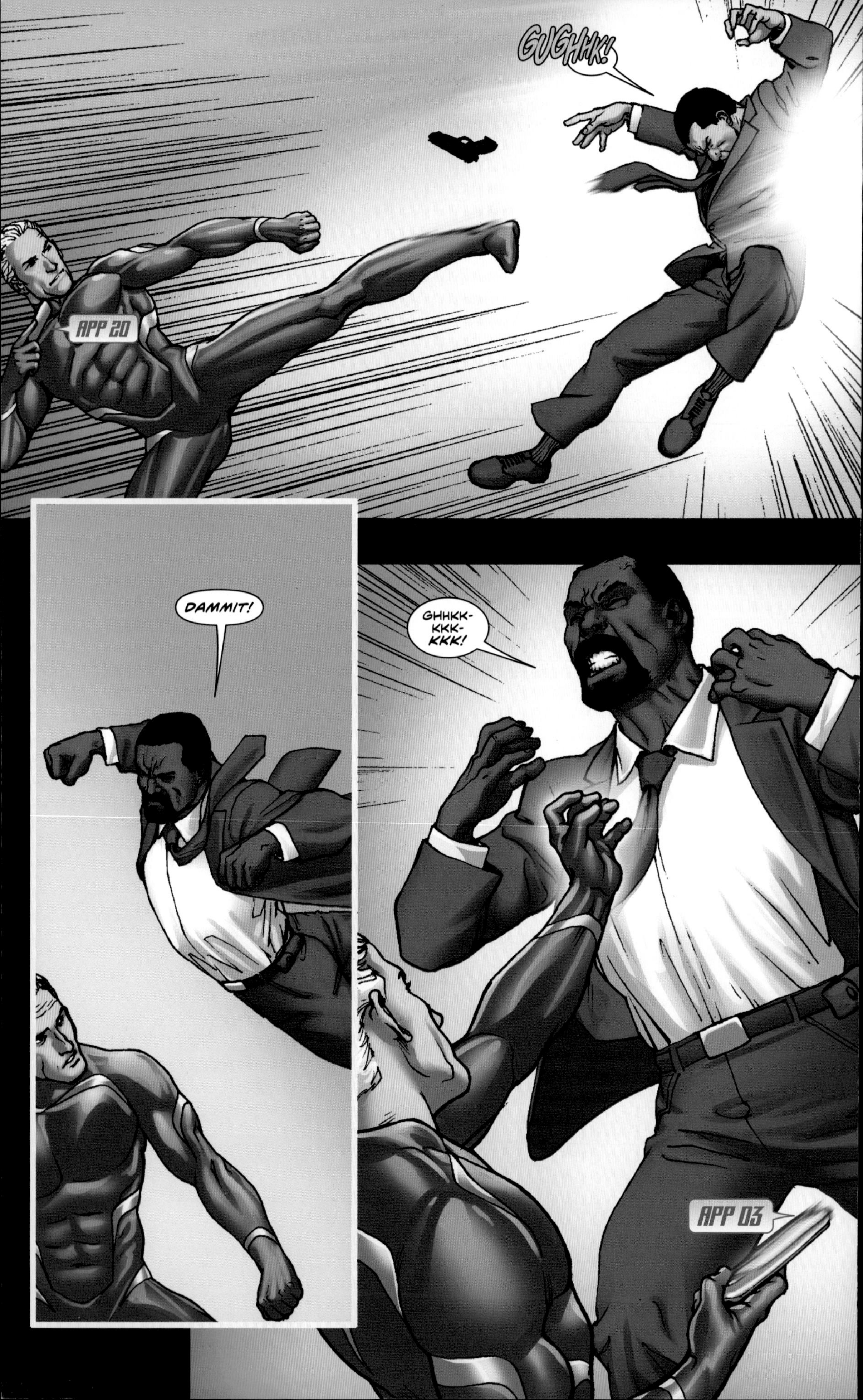
GUGHHK!
APP 20
DAMMIT!
GHHKK-
KKK-
KKK!
APP 03

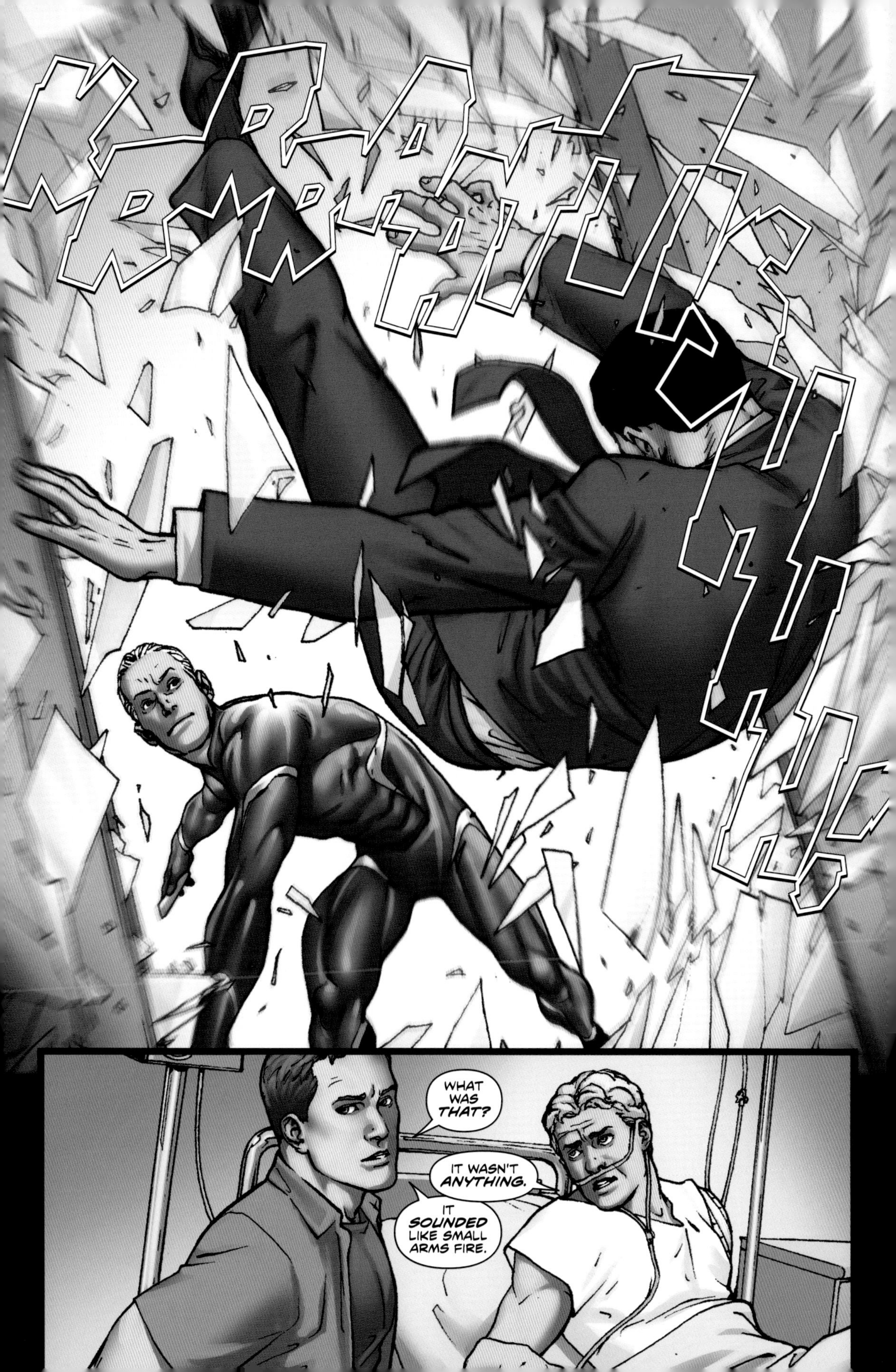
WHAT WAS *THAT?*
IT WASN'T *ANYTHING.*
IT *SOUNDED* LIKE SMALL ARMS FIRE.

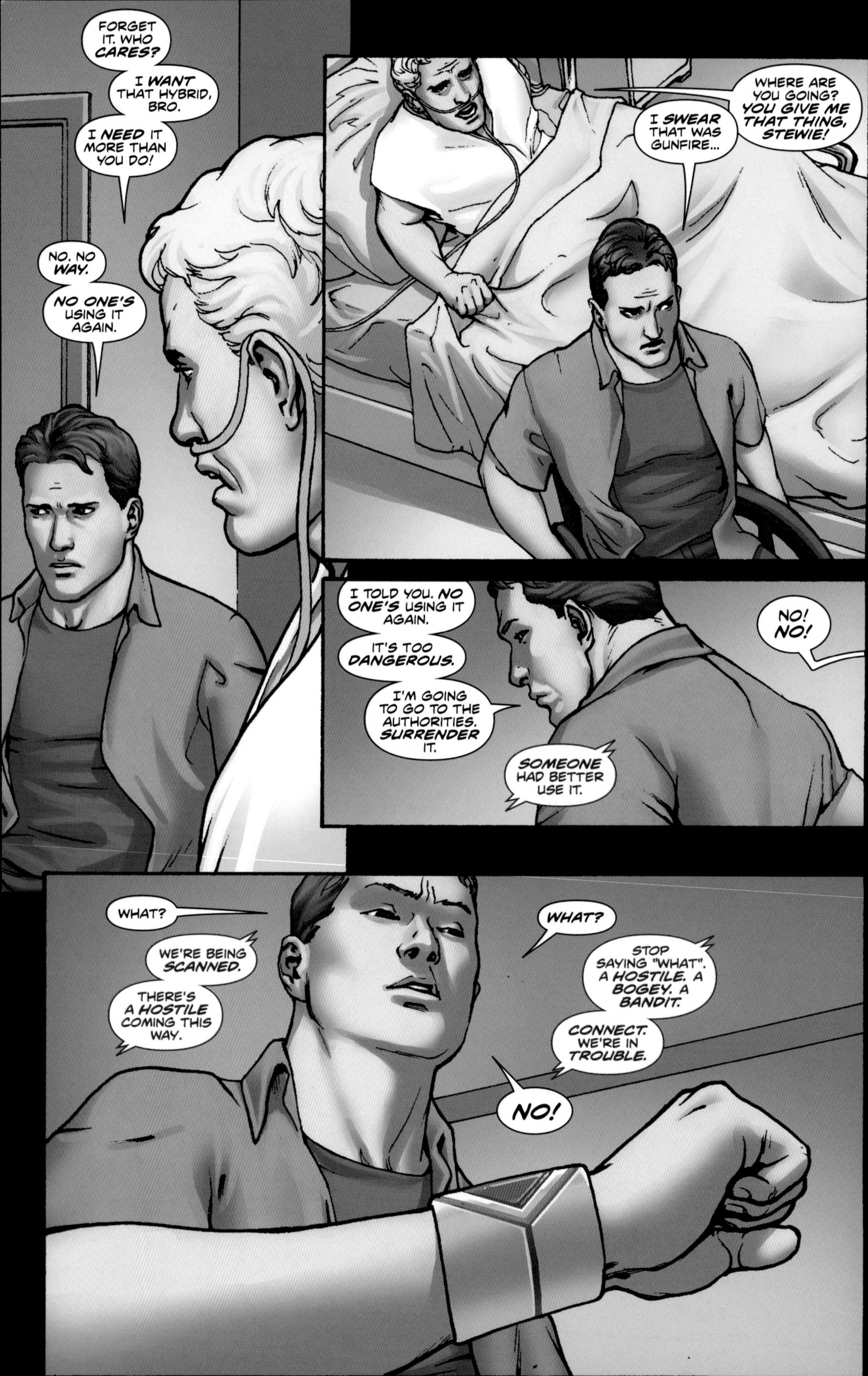
FORGET IT. WHO CARES?
I WANT THAT HYBRID, BRO.
I NEED IT MORE THAN YOU DO!
NO. NO WAY.
NO ONE'S USING IT AGAIN.
WHERE ARE YOU GOING? YOU GIVE ME THAT THING, STEWIE!
I SWEAR THAT WAS GUNFIRE...
I TOLD YOU. NO ONE'S USING IT AGAIN.
IT'S TOO DANGEROUS.
I'M GOING TO GO TO THE AUTHORITIES. SURRENDER IT.
NO! NO!
SOMEONE HAD BETTER USE IT.
WHAT?
WE'RE BEING SCANNED.
THERE'S A HOSTILE COMING THIS WAY.
WHAT?
STOP SAYING "WHAT". A HOSTILE. A BOGEY. A BANDIT.
CONNECT. WE'RE IN TROUBLE.
NO!

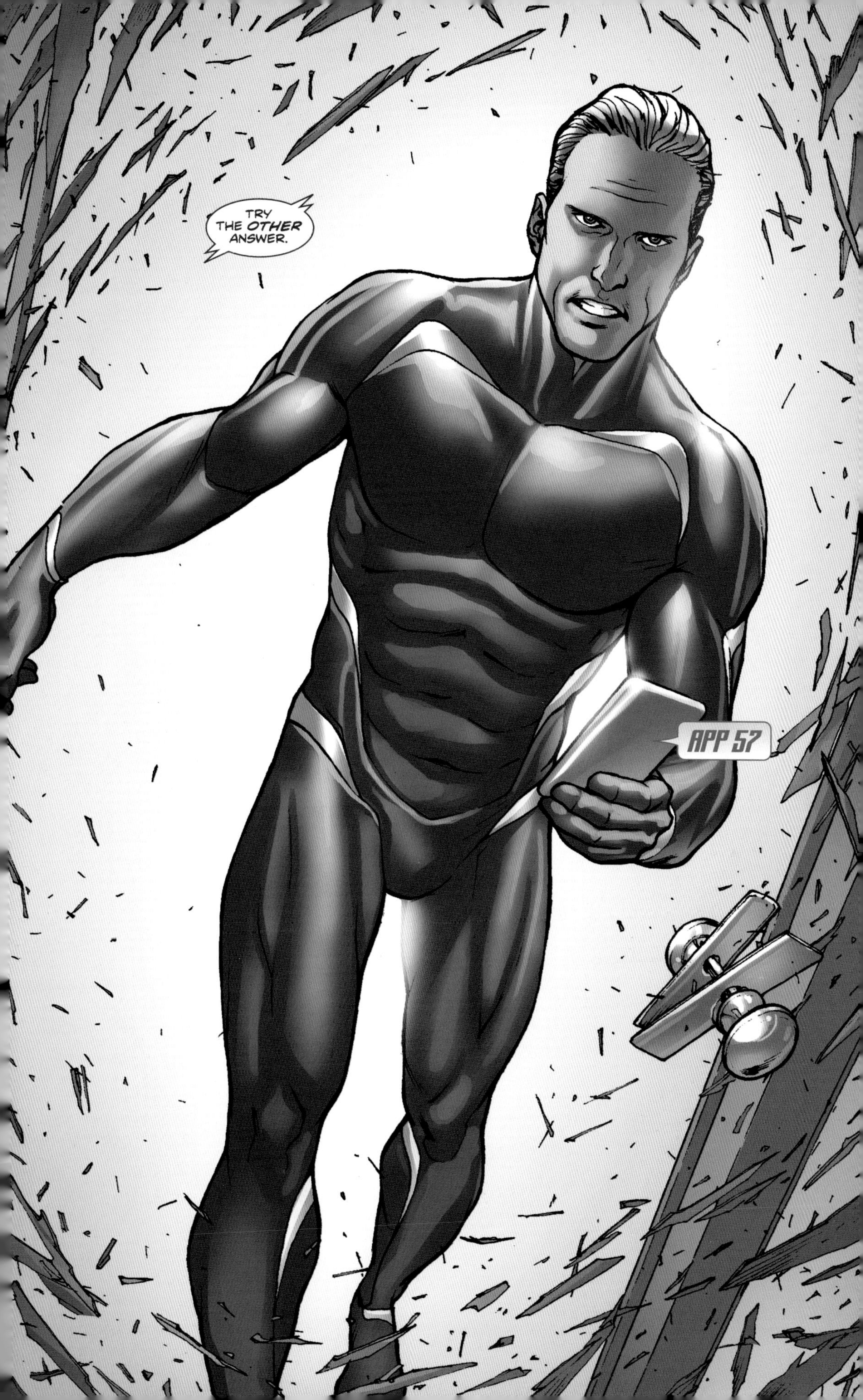
TRY THE OTHER ANSWER.
APP 57

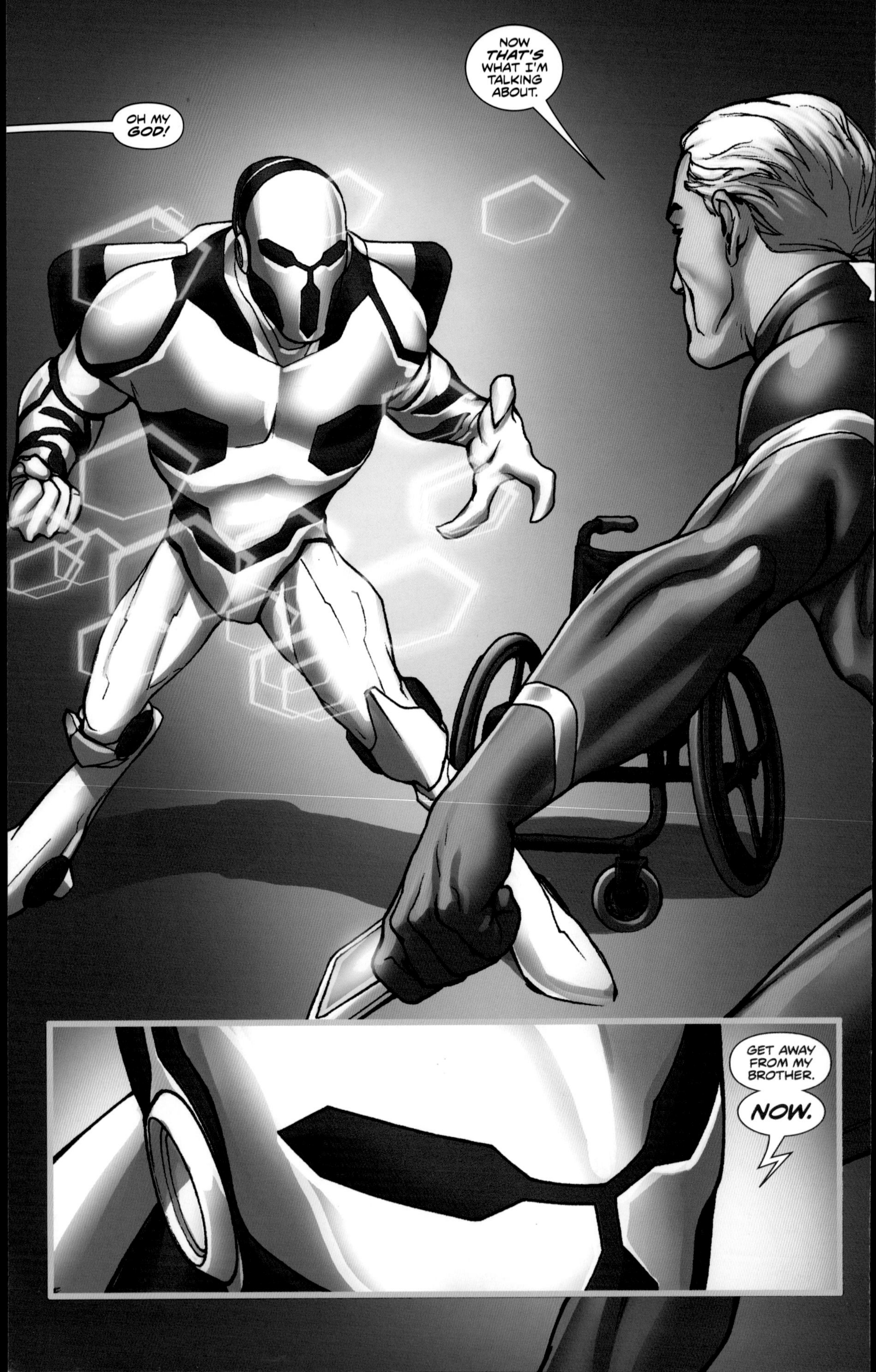
OH MY GOD!
NOW THAT'S WHAT I'M TALKING ABOUT.
GET AWAY FROM MY BROTHER.
NOW.

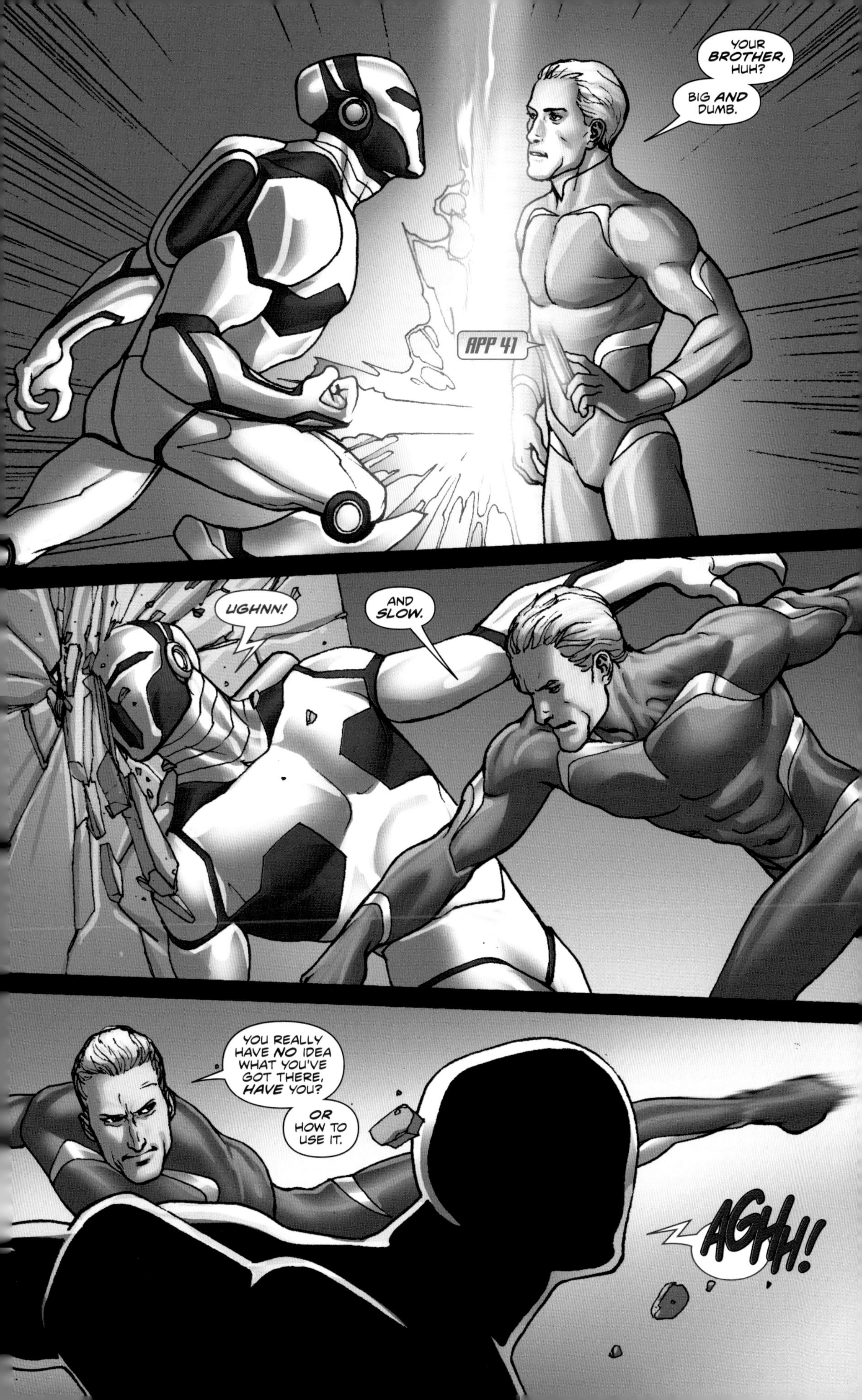
YOUR BROTHER, HUH?
BIG AND DUMB.
APP 41
UGHNN!
AND SLOW.
YOU REALLY HAVE NO IDEA WHAT YOU'VE GOT THERE, HAVE YOU?
OR HOW TO USE IT.
AGHH!

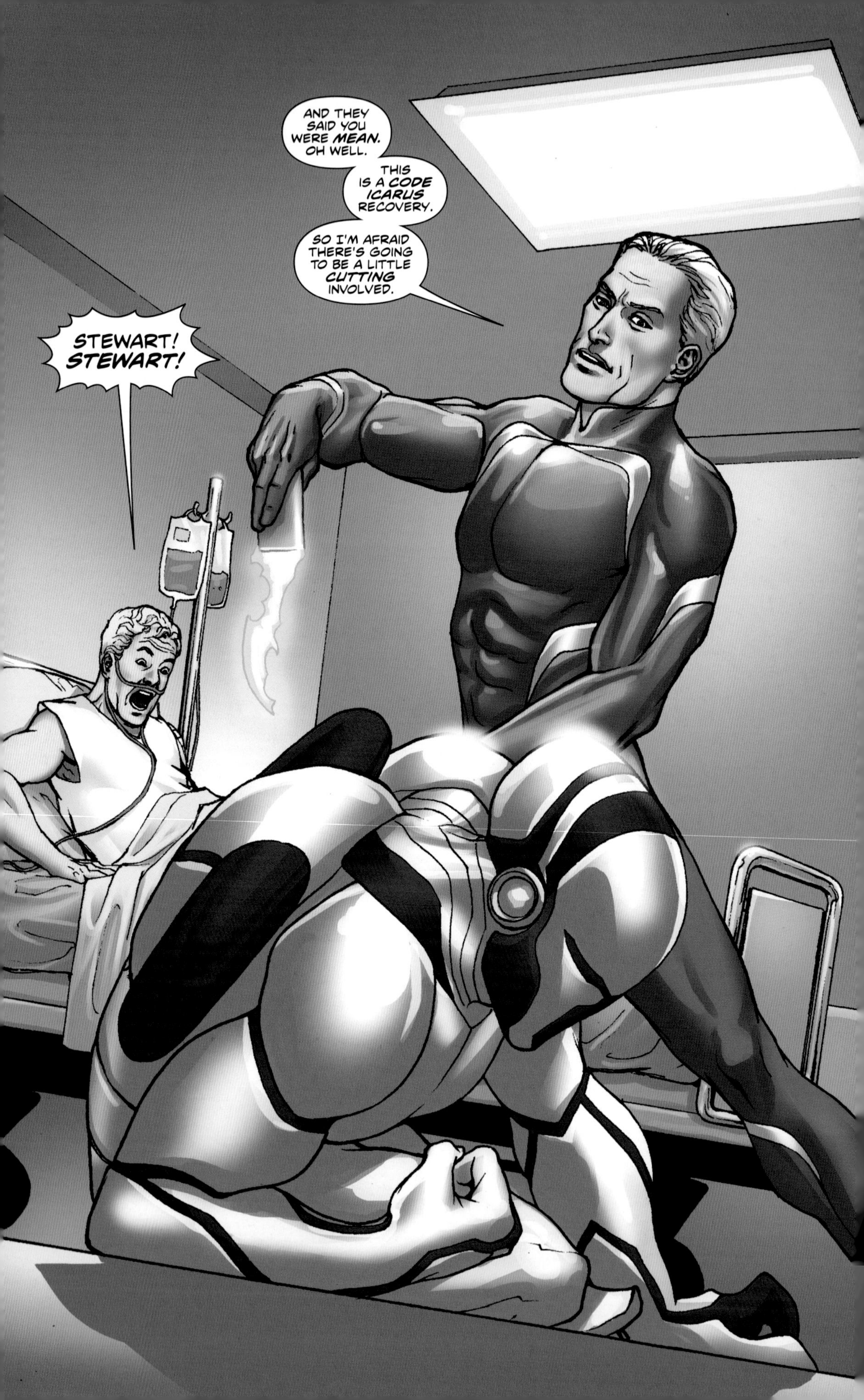
AND THEY SAID YOU WERE MEAN. OH WELL.
THIS IS A CODE ICARUS RECOVERY.
SO I'M AFRAID THERE'S GOING TO BE A LITTLE CUTTING INVOLVED.
STEWART! STEWART!

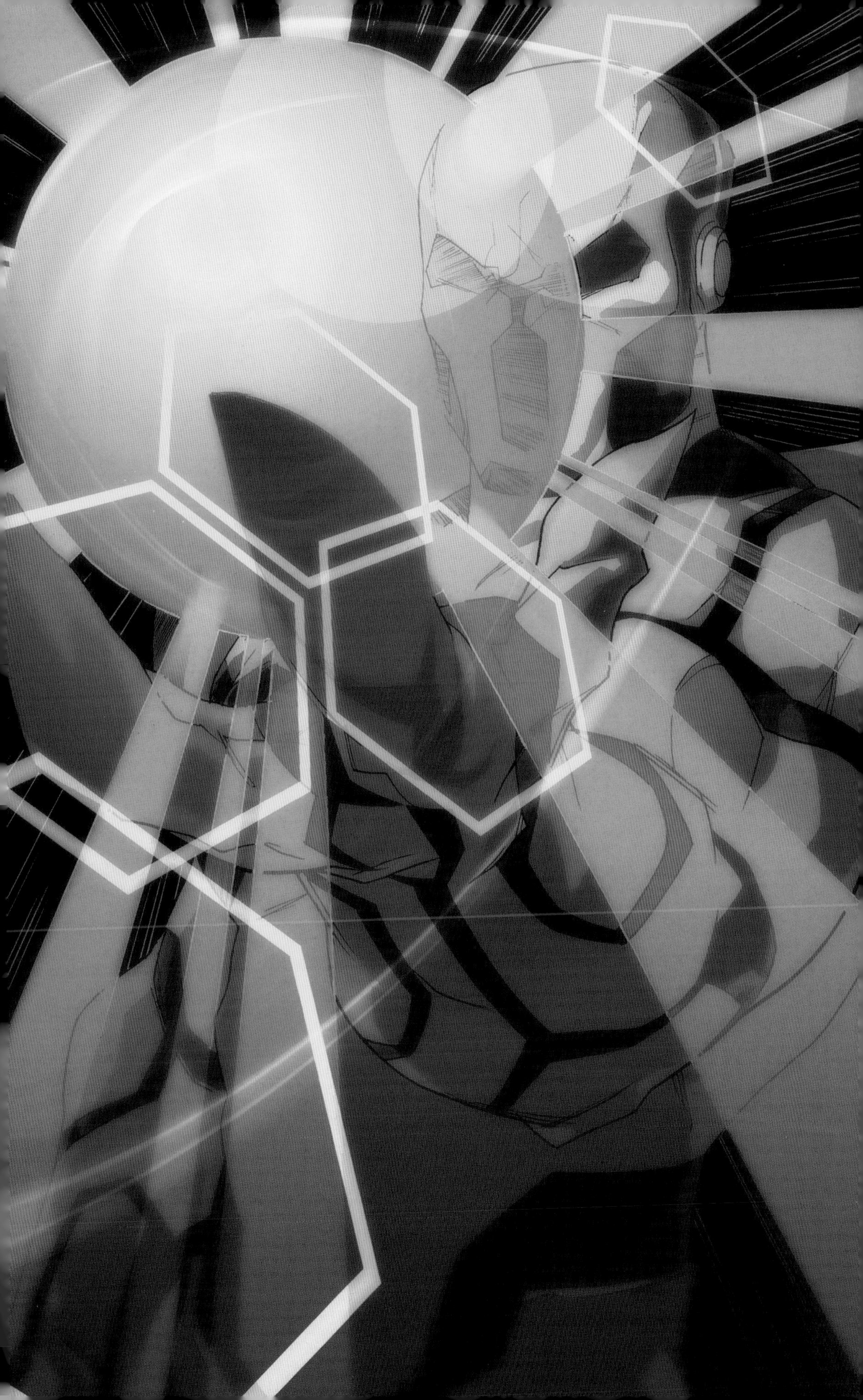

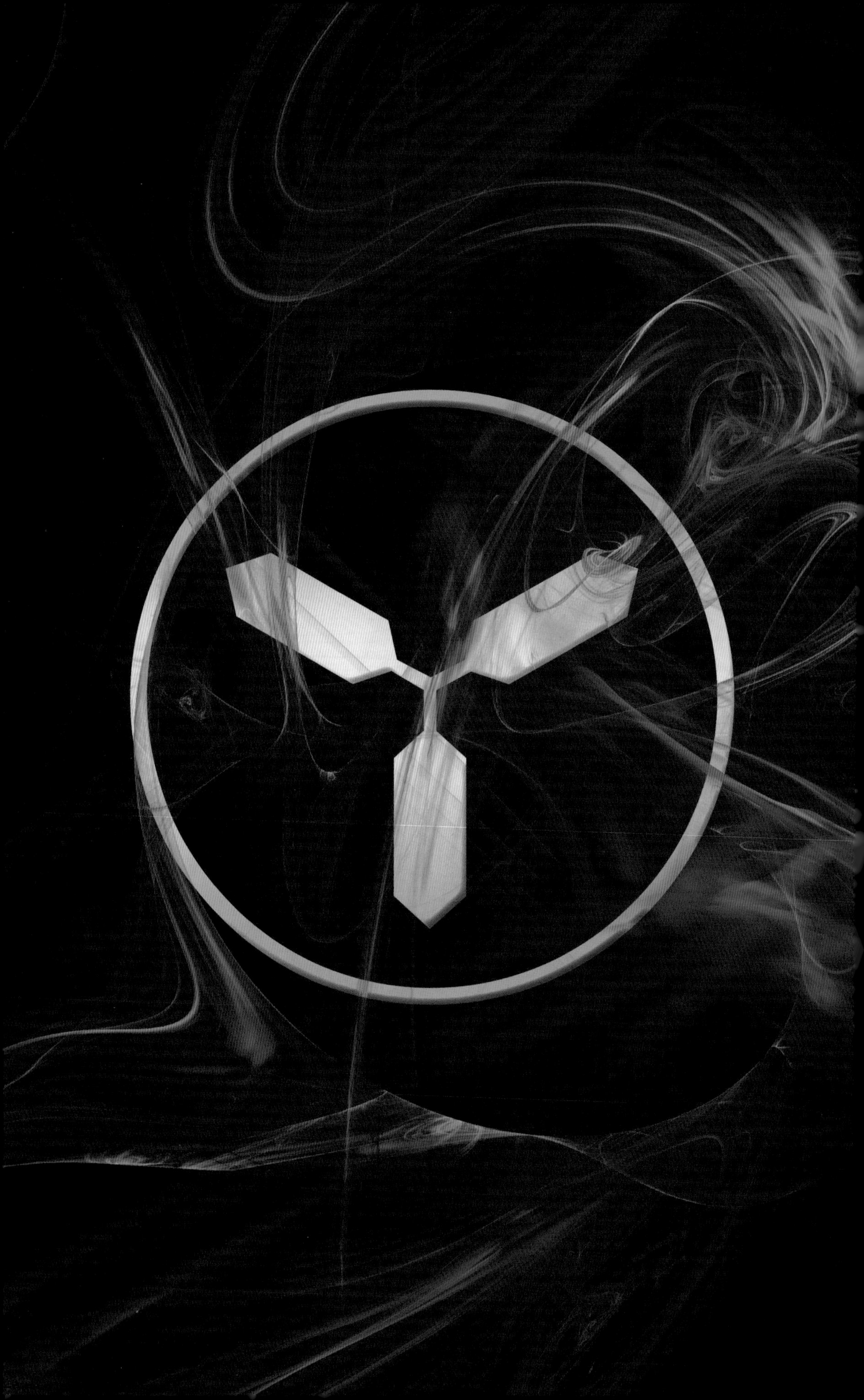

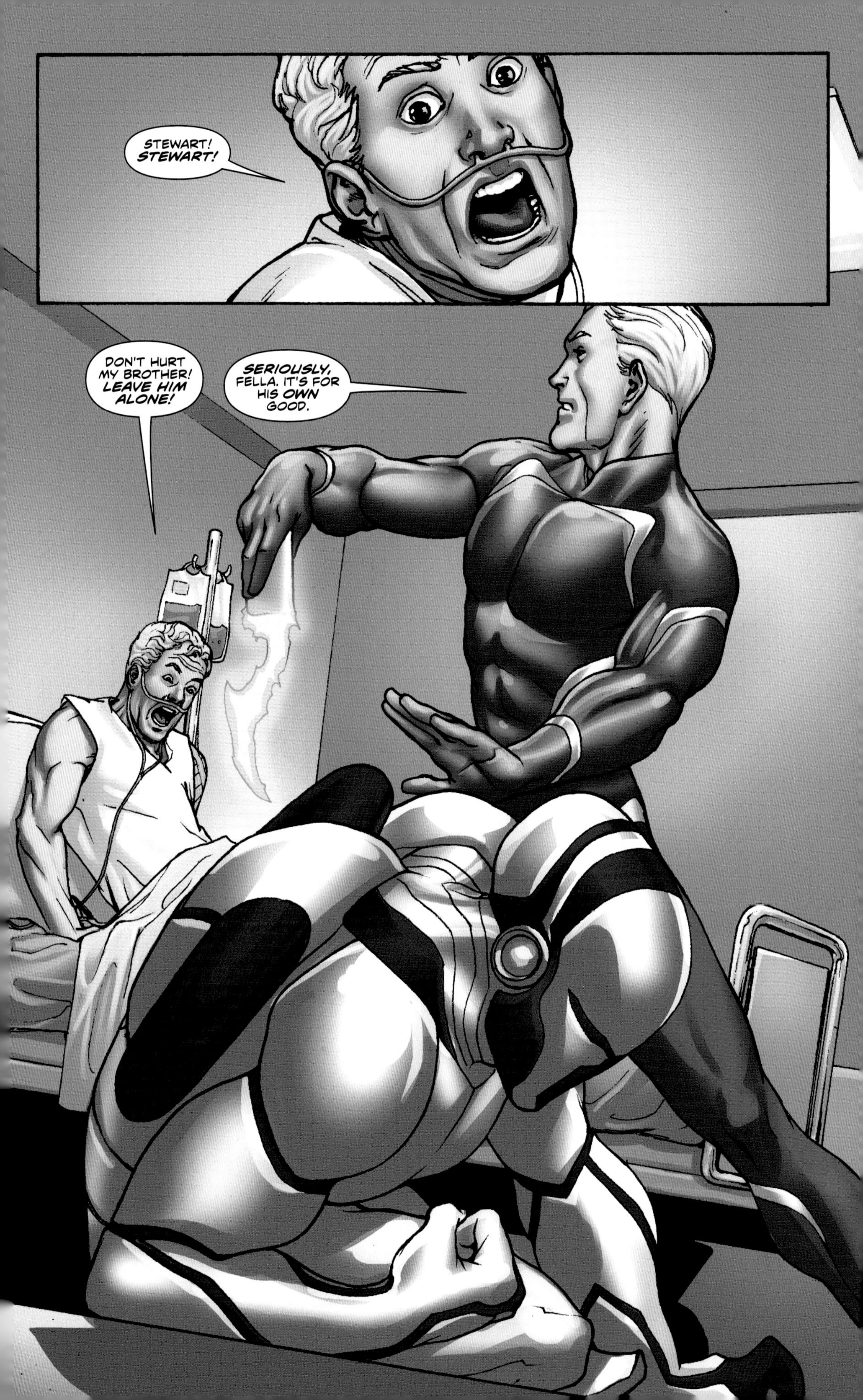
STEWART! STEWART!
DON'T HURT MY BROTHER! LEAVE HIM ALONE!
SERIOUSLY, FELLA. IT'S FOR HIS OWN GOOD.

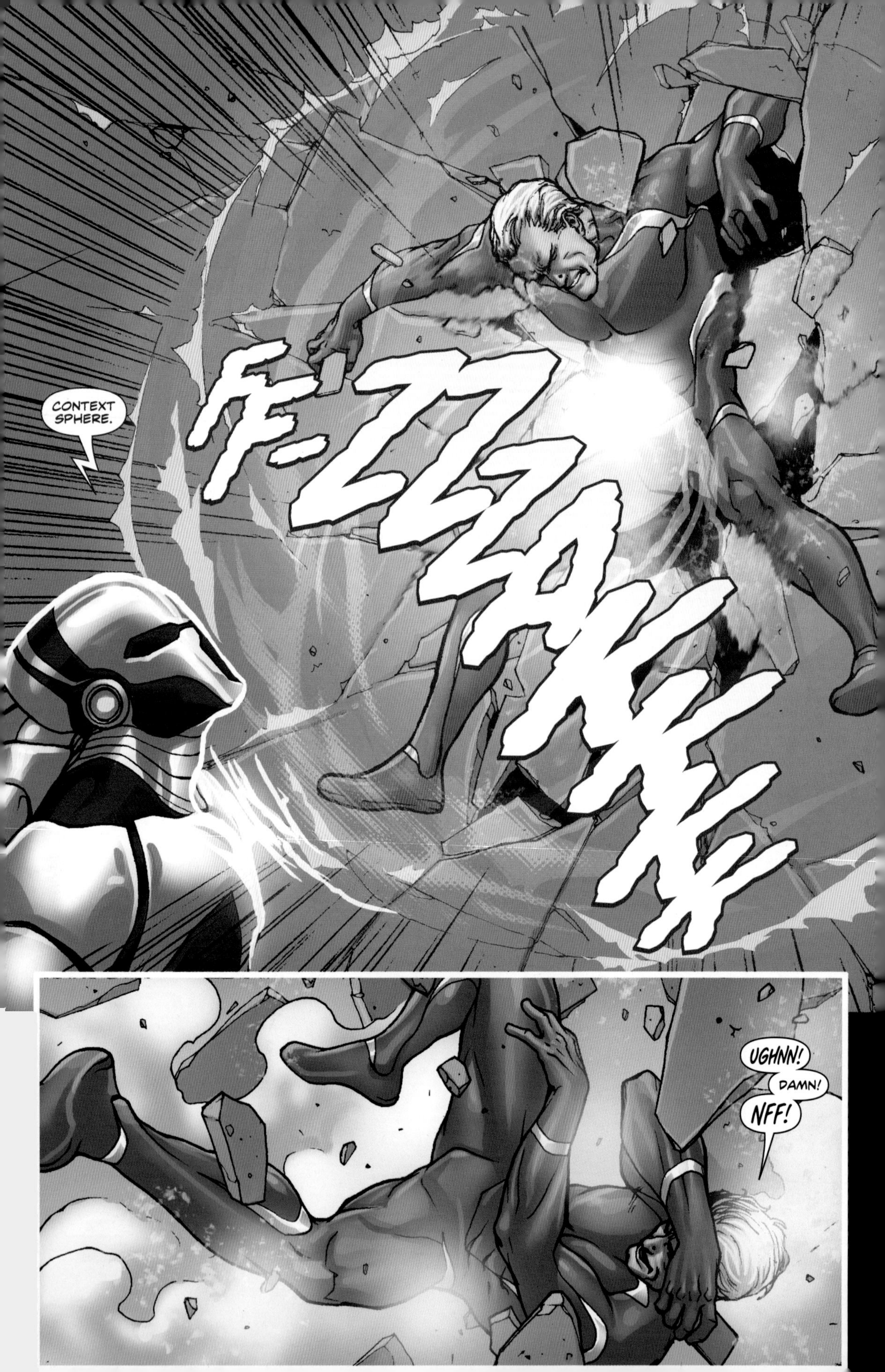
CONTEXT SPHERE.
F-ZZZAKKK
UGHNN!
DAMN!
NFF!

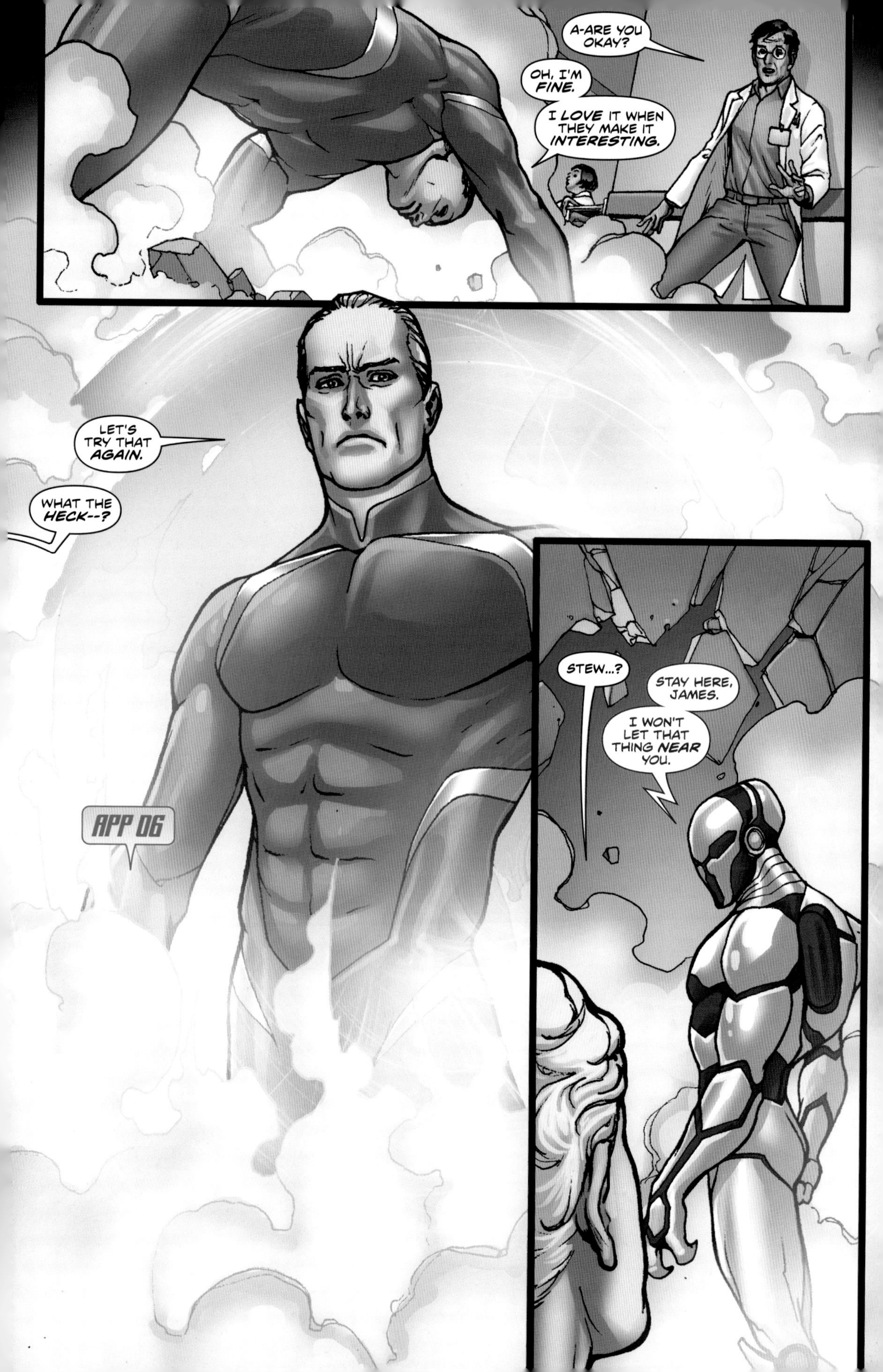
A-ARE YOU OKAY?
OH, I'M FINE.
I LOVE IT WHEN THEY MAKE IT INTERESTING.
LET'S TRY THAT AGAIN.
WHAT THE HECK--?
APP 06
STEW...?
STAY HERE, JAMES.
I WON'T LET THAT THING NEAR YOU.

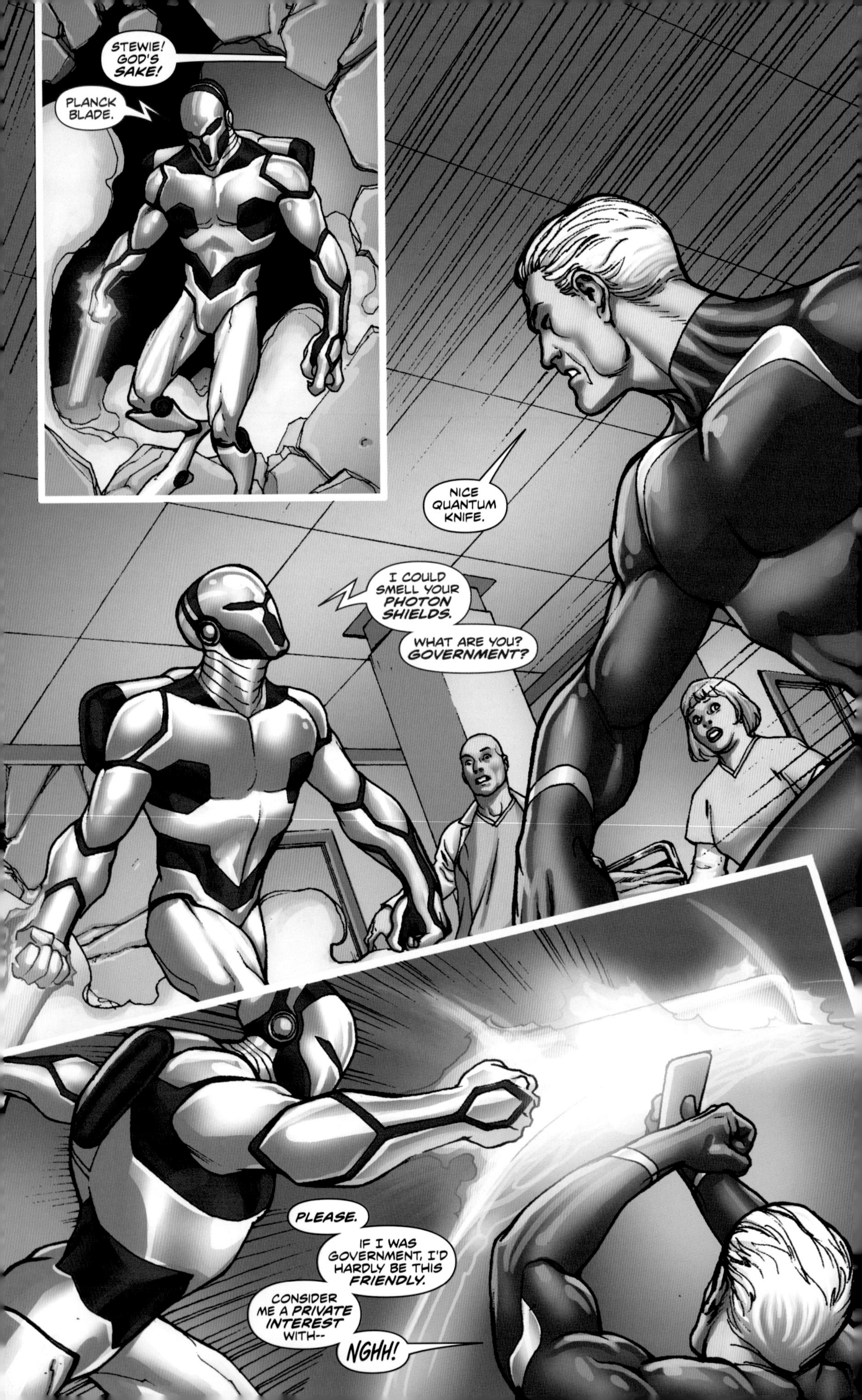
STEWIE! GOD'S SAKE!
PLANCK BLADE.
NICE QUANTUM KNIFE.
I COULD SMELL YOUR PHOTON SHIELDS.
WHAT ARE YOU? GOVERNMENT?
PLEASE.
IF I WAS GOVERNMENT, I'D HARDLY BE THIS FRIENDLY.
CONSIDER ME A PRIVATE INTEREST WITH--
NGHH!

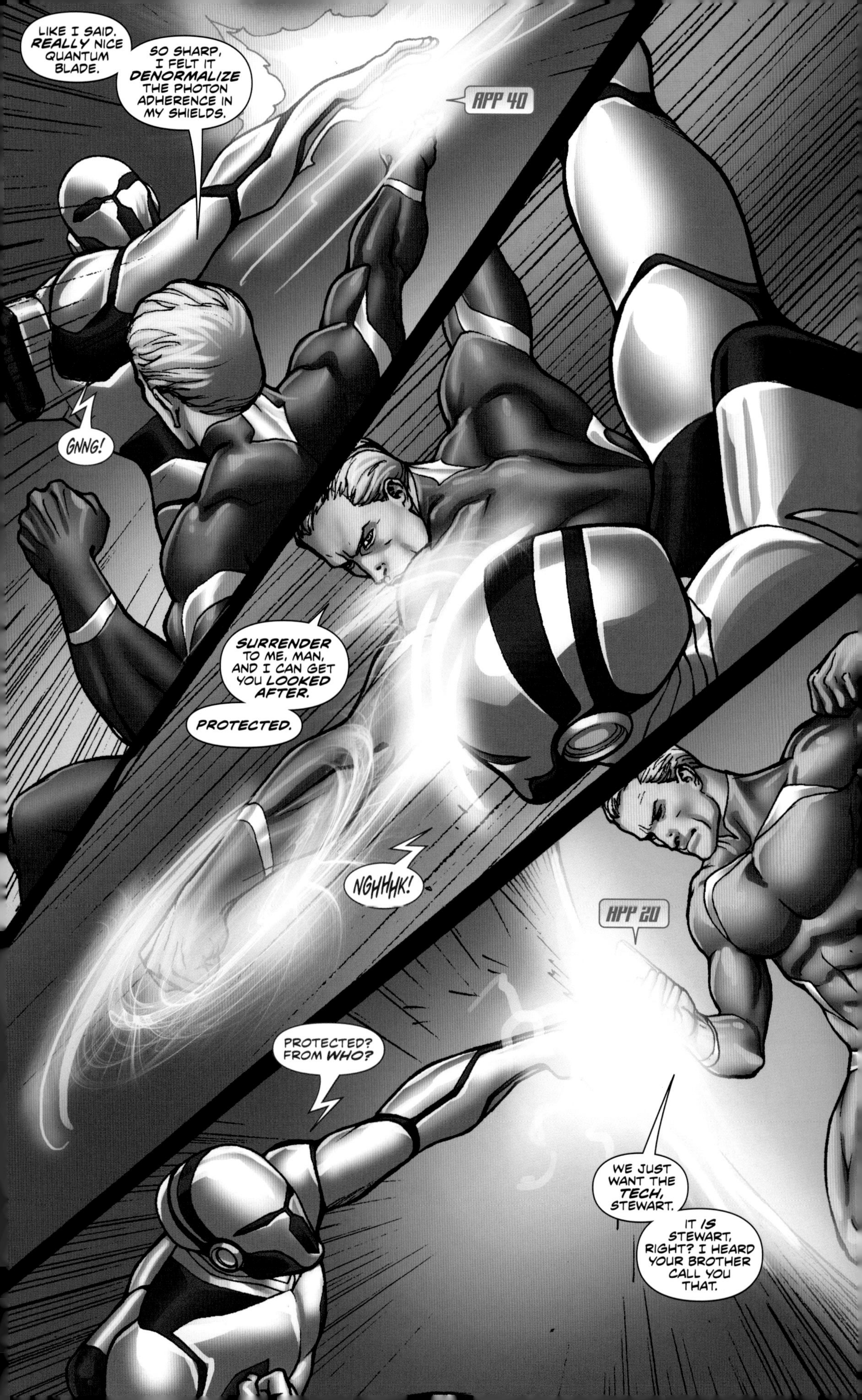
LIKE I SAID. REALLY NICE QUANTUM BLADE.
SO SHARP, I FELT IT DENORMALIZE THE PHOTON ADHERENCE IN MY SHIELDS.
APP 40
GNNG!
SURRENDER TO ME, MAN, AND I CAN GET YOU LOOKED AFTER.
PROTECTED.
NGHHHK!
APP 20
PROTECTED? FROM WHO?
WE JUST WANT THE TECH, STEWART.
IT IS STEWART, RIGHT? I HEARD YOUR BROTHER CALL YOU THAT.

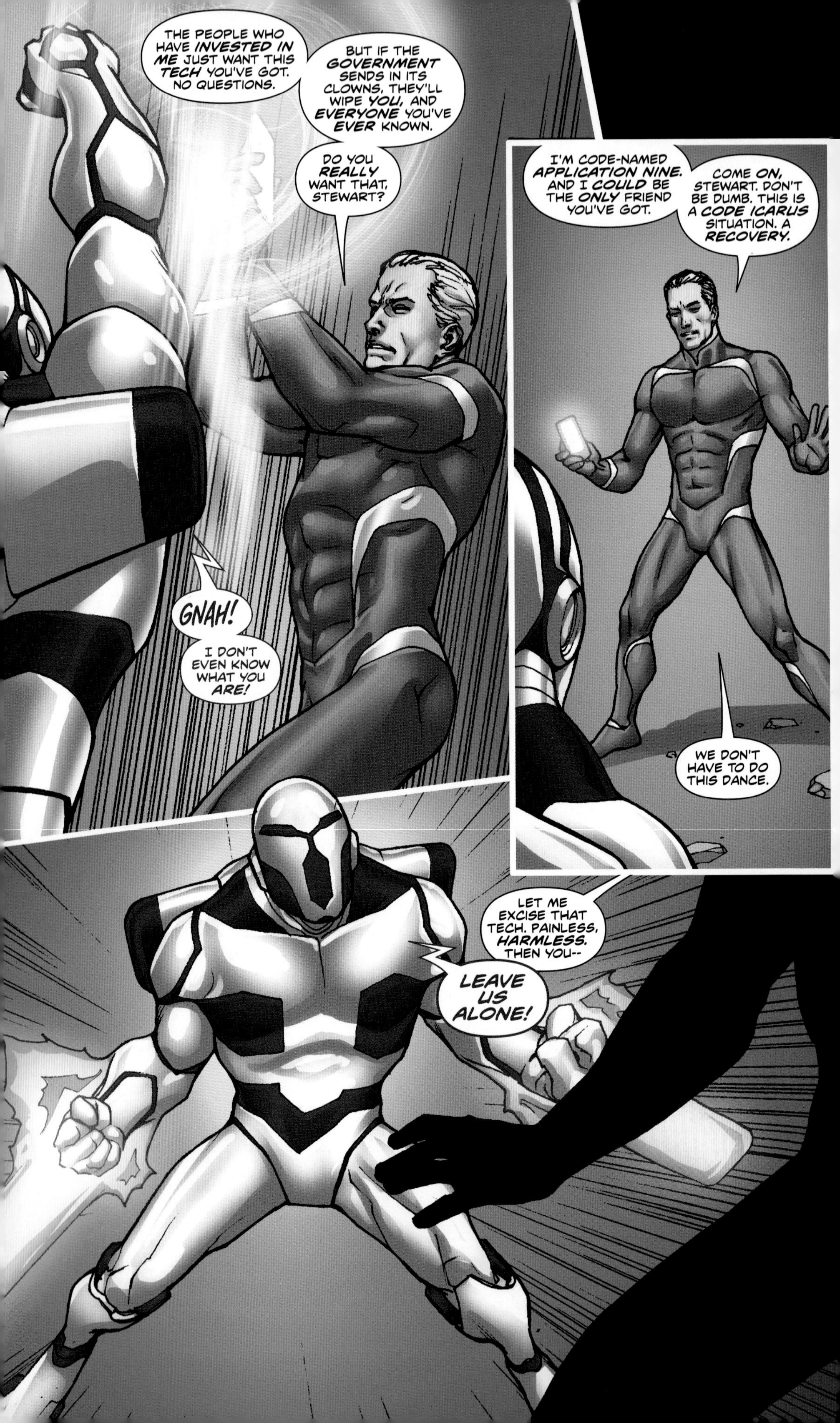
THE PEOPLE WHO HAVE INVESTED IN ME JUST WANT THIS TECH YOU'VE GOT. NO QUESTIONS.
BUT IF THE GOVERNMENT SENDS IN ITS CLOWNS, THEY'LL WIPE YOU, AND EVERYONE YOU'VE EVER KNOWN.
DO YOU REALLY WANT THAT, STEWART?
GNAH!
I DON'T EVEN KNOW WHAT YOU ARE!
I'M CODE-NAMED APPLICATION NINE. AND I COULD BE THE ONLY FRIEND YOU'VE GOT.
COME ON, STEWART. DON'T BE DUMB. THIS IS A CODE ICARUS SITUATION. A RECOVERY.
WE DON'T HAVE TO DO THIS DANCE.
LET ME EXCISE THAT TECH. PAINLESS, HARMLESS. THEN YOU--
LEAVE US ALONE!

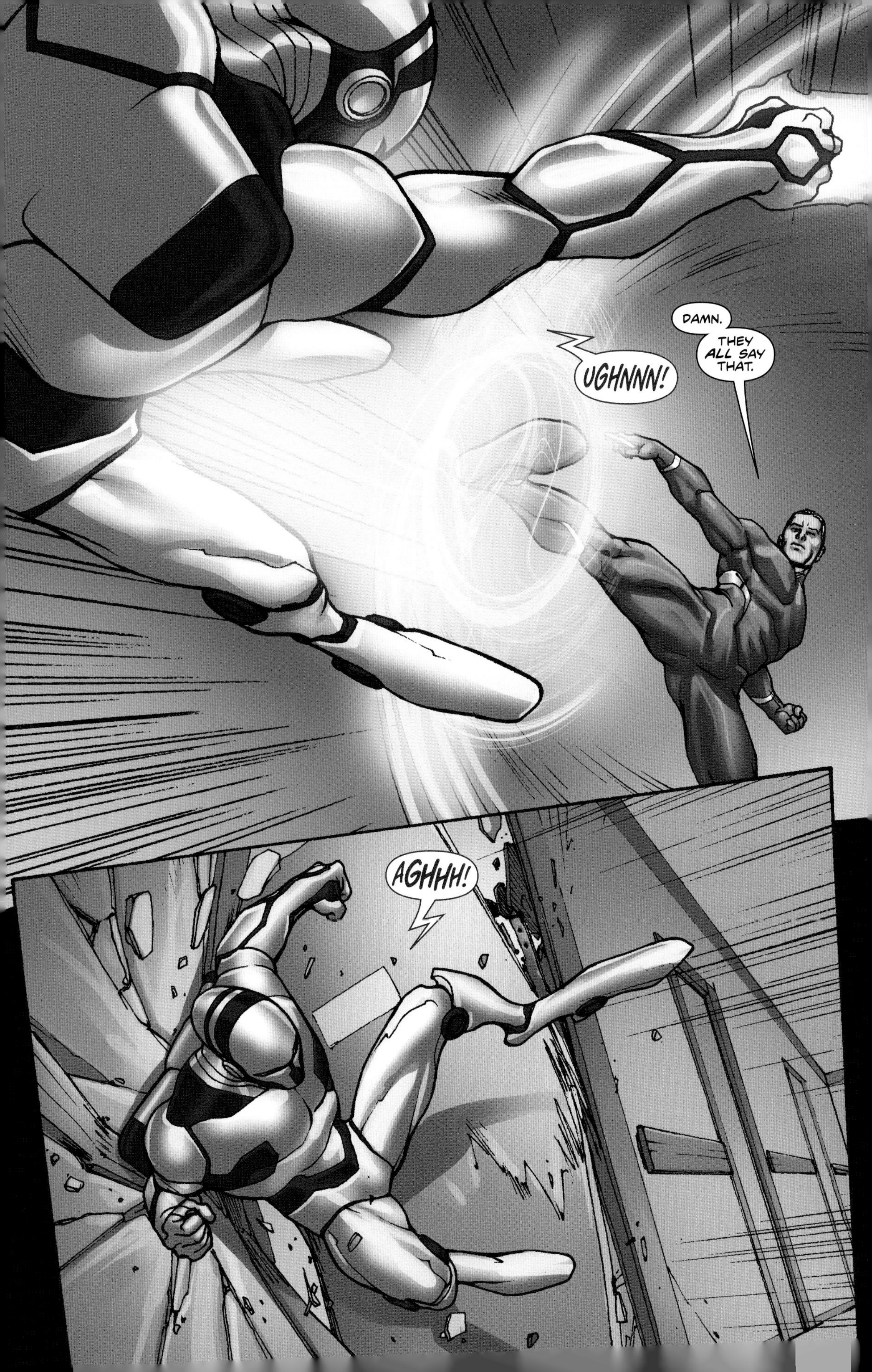
UGHNNN!
DAMN.
THEY ALL SAY THAT.
AGHHH!

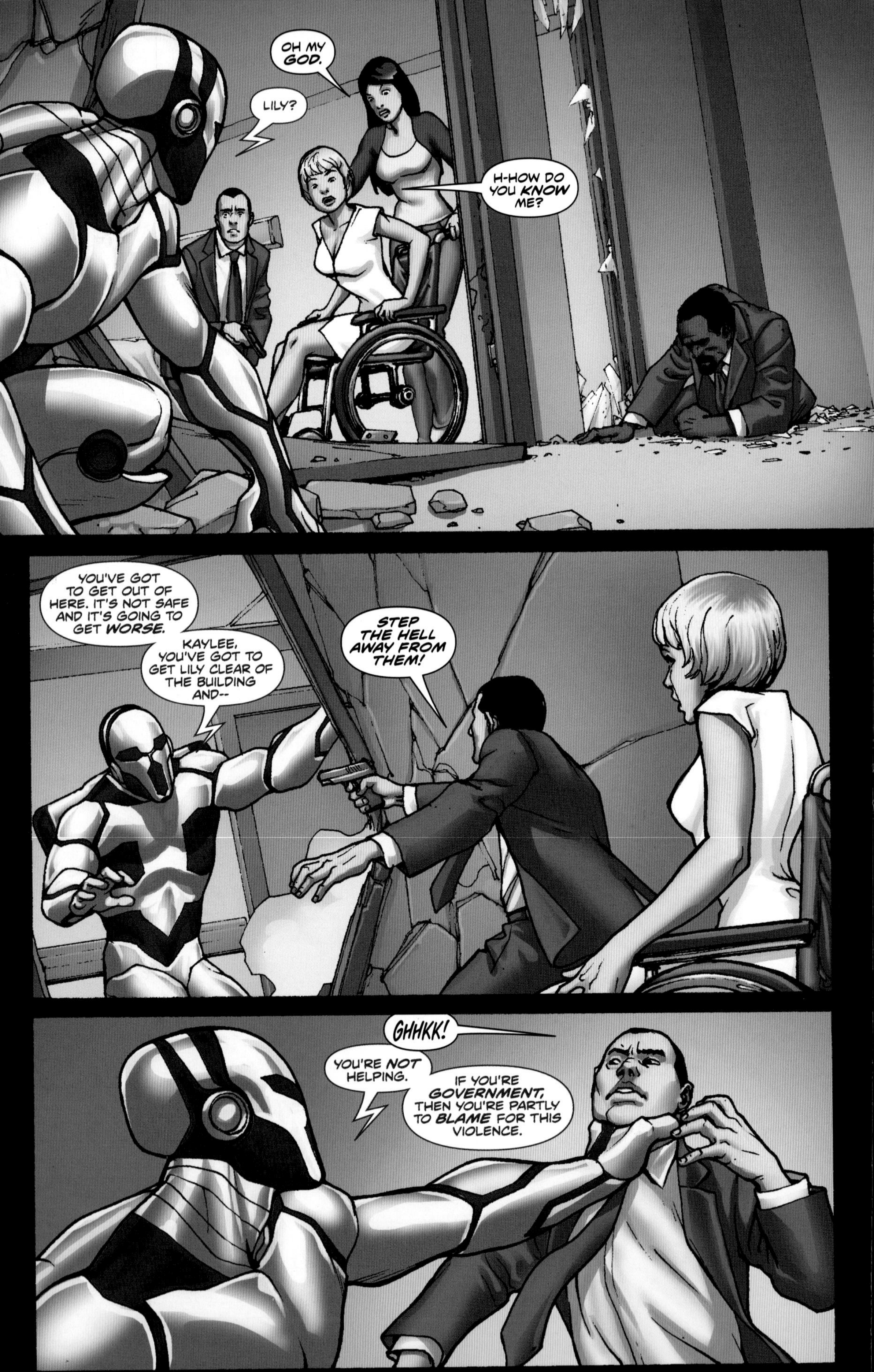
OH MY GOD.
LILY?
H-HOW DO YOU KNOW ME?
YOU'VE GOT TO GET OUT OF HERE. IT'S NOT SAFE AND IT'S GOING TO GET WORSE.
KAYLEE, YOU'VE GOT TO GET LILY CLEAR OF THE BUILDING AND--
STEP THE HELL AWAY FROM THEM!
GHHKK!
YOU'RE NOT HELPING.
IF YOU'RE GOVERNMENT, THEN YOU'RE PARTLY TO BLAME FOR THIS VIOLENCE.

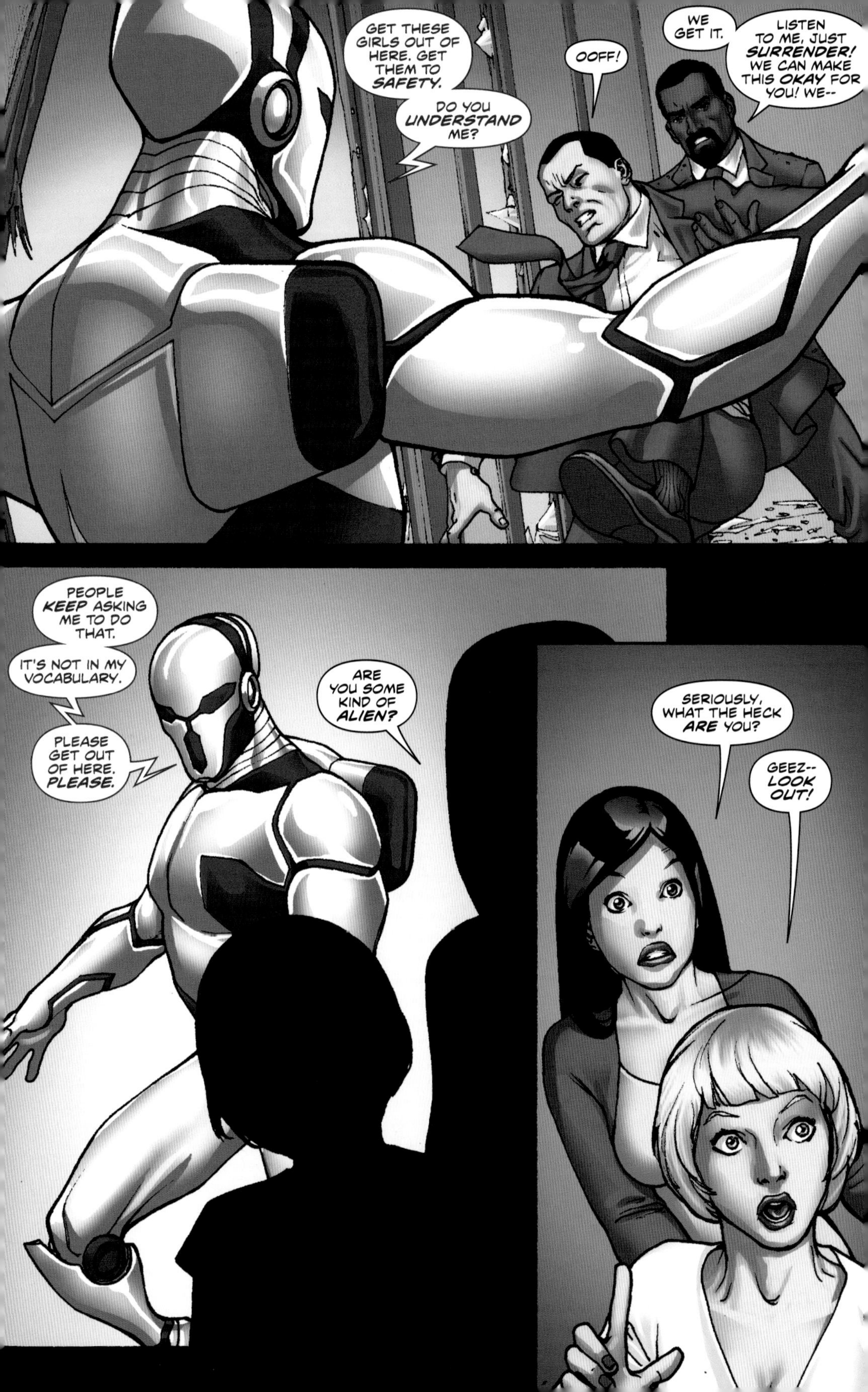

GET THESE GIRLS OUT OF HERE. GET THEM TO SAFETY.
DO YOU UNDERSTAND ME?
OOFF!
WE GET IT.
LISTEN TO ME, JUST SURRENDER! WE CAN MAKE THIS OKAY FOR YOU! WE--
PEOPLE KEEP ASKING ME TO DO THAT.
IT'S NOT IN MY VOCABULARY.
PLEASE GET OUT OF HERE. PLEASE.
ARE YOU SOME KIND OF ALIEN?
SERIOUSLY, WHAT THE HECK ARE YOU?
GEEZ-- LOOK OUT!

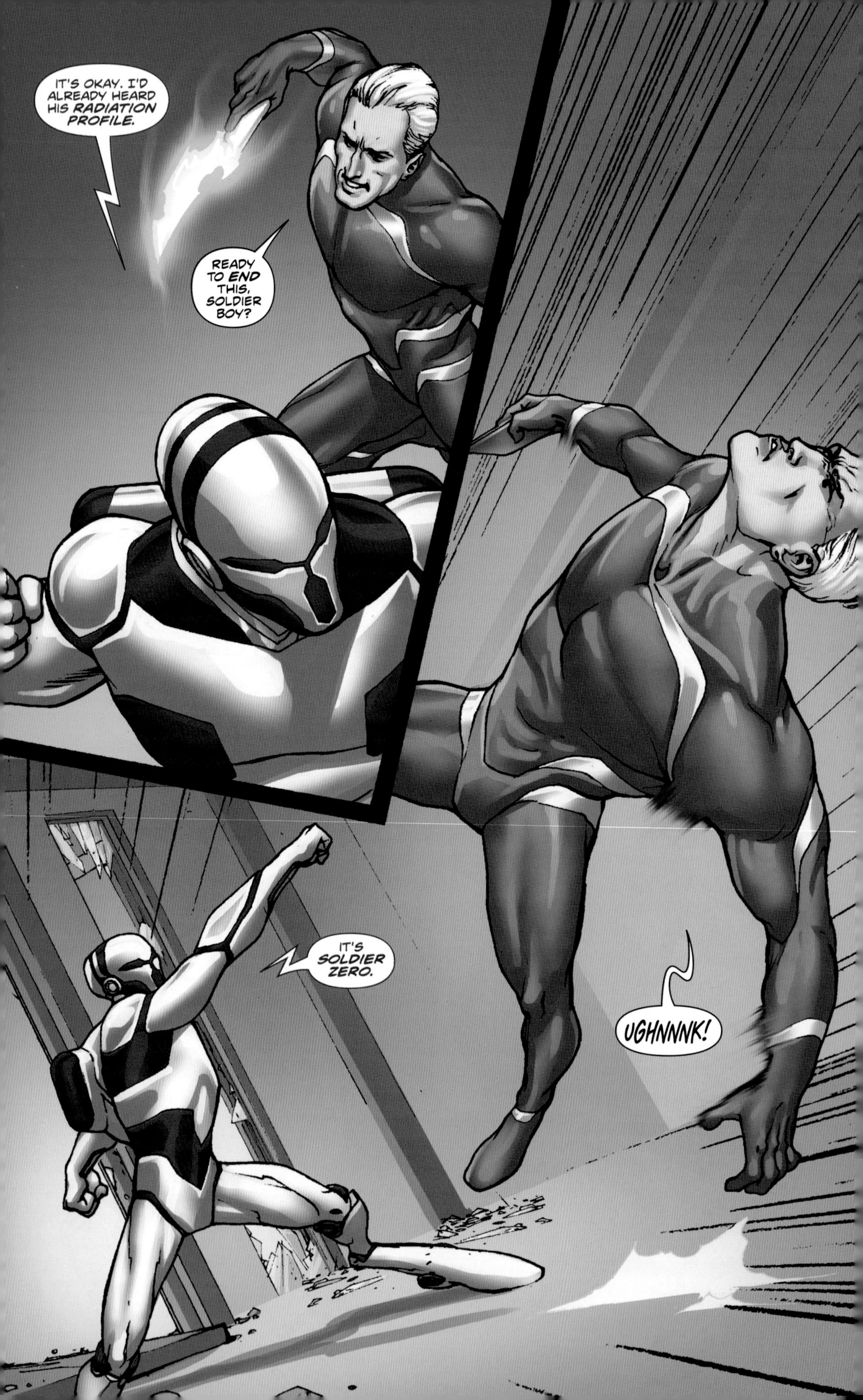
IT'S OKAY. I'D ALREADY HEARD HIS RADIATION PROFILE.
READY TO END THIS, SOLDIER BOY?
IT'S SOLDIER ZERO.
UGHNNNK!

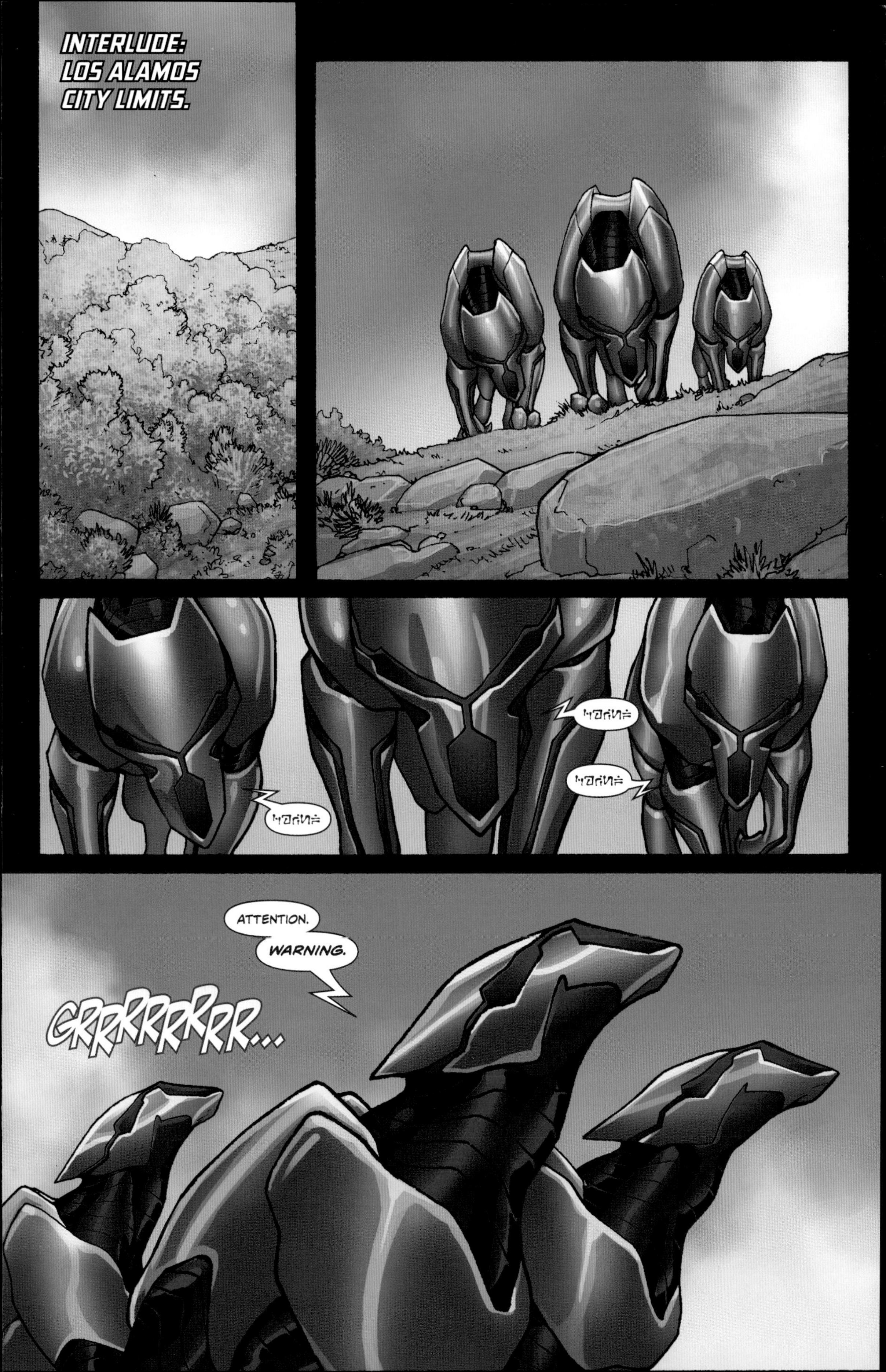
INTERLUDE: LOS ALAMOS CITY LIMITS.
ATTENTION.
WARNING.
GRRRRRRRR...

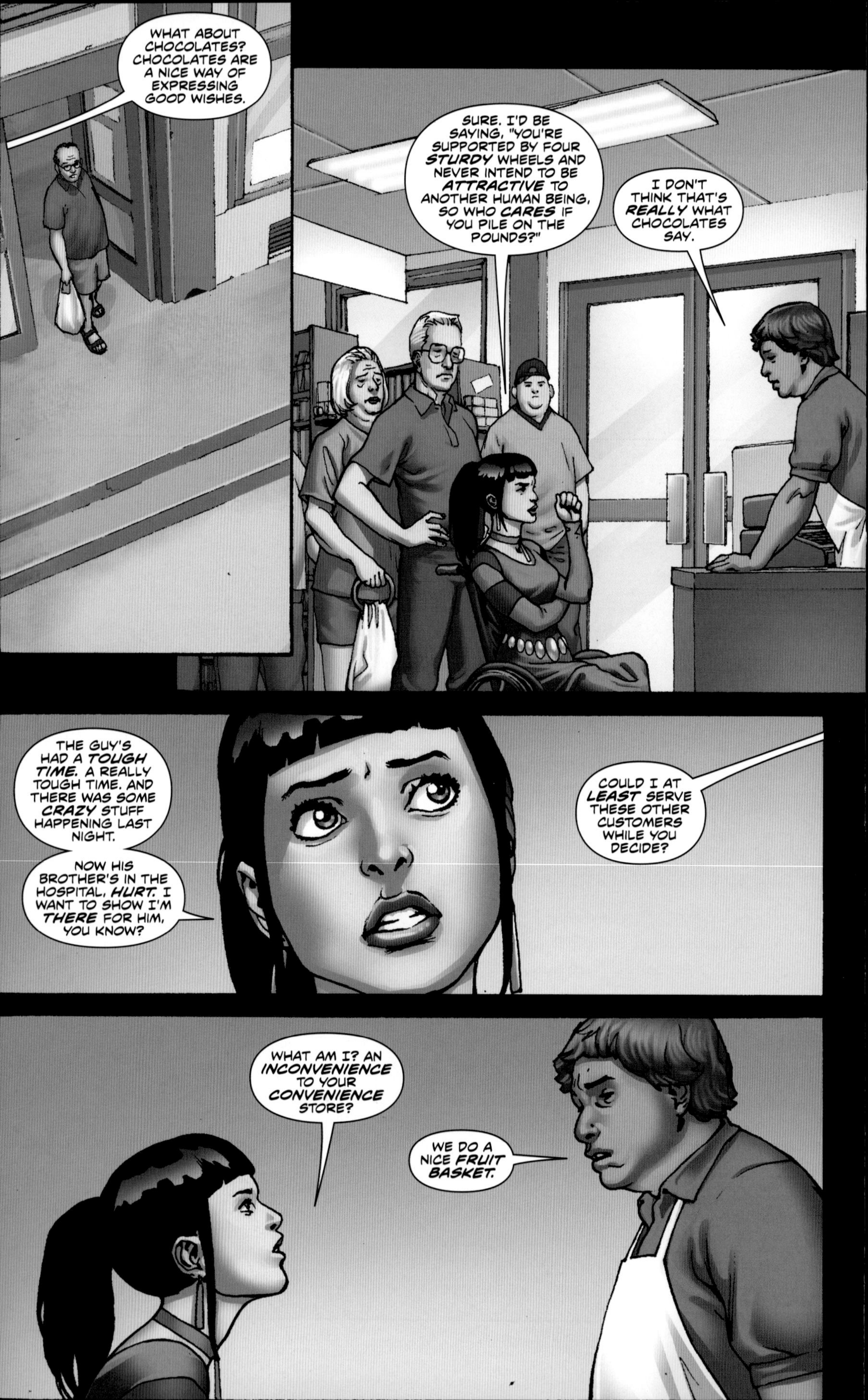
WHAT ABOUT CHOCOLATES? CHOCOLATES ARE A NICE WAY OF EXPRESSING GOOD WISHES.
SURE. I'D BE SAYING, "YOU'RE SUPPORTED BY FOUR STURDY WHEELS AND NEVER INTEND TO BE ATTRACTIVE TO ANOTHER HUMAN BEING, SO WHO CARES IF YOU PILE ON THE POUNDS?"
I DON'T THINK THAT'S REALLY WHAT CHOCOLATES SAY.
THE GUY'S HAD A TOUGH TIME. A REALLY TOUGH TIME. AND THERE WAS SOME CRAZY STUFF HAPPENING LAST NIGHT.
NOW HIS BROTHER'S IN THE HOSPITAL, HURT. I WANT TO SHOW I'M THERE FOR HIM, YOU KNOW?
COULD I AT LEAST SERVE THESE OTHER CUSTOMERS WHILE YOU DECIDE?
WHAT AM I? AN INCONVENIENCE TO YOUR CONVENIENCE STORE?
WE DO A NICE FRUIT BASKET.

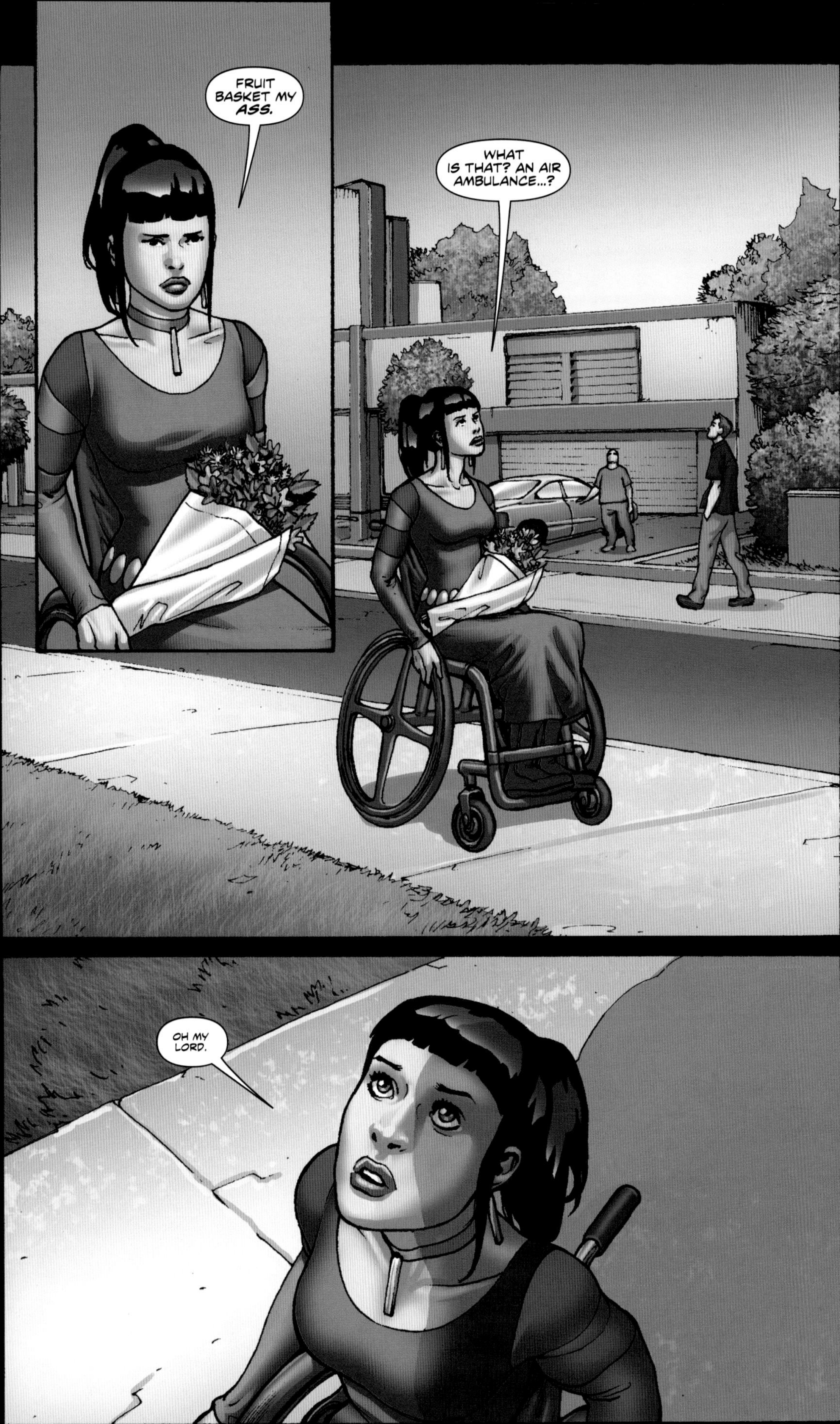
FRUIT BASKET MY ASS.
WHAT IS THAT? AN AIR AMBULANCE...?
OH MY LORD.

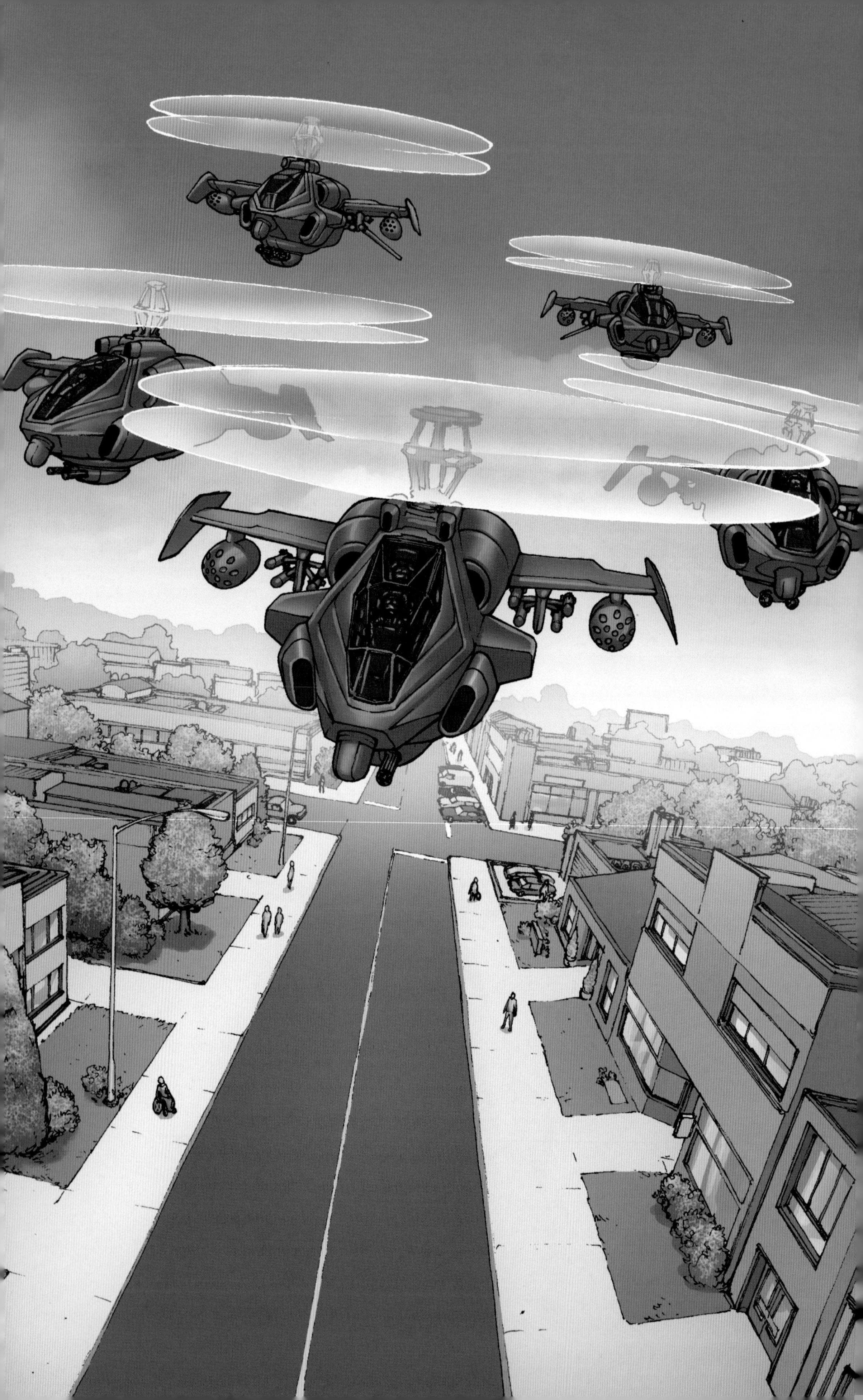

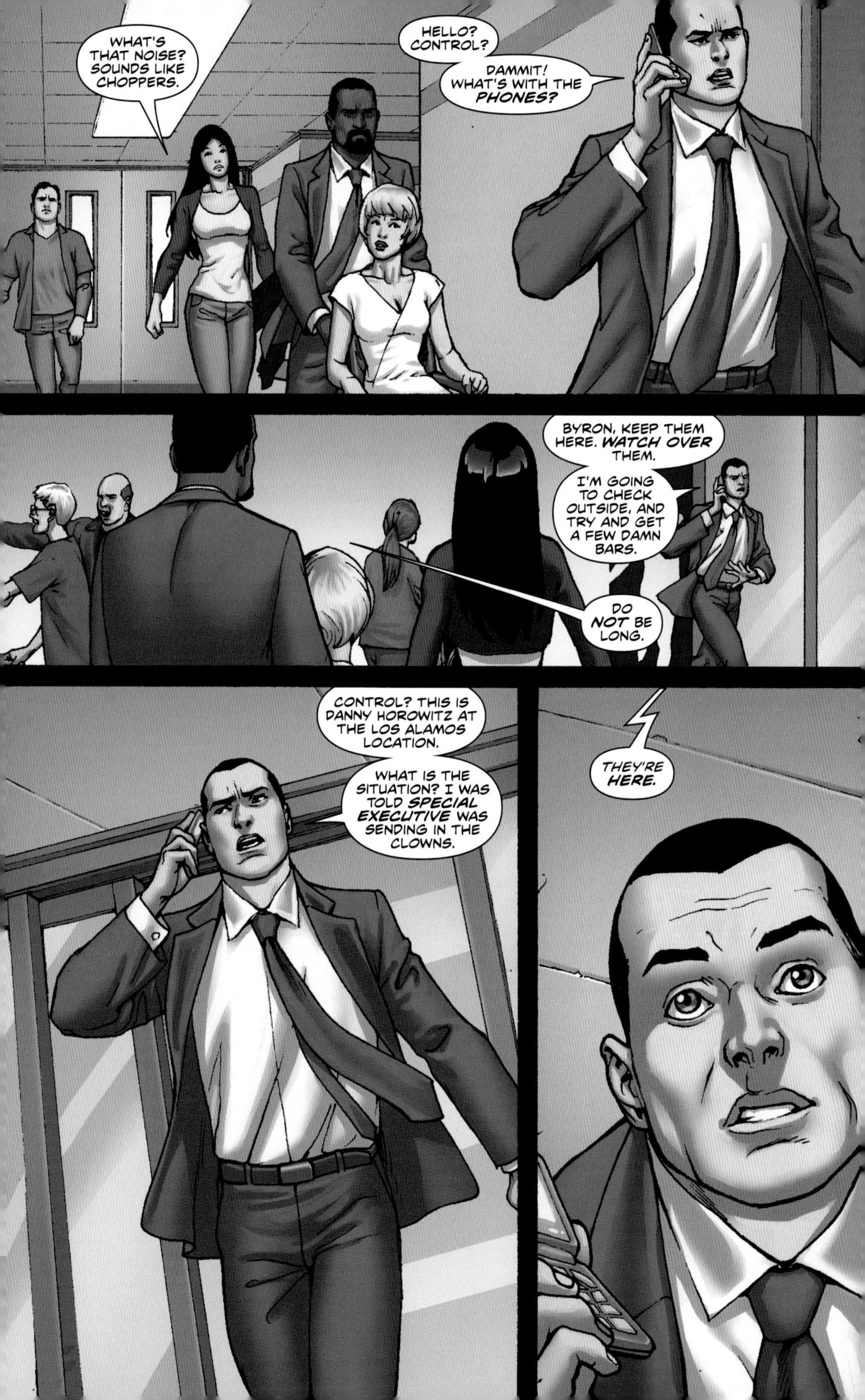
WHAT'S THAT NOISE? SOUNDS LIKE CHOPPERS.
HELLO? CONTROL?
DAMMIT! WHAT'S WITH THE PHONES?
BYRON, KEEP THEM HERE. WATCH OVER THEM.
I'M GOING TO CHECK OUTSIDE, AND TRY AND GET A FEW DAMN BARS.
DO NOT BE LONG.
CONTROL? THIS IS DANNY HOROWITZ AT THE LOS ALAMOS LOCATION.
WHAT IS THE SITUATION? I WAS TOLD SPECIAL EXECUTIVE WAS SENDING IN THE CLOWNS.
THEY'RE HERE.

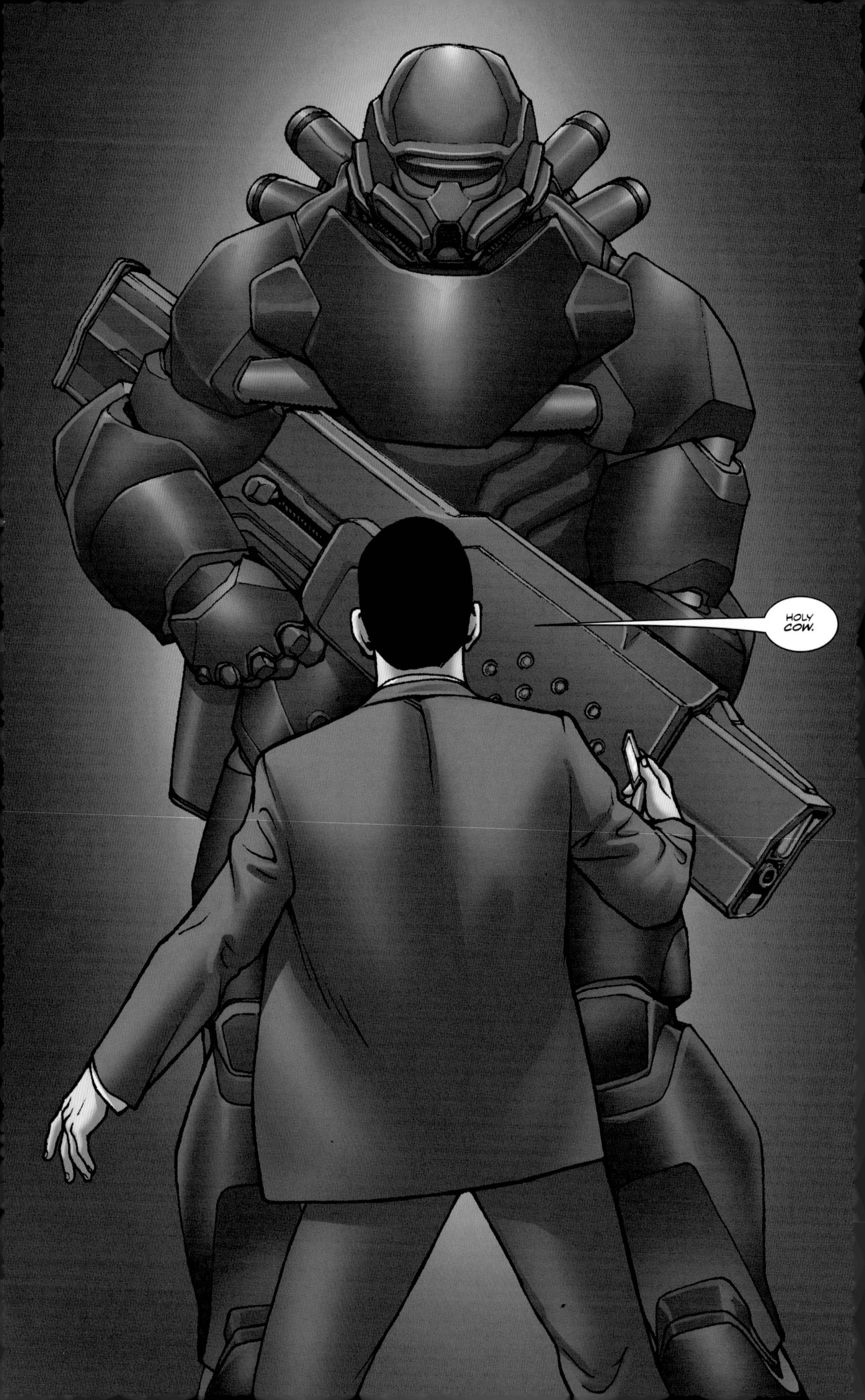
HOLY COW.

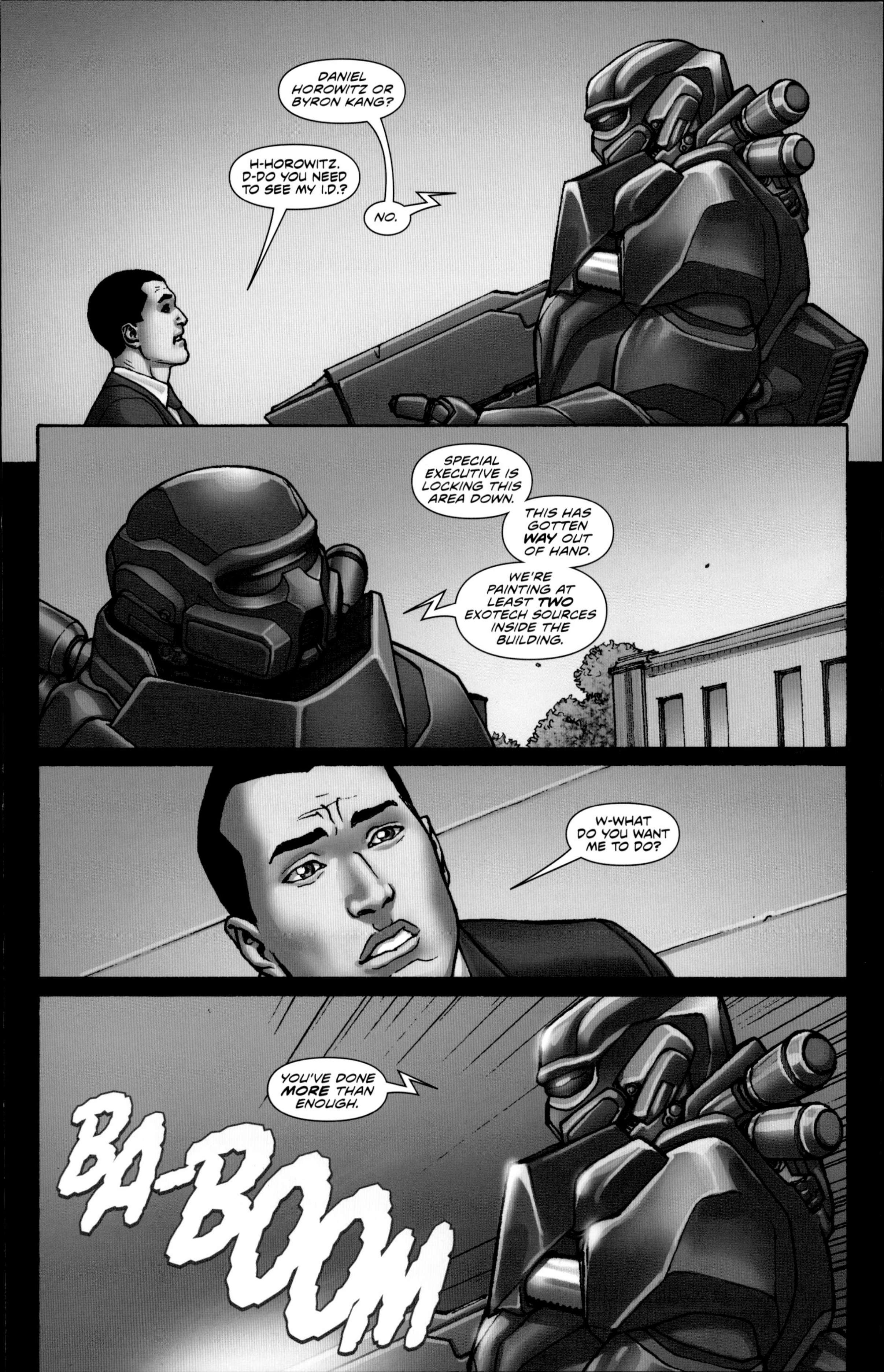
DANIEL HOROWITZ OR BYRON KANG?
H-HOROWITZ. D-DO YOU NEED TO SEE MY I.D.?
NO.
SPECIAL EXECUTIVE IS LOCKING THIS AREA DOWN.
THIS HAS GOTTEN WAY OUT OF HAND.
WE'RE PAINTING AT LEAST TWO EXOTECH SOURCES INSIDE THE BUILDING.
W-WHAT DO YOU WANT ME TO DO?
YOU'VE DONE MORE THAN ENOUGH.
BA-BOOM

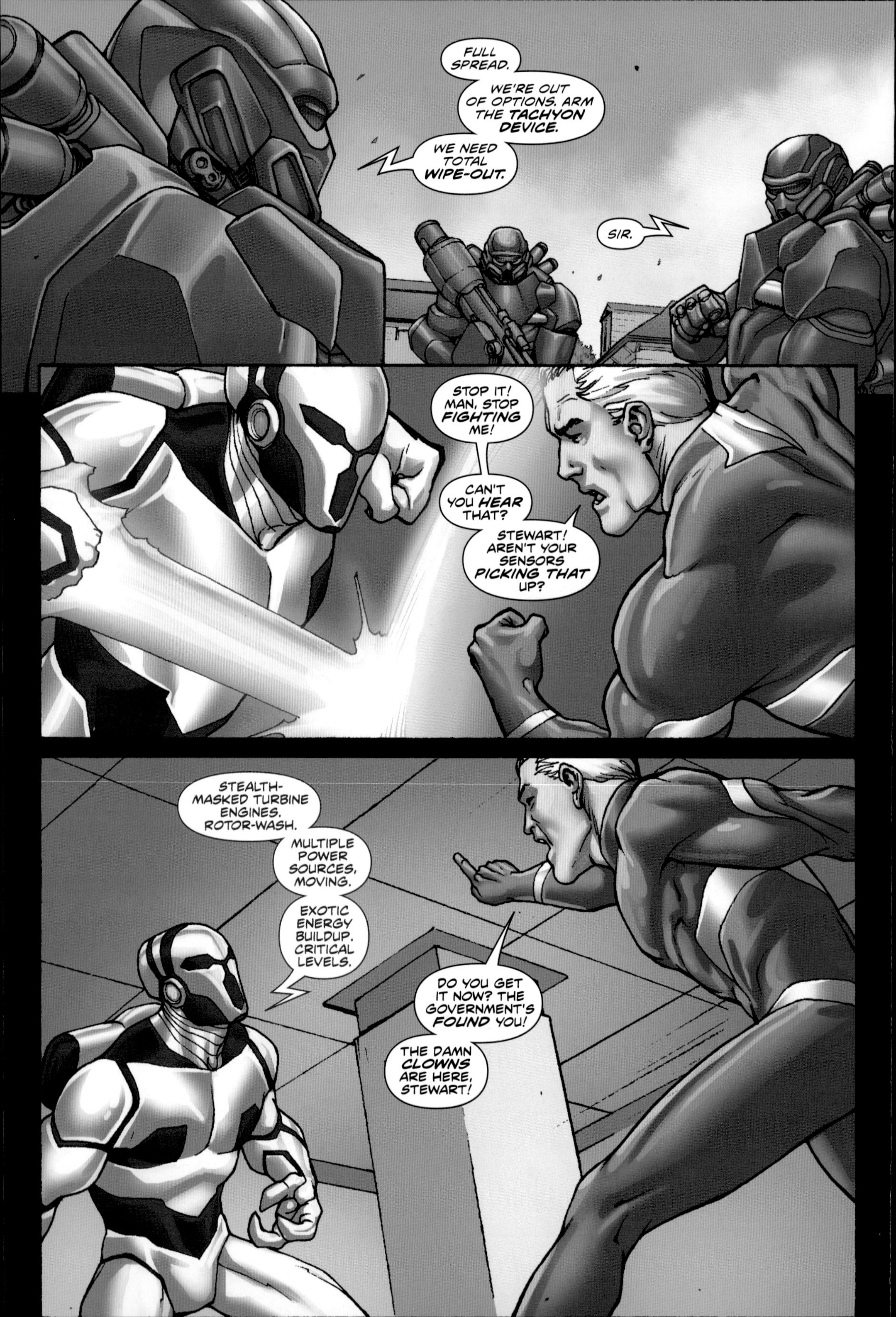
FULL SPREAD.
WE'RE OUT OF OPTIONS. ARM THE TACHYON DEVICE.
WE NEED TOTAL WIPE-OUT.
SIR.
STOP IT! MAN, STOP FIGHTING ME!
CAN'T YOU HEAR THAT?
STEWART! AREN'T YOUR SENSORS PICKING THAT UP?
STEALTH-MASKED TURBINE ENGINES. ROTOR-WASH.
MULTIPLE POWER SOURCES, MOVING.
EXOTIC ENERGY BUILDUP. CRITICAL LEVELS.
DO YOU GET IT NOW? THE GOVERNMENT'S FOUND YOU!
THE DAMN CLOWNS ARE HERE, STEWART!

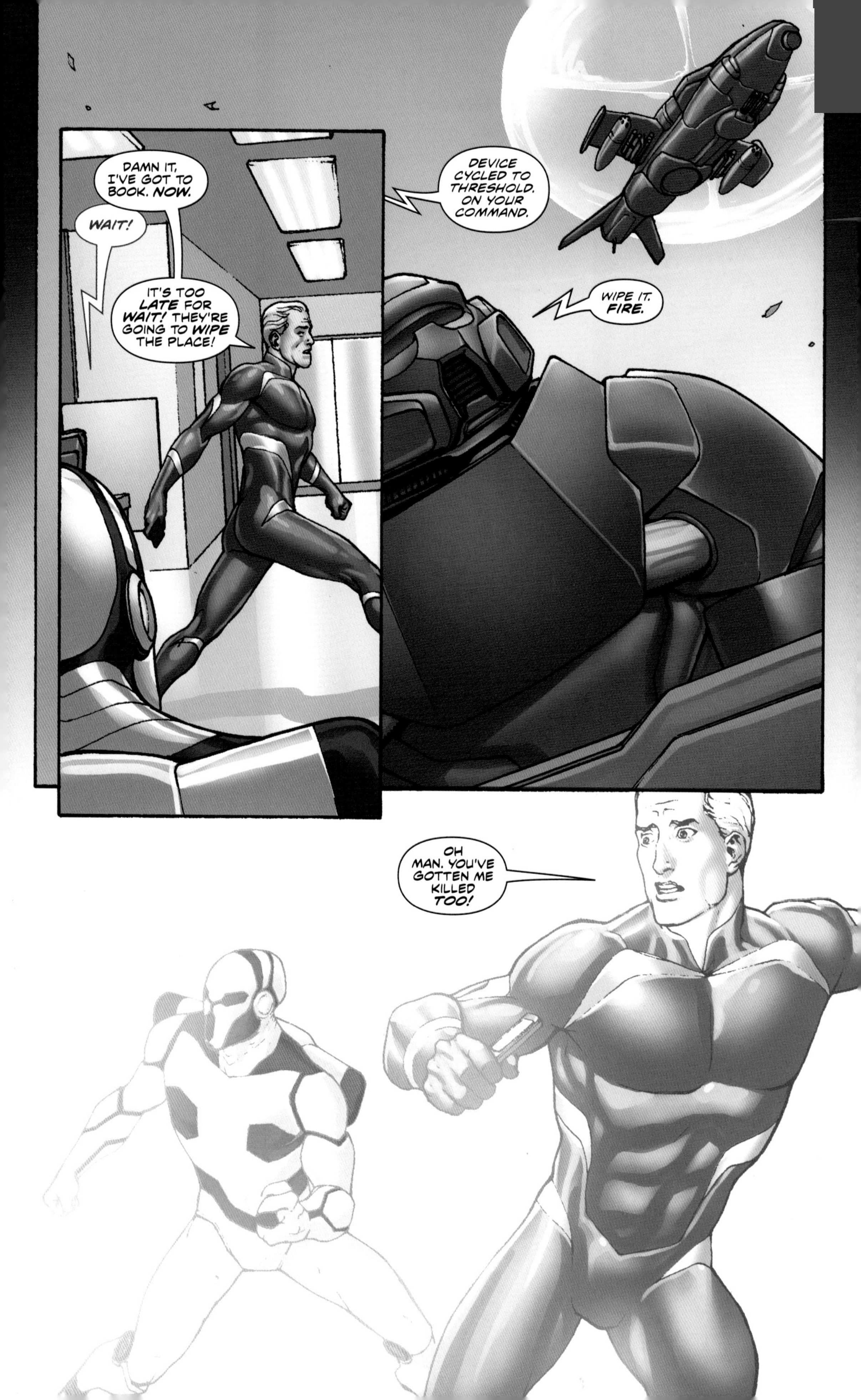
DAMN IT, I'VE GOT TO BOOK. NOW.
WAIT!
IT'S TOO LATE FOR WAIT! THEY'RE GOING TO WIPE THE PLACE!
DEVICE CYCLED TO THRESHOLD. ON YOUR COMMAND.
WIPE IT. FIRE.
OH MAN. YOU'VE GOTTEN ME KILLED TOO!

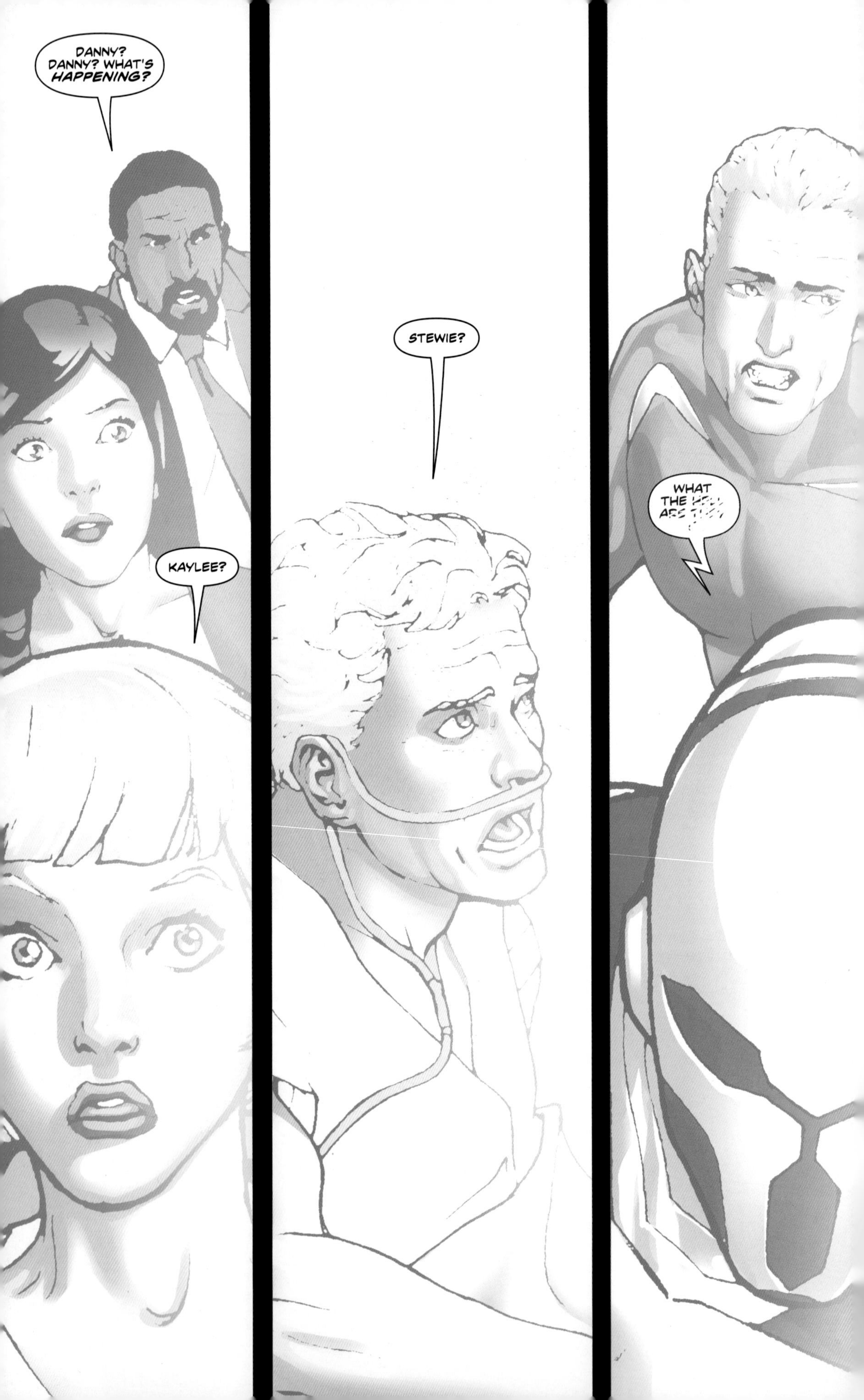
DANNY?
DANNY? WHAT'S *HAPPENING?*
KAYLEE?
STEWIE?
WHAT THE

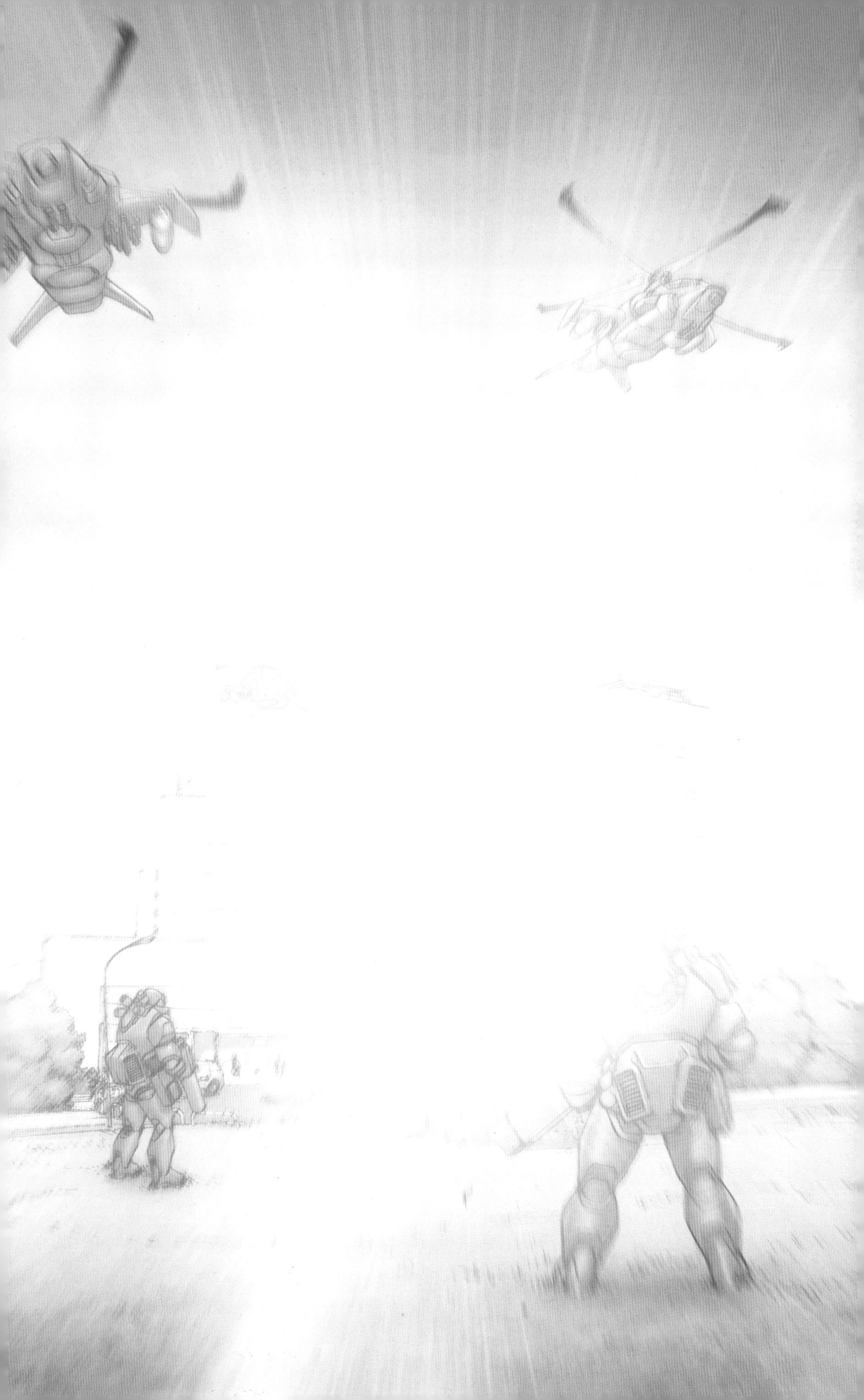

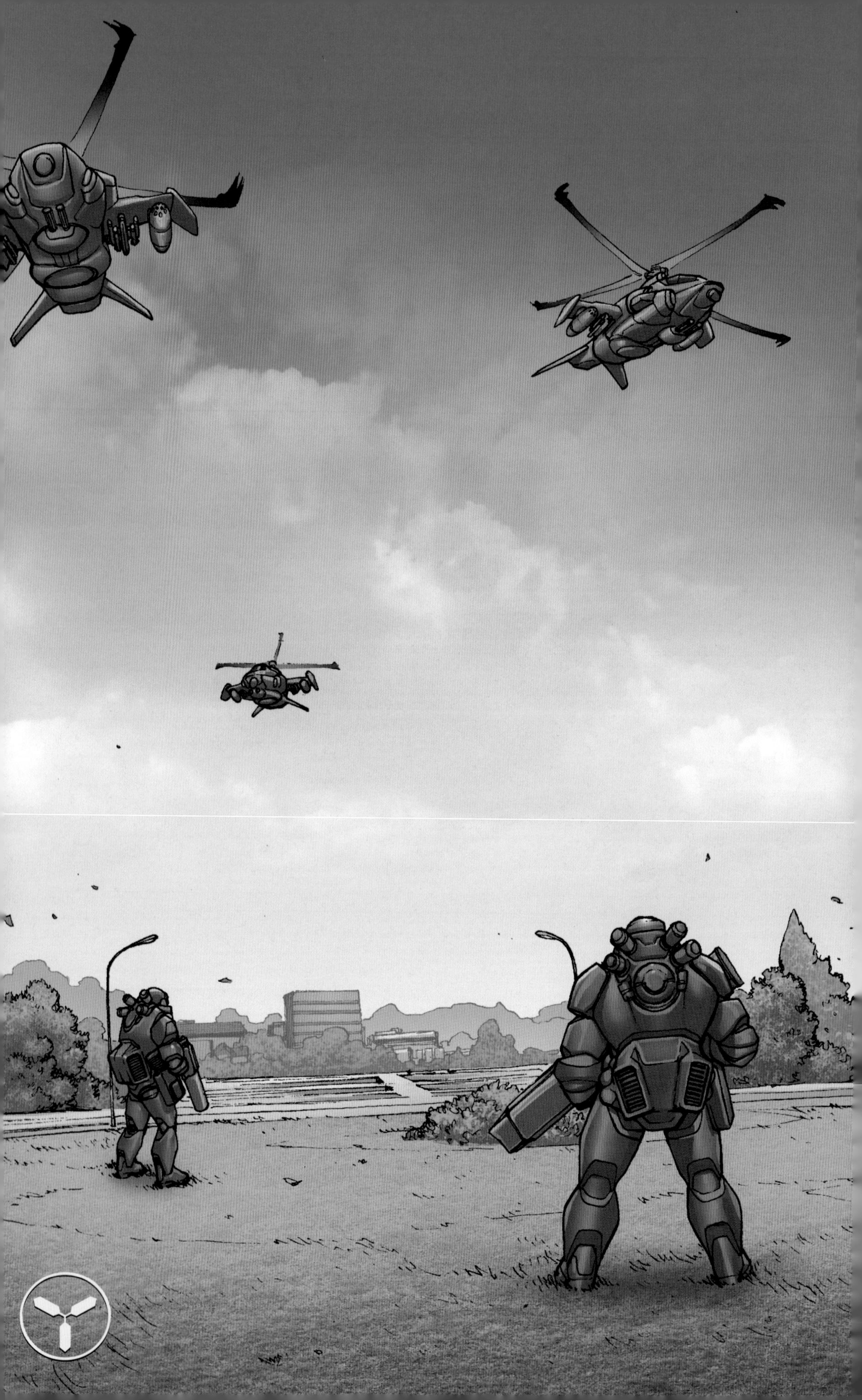

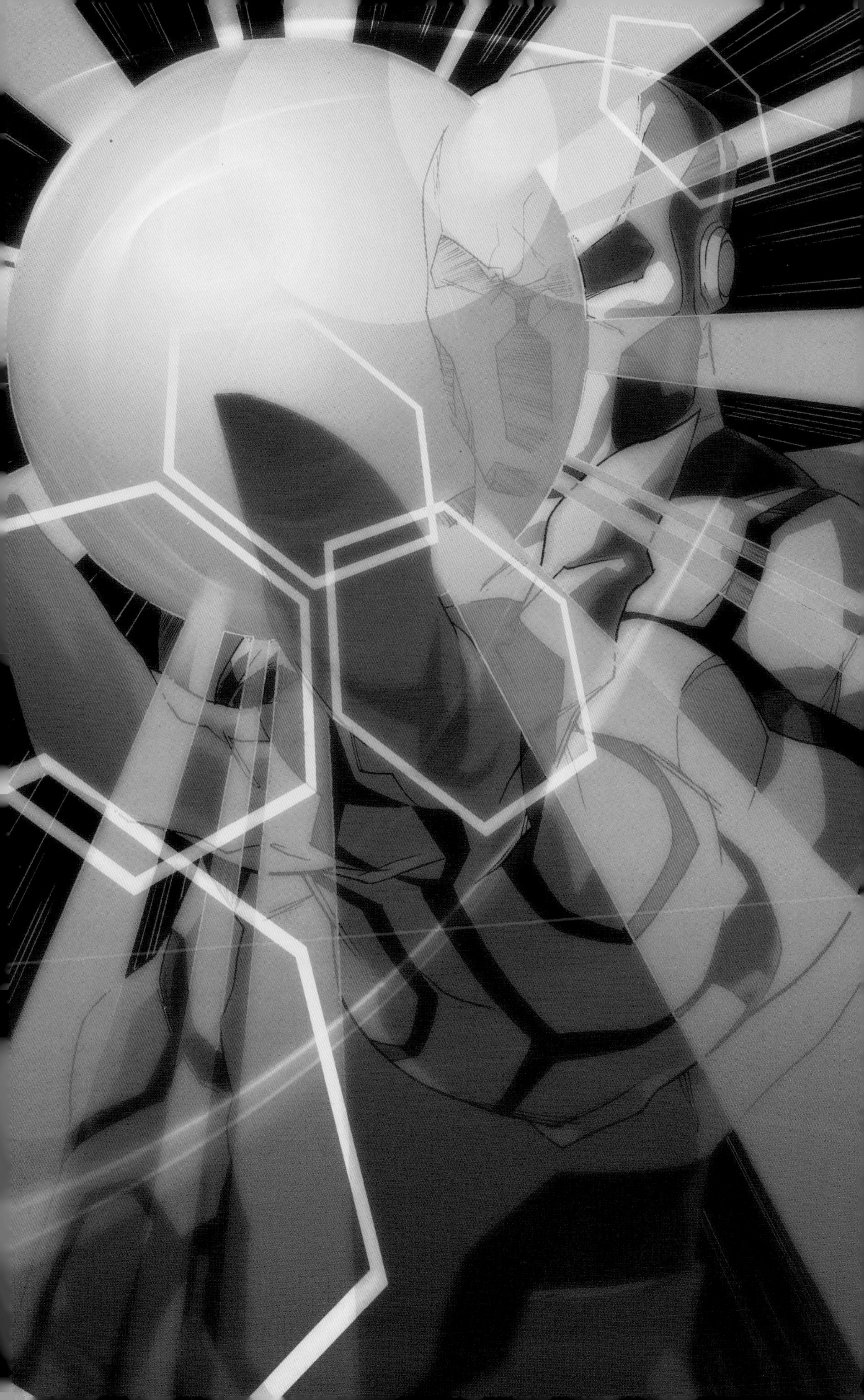

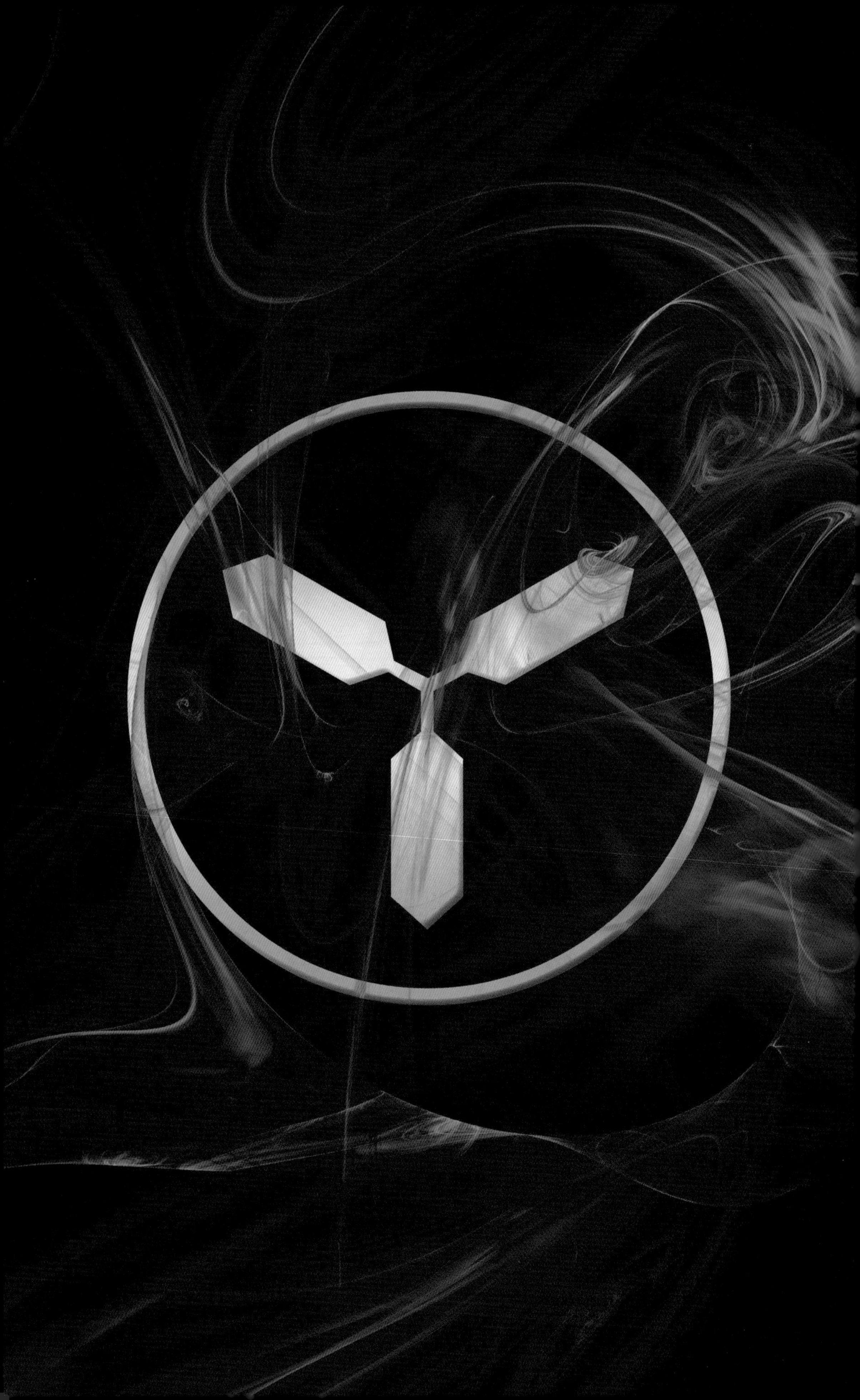

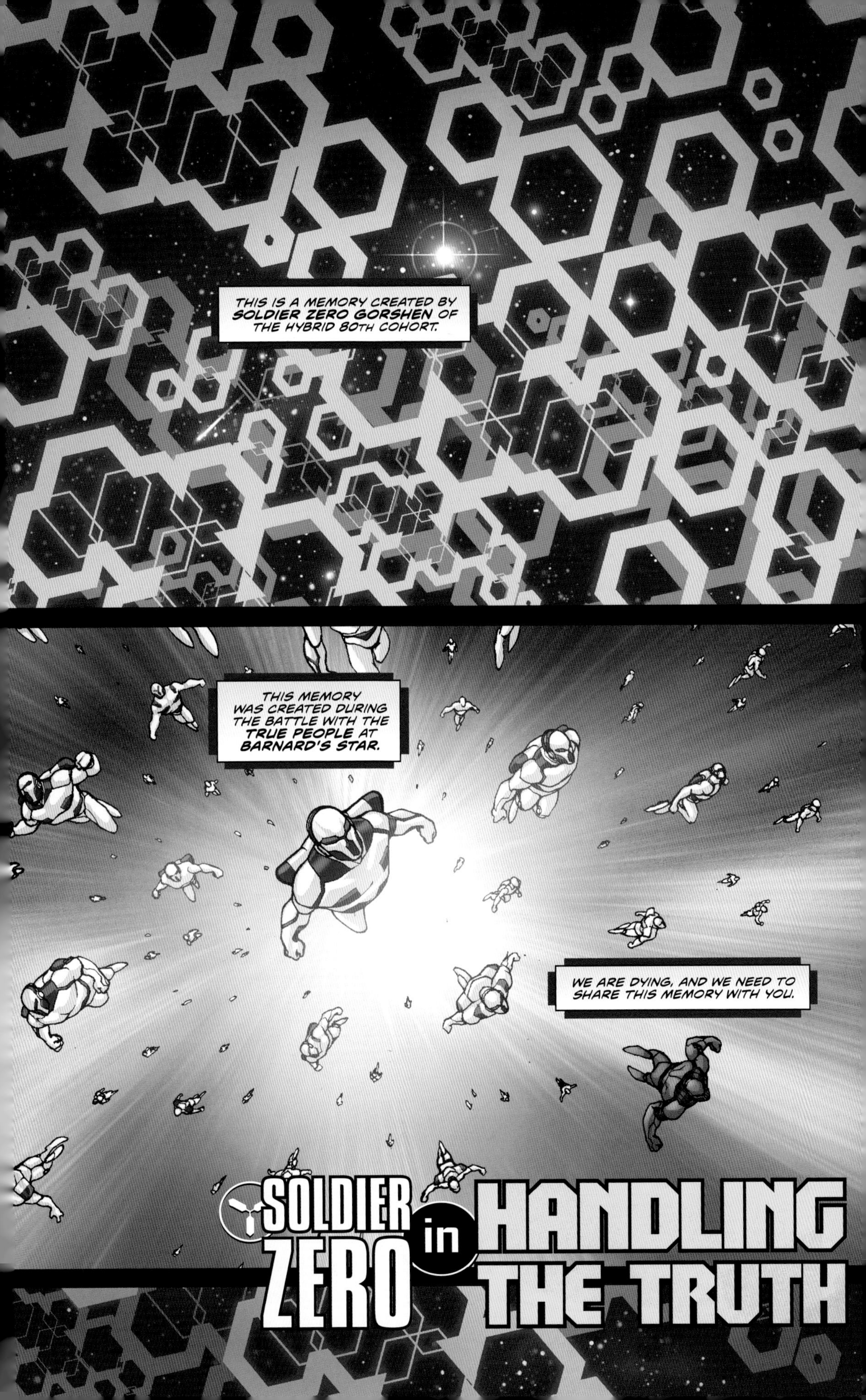
THIS IS A MEMORY CREATED BY SOLDIER ZERO GORSHEN OF THE HYBRID 80TH COHORT.
THIS MEMORY WAS CREATED DURING THE BATTLE WITH THE TRUE PEOPLE AT BARNARD'S STAR.
WE ARE DYING, AND WE NEED TO SHARE THIS MEMORY WITH YOU.
SOLDIER ZERO in HANDLING THE TRUTH

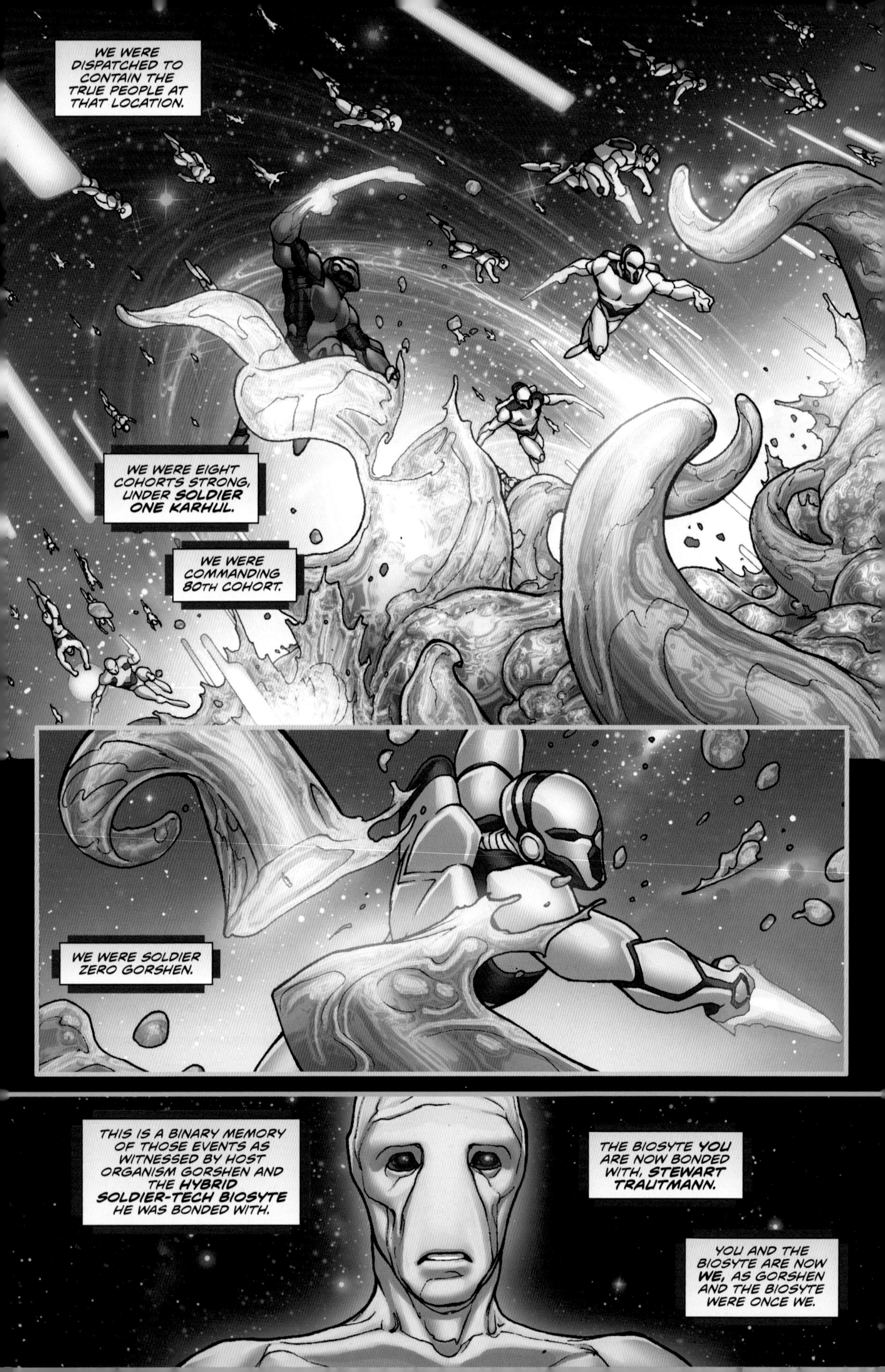

WE WERE DISPATCHED TO CONTAIN THE TRUE PEOPLE AT THAT LOCATION.
WE WERE EIGHT COHORTS STRONG, UNDER SOLDIER ONE KARHUL.
WE WERE COMMANDING 80TH COHORT.
WE WERE SOLDIER ZERO GORSHEN.
THIS IS A BINARY MEMORY OF THOSE EVENTS AS WITNESSED BY HOST ORGANISM GORSHEN AND THE HYBRID SOLDIER-TECH BIOSYTE HE WAS BONDED WITH.
THE BIOSYTE YOU ARE NOW BONDED WITH, STEWART TRAUTMANN.
YOU AND THE BIOSYTE ARE NOW WE, AS GORSHEN AND THE BIOSYTE WERE ONCE WE.

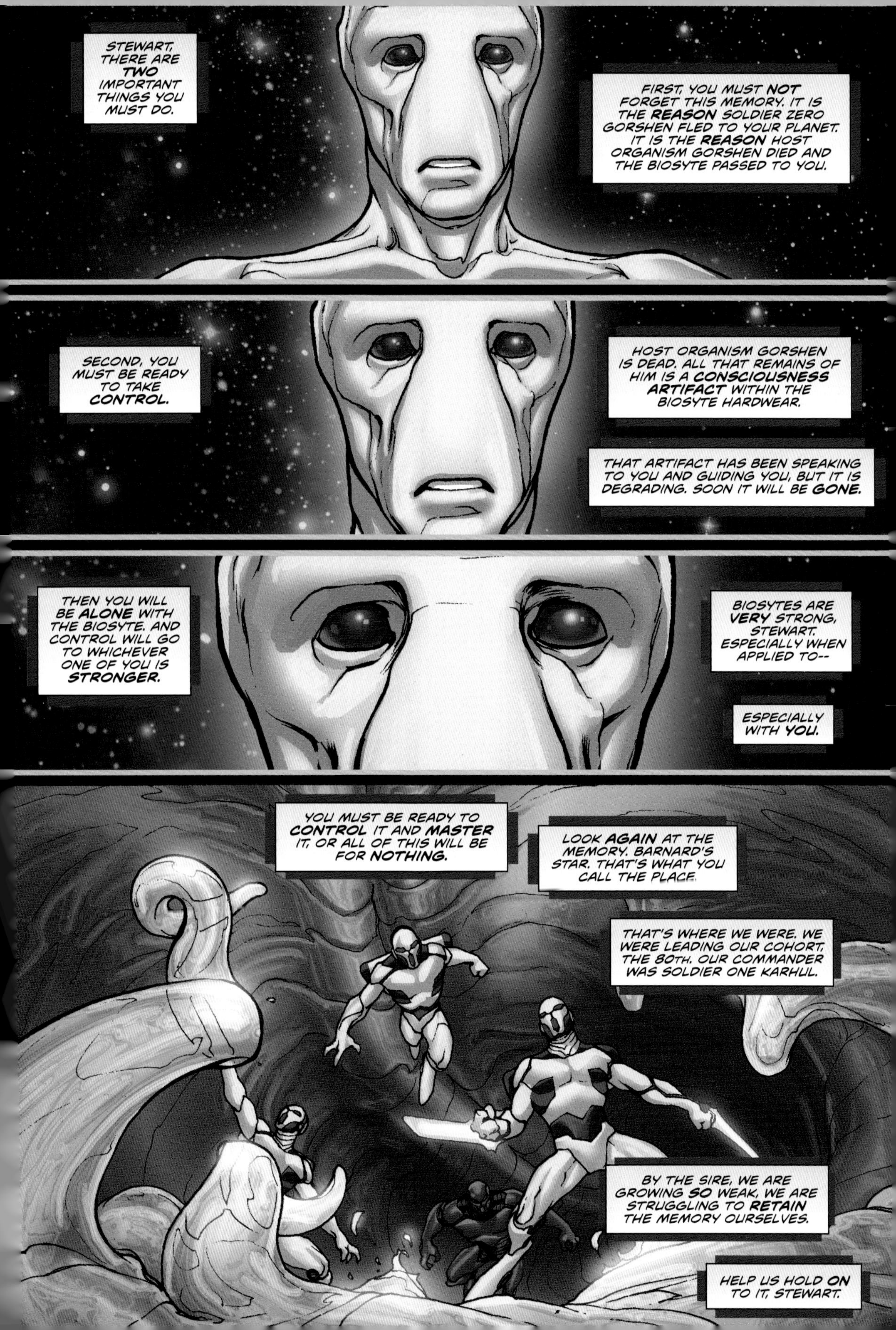
STEWART, THERE ARE TWO IMPORTANT THINGS YOU MUST DO.
FIRST, YOU MUST NOT FORGET THIS MEMORY. IT IS THE REASON SOLDIER ZERO GORSHEN FLED TO YOUR PLANET. IT IS THE REASON HOST ORGANISM GORSHEN DIED AND THE BIOSYTE PASSED TO YOU.
SECOND, YOU MUST BE READY TO TAKE CONTROL.
HOST ORGANISM GORSHEN IS DEAD. ALL THAT REMAINS OF HIM IS A CONSCIOUSNESS ARTIFACT WITHIN THE BIOSYTE HARDWEAR.
THAT ARTIFACT HAS BEEN SPEAKING TO YOU AND GUIDING YOU, BUT IT IS DEGRADING. SOON IT WILL BE GONE.
THEN YOU WILL BE ALONE WITH THE BIOSYTE. AND CONTROL WILL GO TO WHICHEVER ONE OF YOU IS STRONGER.
BIOSYTES ARE VERY STRONG, STEWART. ESPECIALLY WHEN APPLIED TO--
ESPECIALLY WITH YOU.
YOU MUST BE READY TO CONTROL IT AND MASTER IT, OR ALL OF THIS WILL BE FOR NOTHING.
LOOK AGAIN AT THE MEMORY. BARNARD'S STAR. THAT'S WHAT YOU CALL THE PLACE.
THAT'S WHERE WE WERE. WE WERE LEADING OUR COHORT, THE 80TH. OUR COMMANDER WAS SOLDIER ONE KARHUL.
BY THE SIRE, WE ARE GROWING SO WEAK, WE ARE STRUGGLING TO RETAIN THE MEMORY OURSELVES.
HELP US HOLD ON TO IT, STEWART.

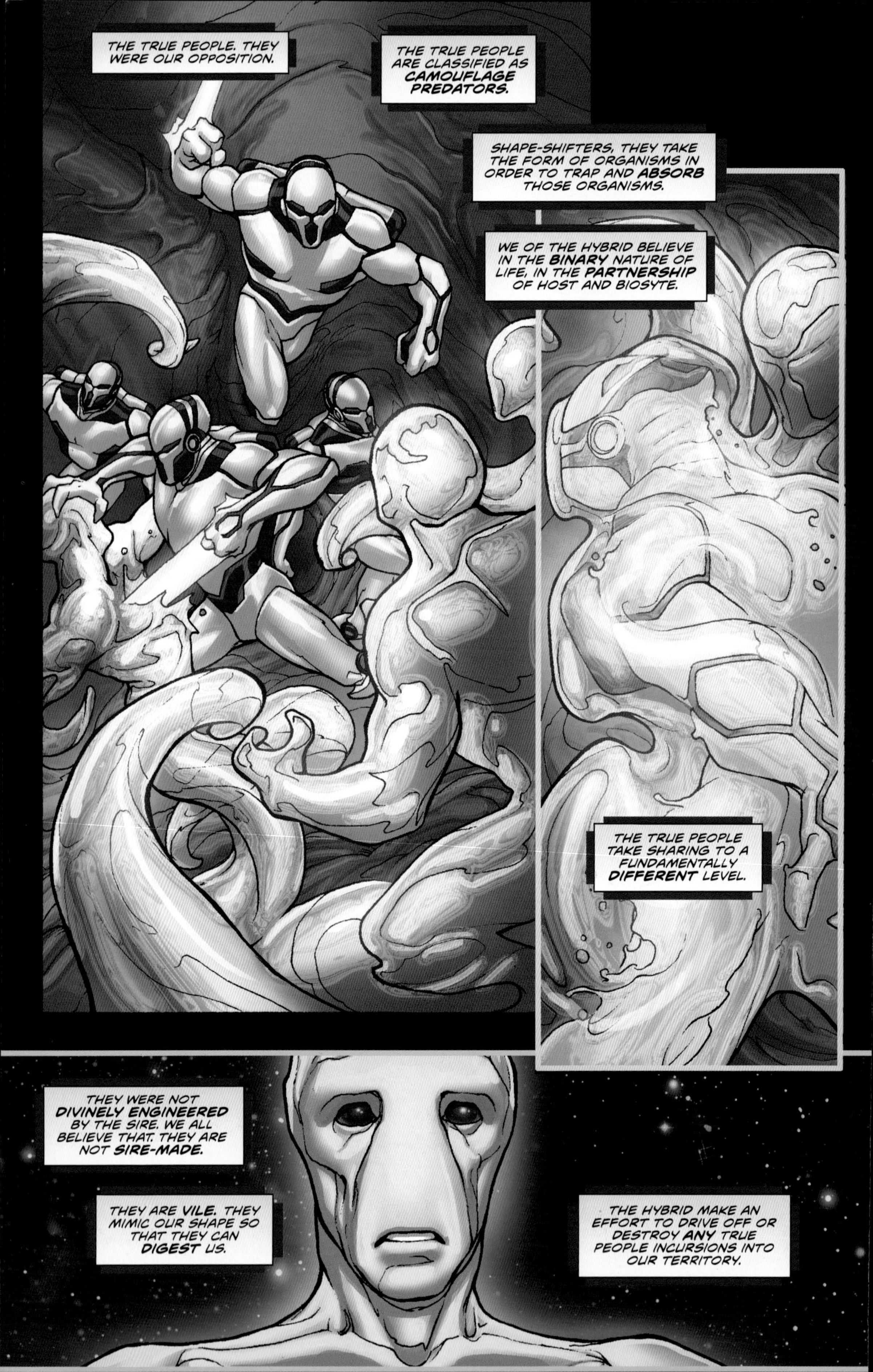
THE TRUE PEOPLE. THEY WERE OUR OPPOSITION.
THE TRUE PEOPLE ARE CLASSIFIED AS CAMOUFLAGE PREDATORS.
SHAPE-SHIFTERS, THEY TAKE THE FORM OF ORGANISMS IN ORDER TO TRAP AND ABSORB THOSE ORGANISMS.
WE OF THE HYBRID BELIEVE IN THE BINARY NATURE OF LIFE, IN THE PARTNERSHIP OF HOST AND BIOSYTE.
THE TRUE PEOPLE TAKE SHARING TO A FUNDAMENTALLY DIFFERENT LEVEL.
THEY WERE NOT DIVINELY ENGINEERED BY THE SIRE. WE ALL BELIEVE THAT. THEY ARE NOT SIRE-MADE.
THEY ARE VILE. THEY MIMIC OUR SHAPE SO THAT THEY CAN DIGEST US.
THE HYBRID MAKE AN EFFORT TO DRIVE OFF OR DESTROY ANY TRUE PEOPLE INCURSIONS INTO OUR TERRITORY.

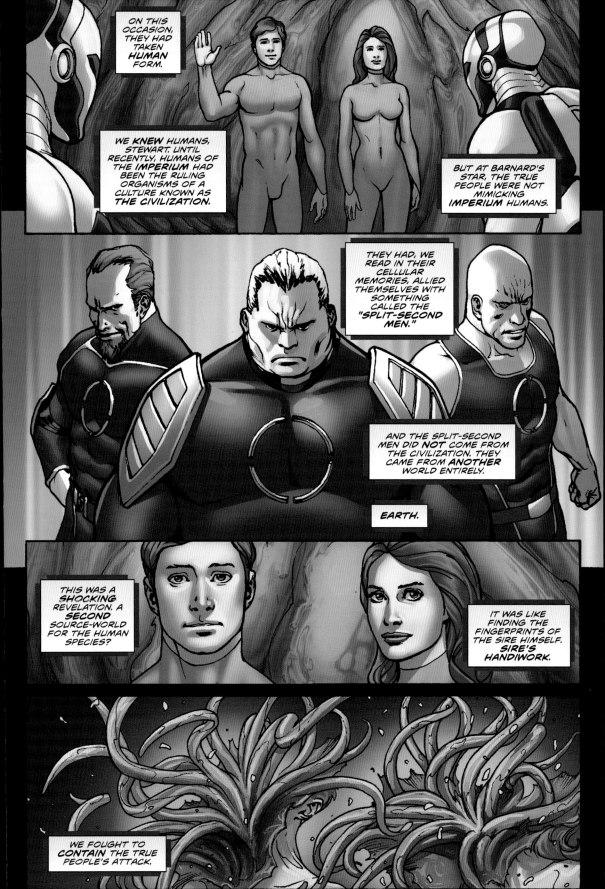

ON THIS OCCASION, THEY HAD TAKEN **HUMAN** FORM.

WE **KNEW** HUMANS, STEWART. UNTIL RECENTLY, HUMANS OF THE **IMPERIUM** HAD BEEN THE RULING ORGANISMS OF A CULTURE KNOWN AS **THE CIVILIZATION.**

BUT AT BARNARD'S STAR, THE TRUE PEOPLE WERE NOT MIMICKING **IMPERIUM** HUMANS.

THEY HAD, WE READ IN THEIR CELLULAR MEMORIES, ALLIED THEMSELVES WITH SOMETHING CALLED THE "SPLIT-SECOND MEN."

AND THE SPLIT-SECOND MEN DID **NOT** COME FROM THE CIVILIZATION. THEY CAME FROM **ANOTHER** WORLD ENTIRELY.

EARTH.

THIS WAS A **SHOCKING** REVELATION. A **SECOND** SOURCE-WORLD FOR THE HUMAN SPECIES?

IT WAS LIKE FINDING THE FINGERPRINTS OF THE SIRE HIMSELF. **SIRE'S** HANDIWORK.

WE FOUGHT TO **CONTAIN** THE TRUE PEOPLE'S ATTACK.

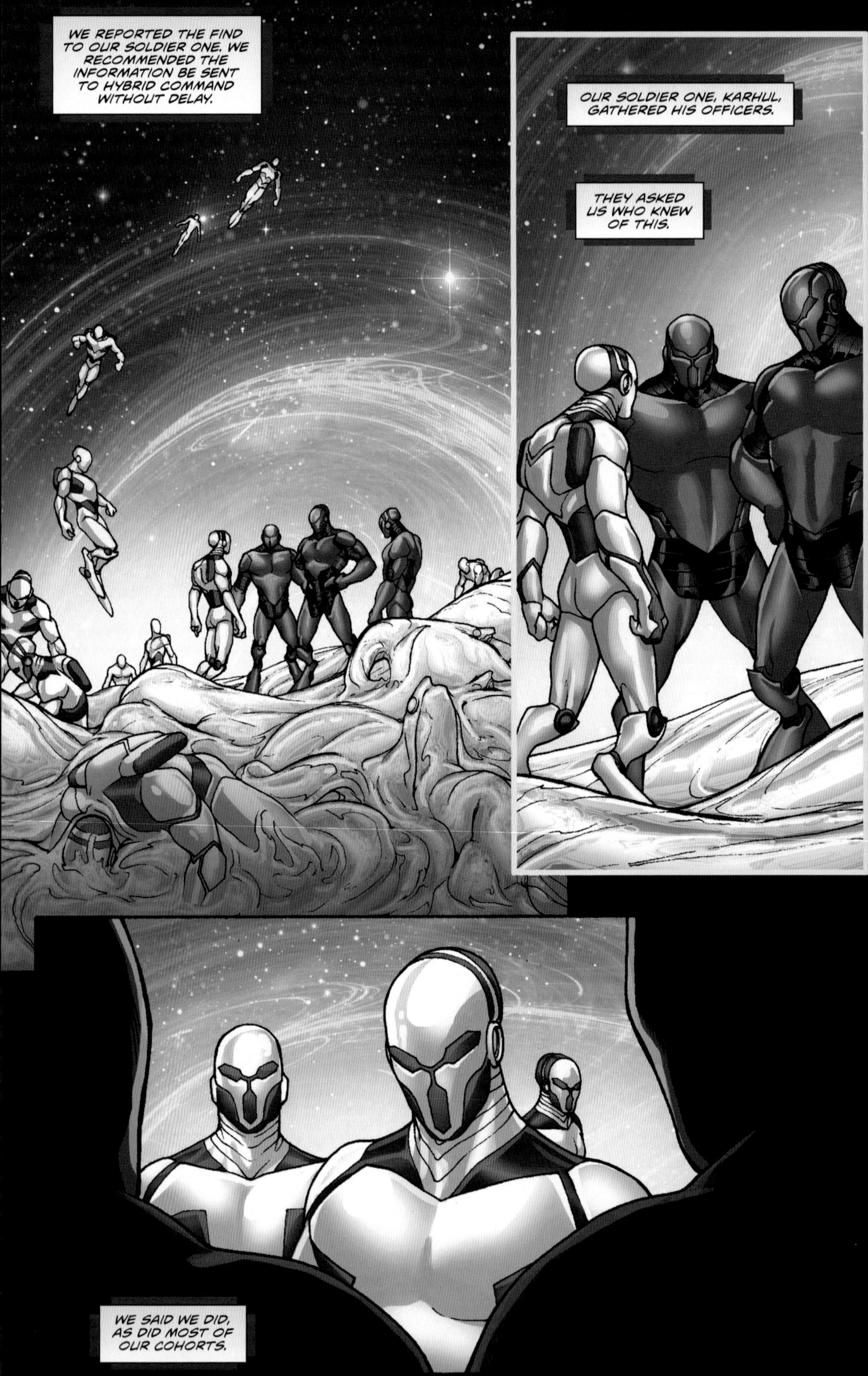
WE REPORTED THE FIND TO OUR SOLDIER ONE. WE RECOMMENDED THE INFORMATION BE SENT TO HYBRID COMMAND WITHOUT DELAY.
OUR SOLDIER ONE, KARHUL, GATHERED HIS OFFICERS.
THEY ASKED US WHO KNEW OF THIS.
WE SAID WE DID, AS DID MOST OF OUR COHORTS.

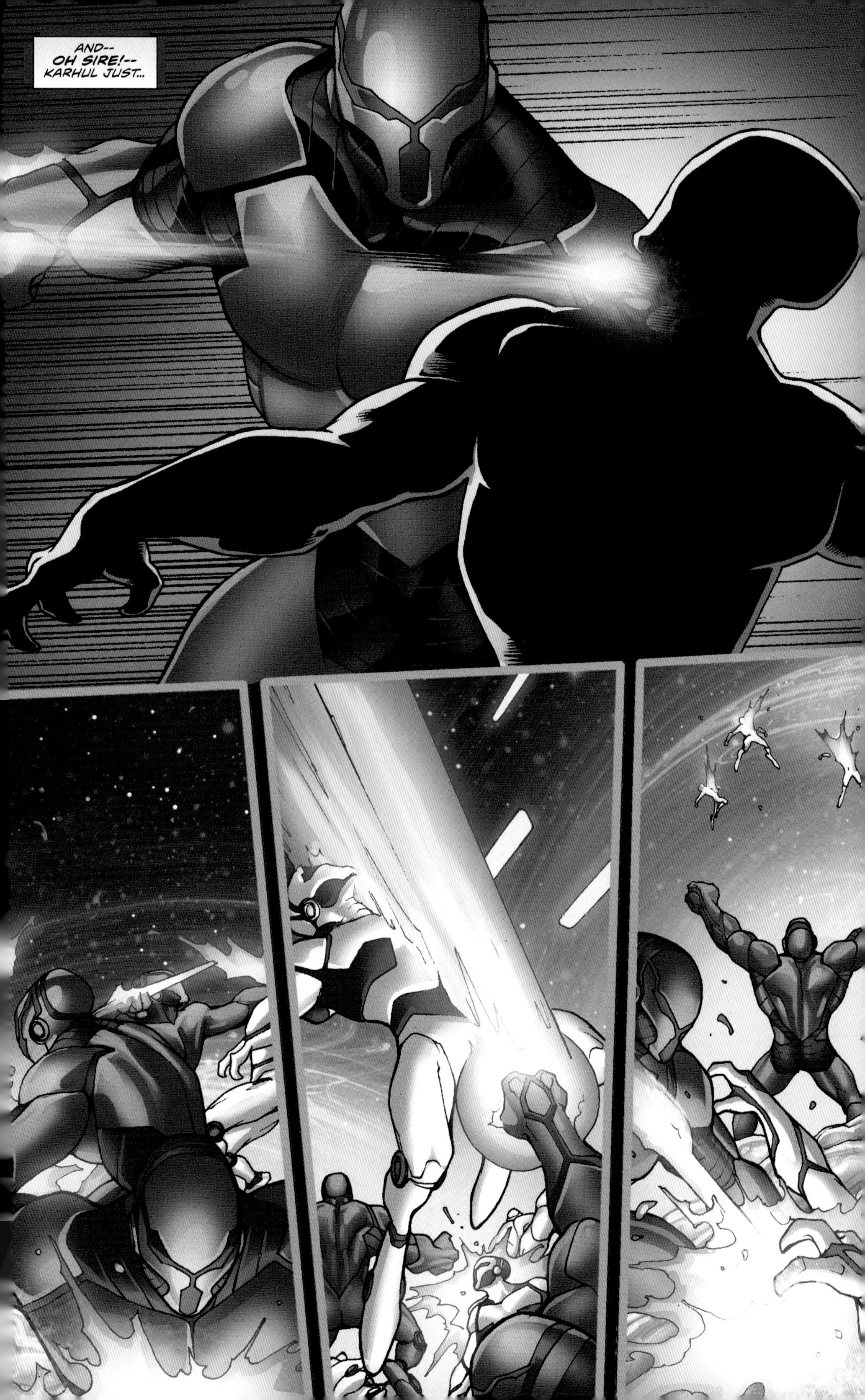
AND--
OH SIRE!--
KARHUL JUST...

WE DID THE ONLY THING WE COULD DO, STEWART. WE RAN...

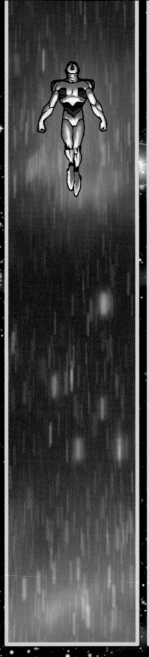

...AND THEY CAME AFTER US.

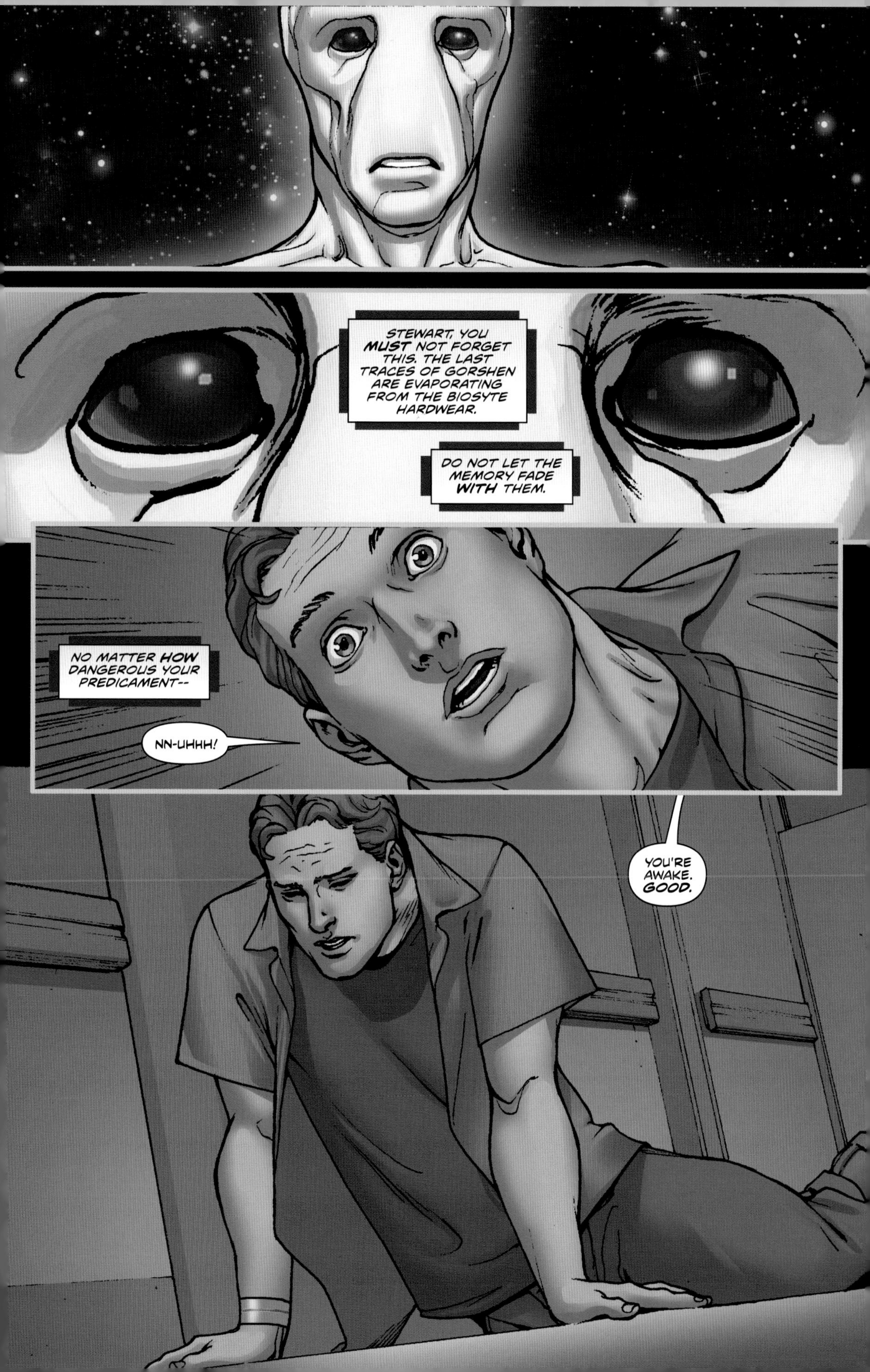
STEWART, YOU MUST NOT FORGET THIS. THE LAST TRACES OF GORSHEN ARE EVAPORATING FROM THE BIOSYTE HARDWEAR.
DO NOT LET THE MEMORY FADE WITH THEM.
NO MATTER HOW DANGEROUS YOUR PREDICAMENT--
NN-UHHH!
YOU'RE AWAKE. GOOD.

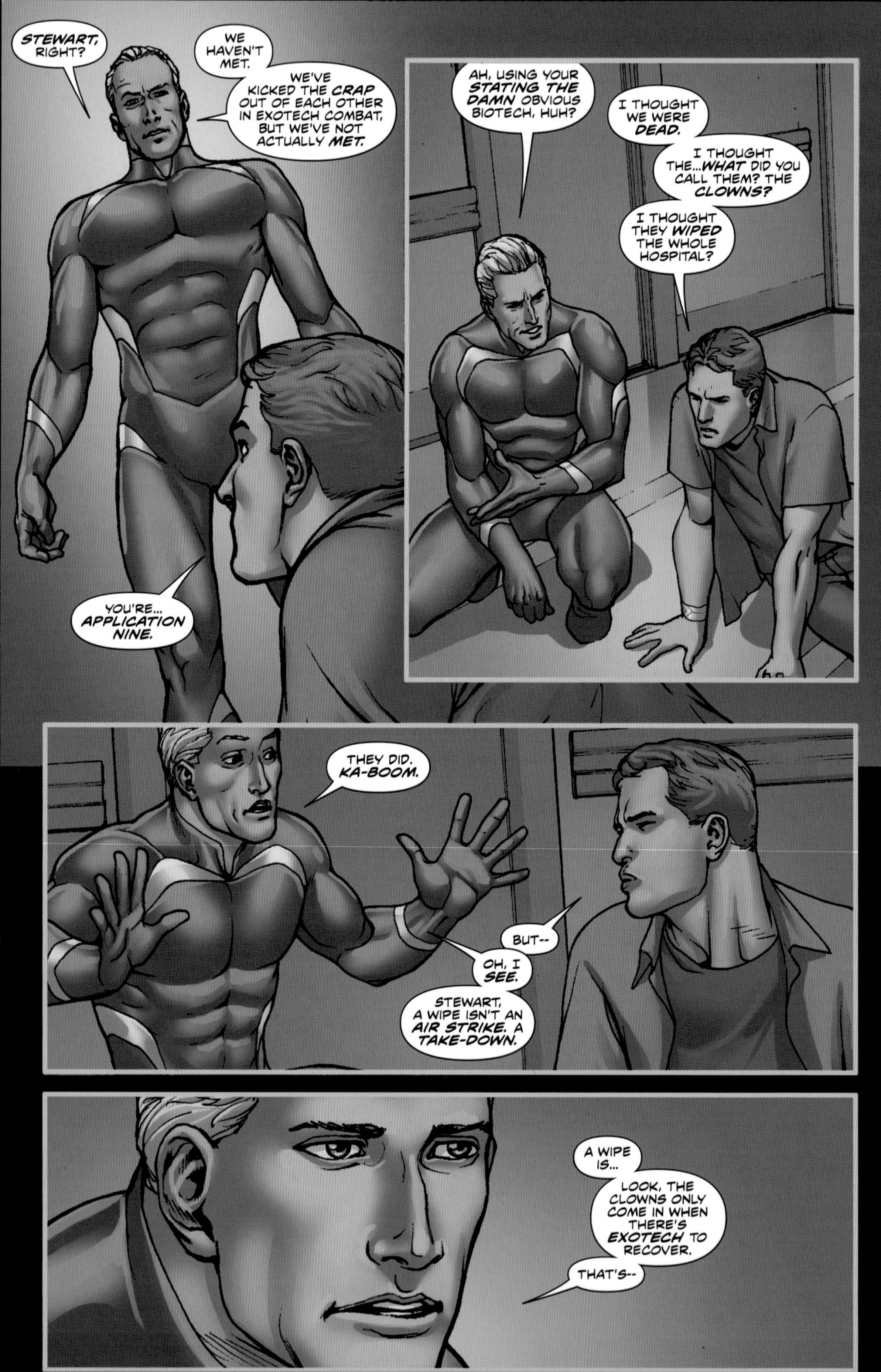
STEWART, RIGHT?
WE HAVEN'T MET.
WE'VE KICKED THE CRAP OUT OF EACH OTHER IN EXOTECH COMBAT, BUT WE'VE NOT ACTUALLY MET.
YOU'RE... APPLICATION NINE.
AH, USING YOUR STATING THE DAMN OBVIOUS BIOTECH, HUH?
I THOUGHT WE WERE DEAD.
I THOUGHT THE...WHAT DID YOU CALL THEM? THE CLOWNS?
I THOUGHT THEY WIPED THE WHOLE HOSPITAL?
THEY DID. KA-BOOM.
BUT--
OH, I SEE.
STEWART, A WIPE ISN'T AN AIR STRIKE. A TAKE-DOWN.
A WIPE IS...
LOOK, THE CLOWNS ONLY COME IN WHEN THERE'S EXOTECH TO RECOVER.
THAT'S--

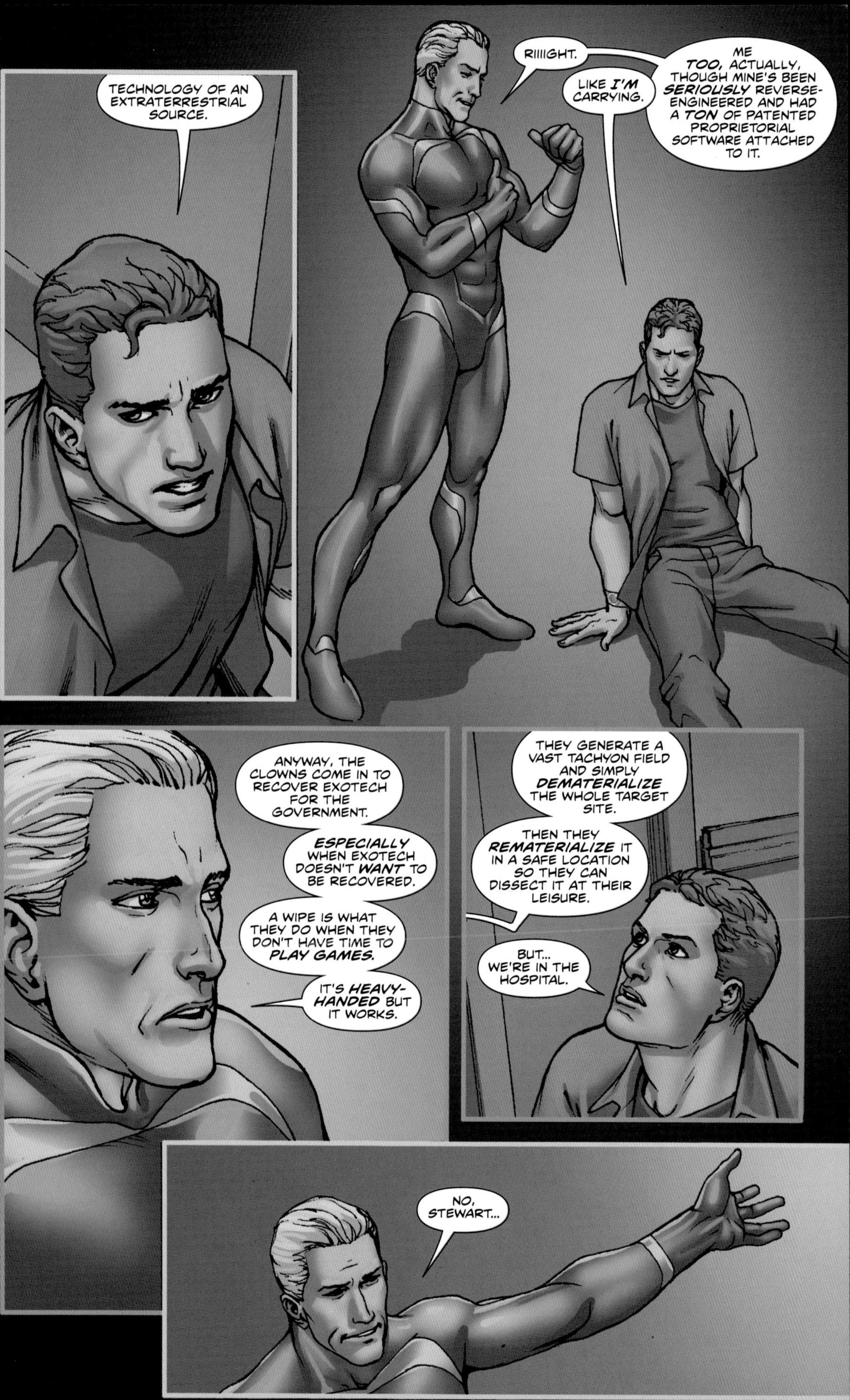
TECHNOLOGY OF AN EXTRATERRESTRIAL SOURCE.
RIIIIGHT.
LIKE *I'M* CARRYING.
ME *TOO,* ACTUALLY, THOUGH MINE'S BEEN *SERIOUSLY* REVERSE-ENGINEERED AND HAD A *TON* OF PATENTED PROPRIETORIAL SOFTWARE ATTACHED TO IT.
ANYWAY, THE CLOWNS COME IN TO RECOVER EXOTECH FOR THE GOVERNMENT.
*ESPECIALLY* WHEN EXOTECH DOESN'T *WANT* TO BE RECOVERED.
A WIPE IS WHAT THEY DO WHEN THEY DON'T HAVE TIME TO *PLAY GAMES.*
IT'S *HEAVY-HANDED* BUT IT WORKS.
THEY GENERATE A VAST TACHYON FIELD AND SIMPLY *DEMATERIALIZE* THE WHOLE TARGET SITE.
THEN THEY *REMATERIALIZE* IT IN A SAFE LOCATION SO THEY CAN DISSECT IT AT THEIR LEISURE.
BUT... WE'RE IN THE HOSPITAL.
NO, STEWART...

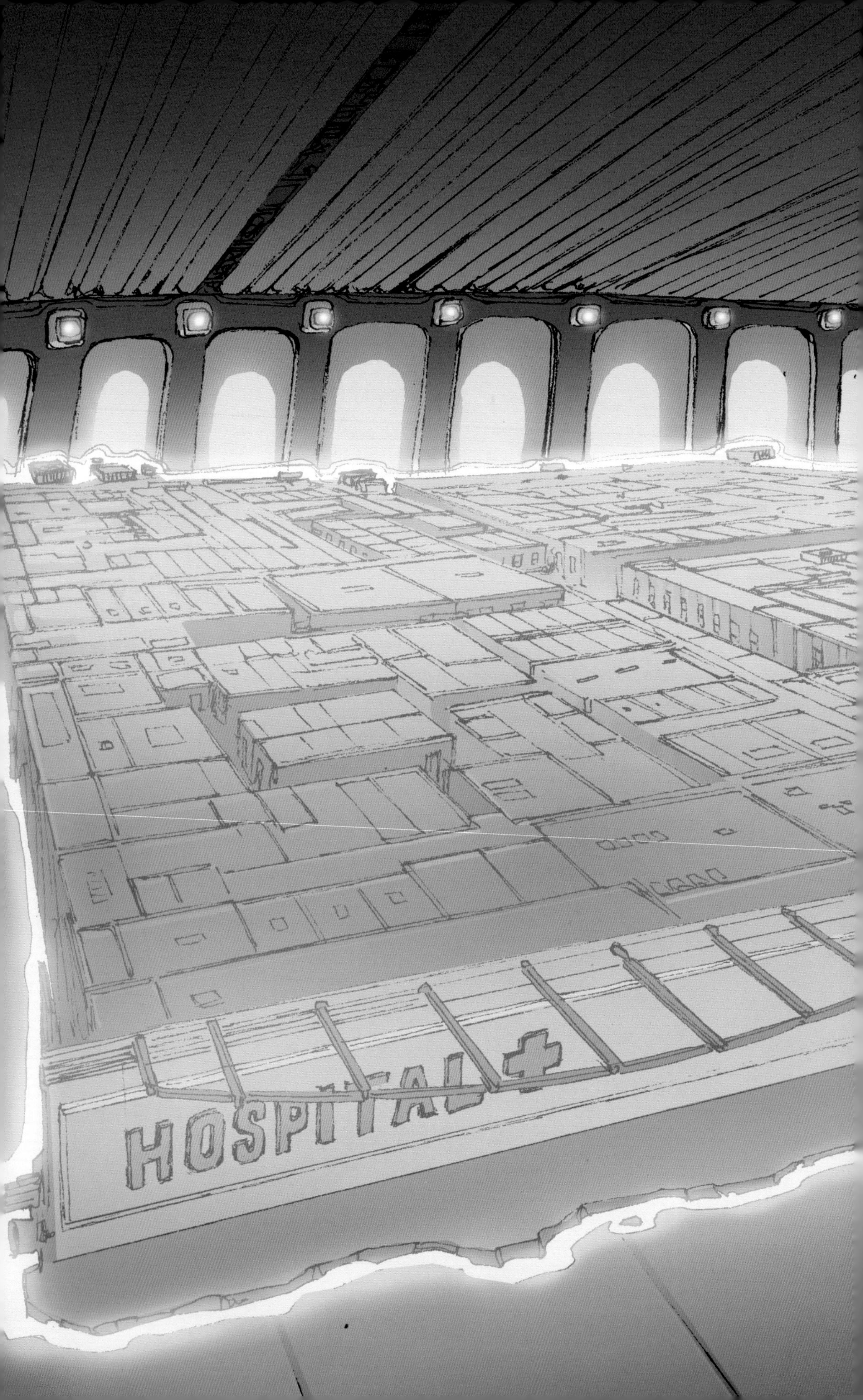
HOSPITAL

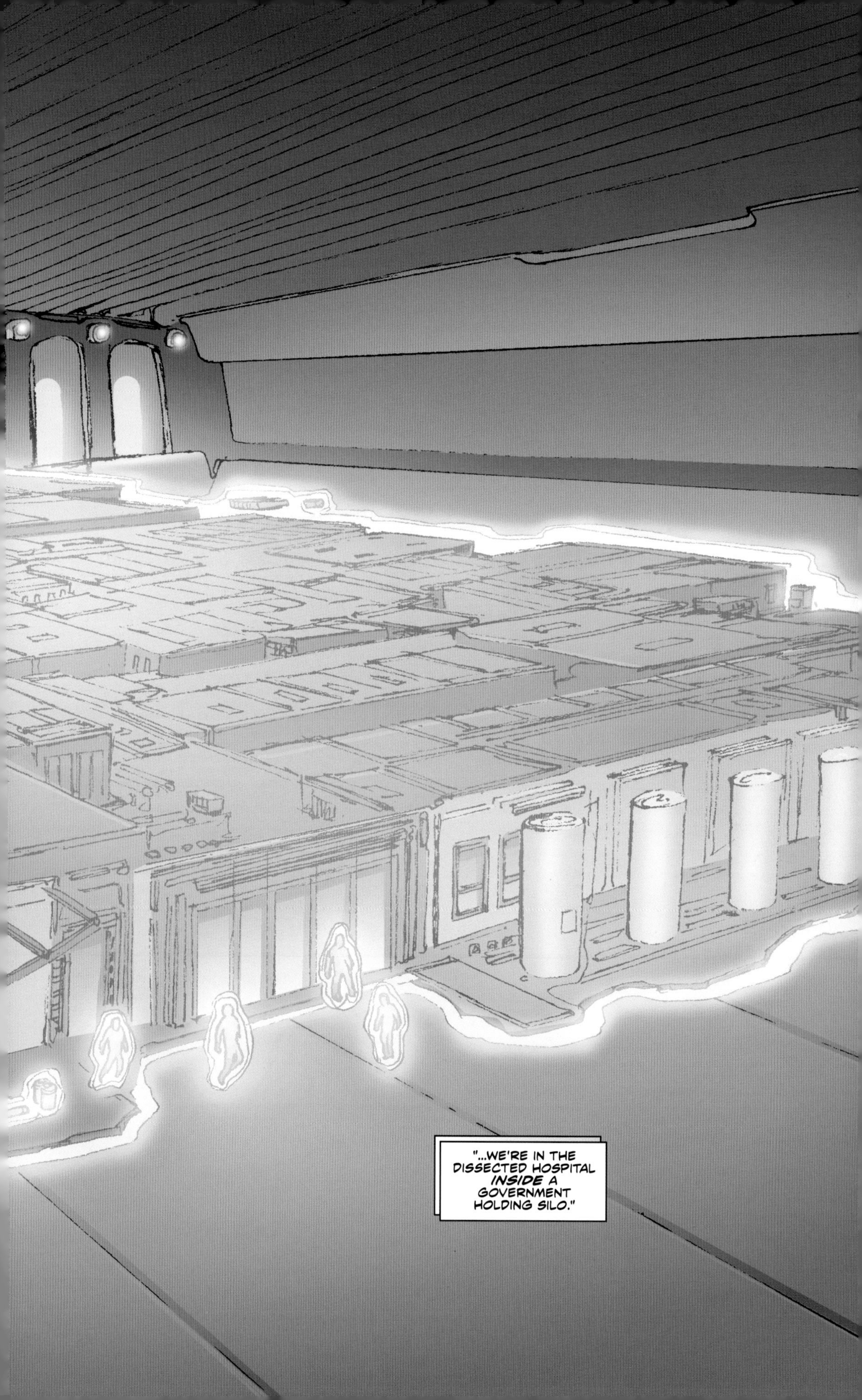
"...WE'RE IN THE DISSECTED HOSPITAL *INSIDE* A GOVERNMENT HOLDING SILO."

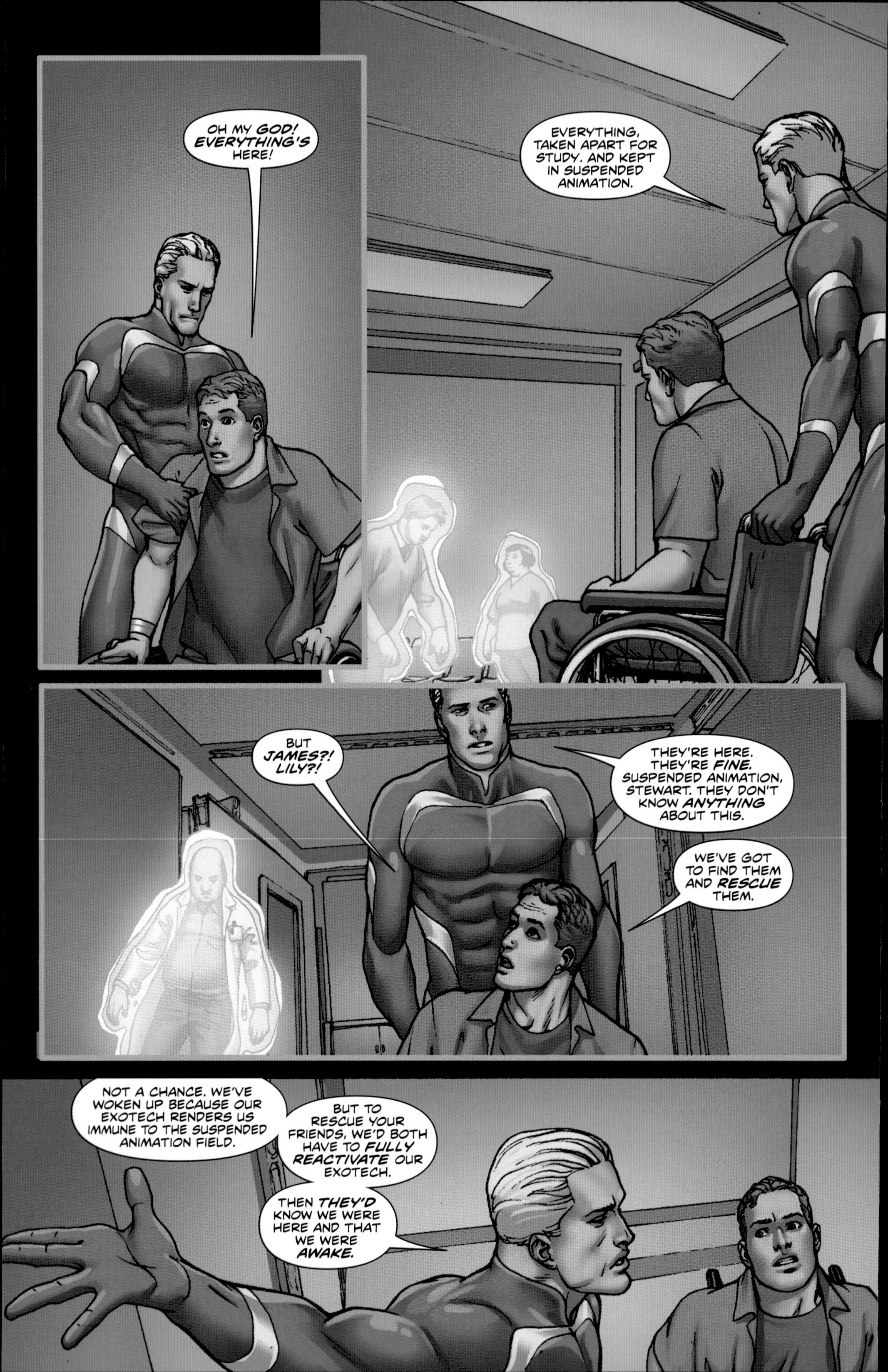
OH MY GOD! EVERYTHING'S HERE!
EVERYTHING, TAKEN APART FOR STUDY. AND KEPT IN SUSPENDED ANIMATION.
BUT JAMES?! LILY?!
THEY'RE HERE. THEY'RE FINE. SUSPENDED ANIMATION, STEWART. THEY DON'T KNOW ANYTHING ABOUT THIS.
WE'VE GOT TO FIND THEM AND RESCUE THEM.
NOT A CHANCE. WE'VE WOKEN UP BECAUSE OUR EXOTECH RENDERS US IMMUNE TO THE SUSPENDED ANIMATION FIELD.
BUT TO RESCUE YOUR FRIENDS, WE'D BOTH HAVE TO FULLY REACTIVATE OUR EXOTECH.
THEN THEY'D KNOW WE WERE HERE AND THAT WE WERE AWAKE.

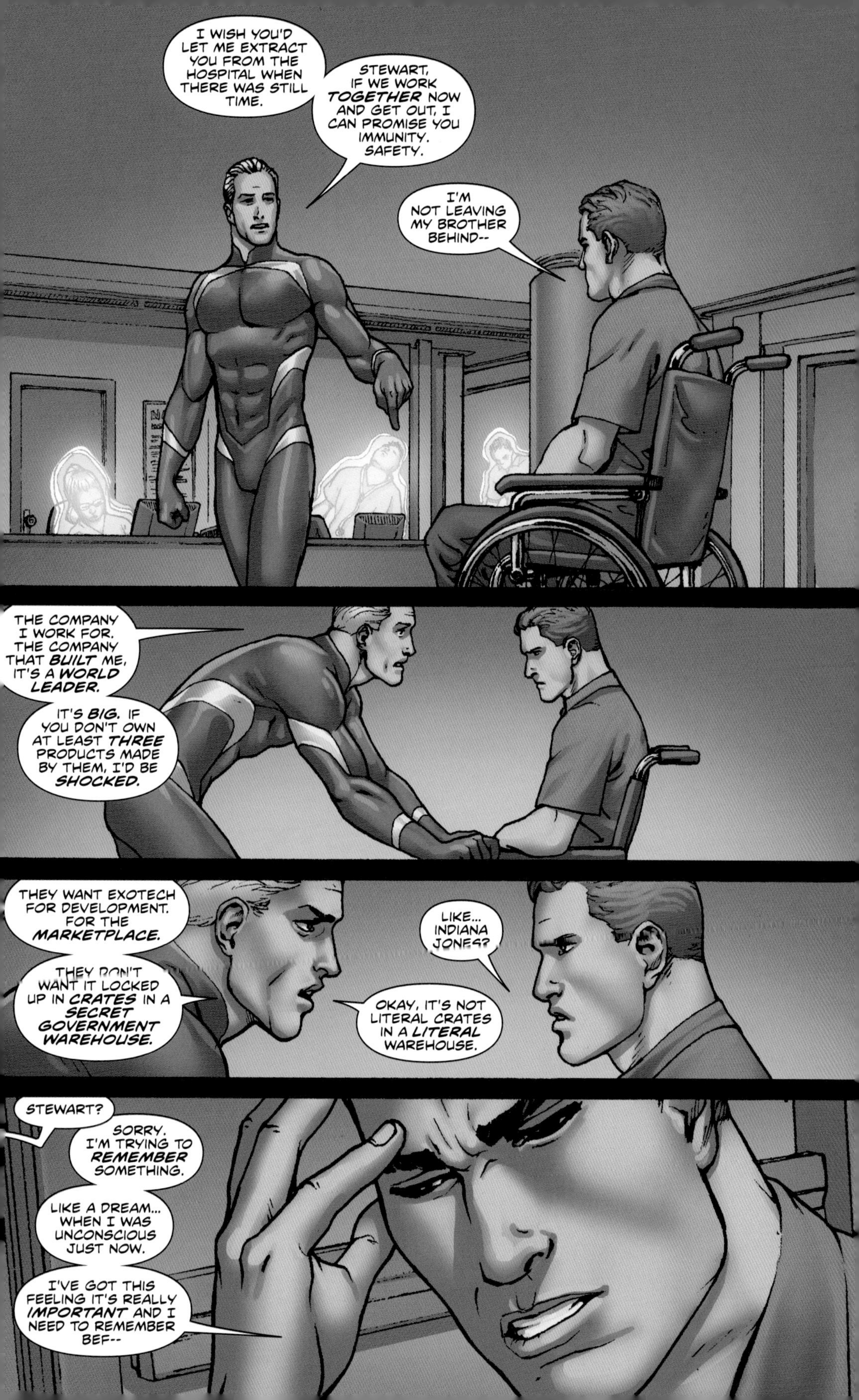
I WISH YOU'D LET ME EXTRACT YOU FROM THE HOSPITAL WHEN THERE WAS STILL TIME.
STEWART, IF WE WORK **TOGETHER** NOW AND GET OUT, I CAN PROMISE YOU IMMUNITY. SAFETY.
I'M NOT LEAVING MY BROTHER BEHIND--
THE COMPANY I WORK FOR. THE COMPANY THAT **BUILT** ME, IT'S A **WORLD LEADER.**
IT'S **BIG.** IF YOU DON'T OWN AT LEAST **THREE** PRODUCTS MADE BY THEM, I'D BE **SHOCKED.**
THEY WANT EXOTECH FOR DEVELOPMENT. FOR THE **MARKETPLACE.**
THEY DON'T WANT IT LOCKED UP IN **CRATES** IN A **SECRET GOVERNMENT WAREHOUSE.**
LIKE... INDIANA JONES?
OKAY, IT'S NOT LITERAL CRATES IN A **LITERAL** WAREHOUSE.
STEWART?
SORRY. I'M TRYING TO **REMEMBER** SOMETHING.
LIKE A DREAM... WHEN I WAS UNCONSCIOUS JUST NOW.
I'VE GOT THIS FEELING IT'S REALLY **IMPORTANT** AND I NEED TO REMEMBER BEF--

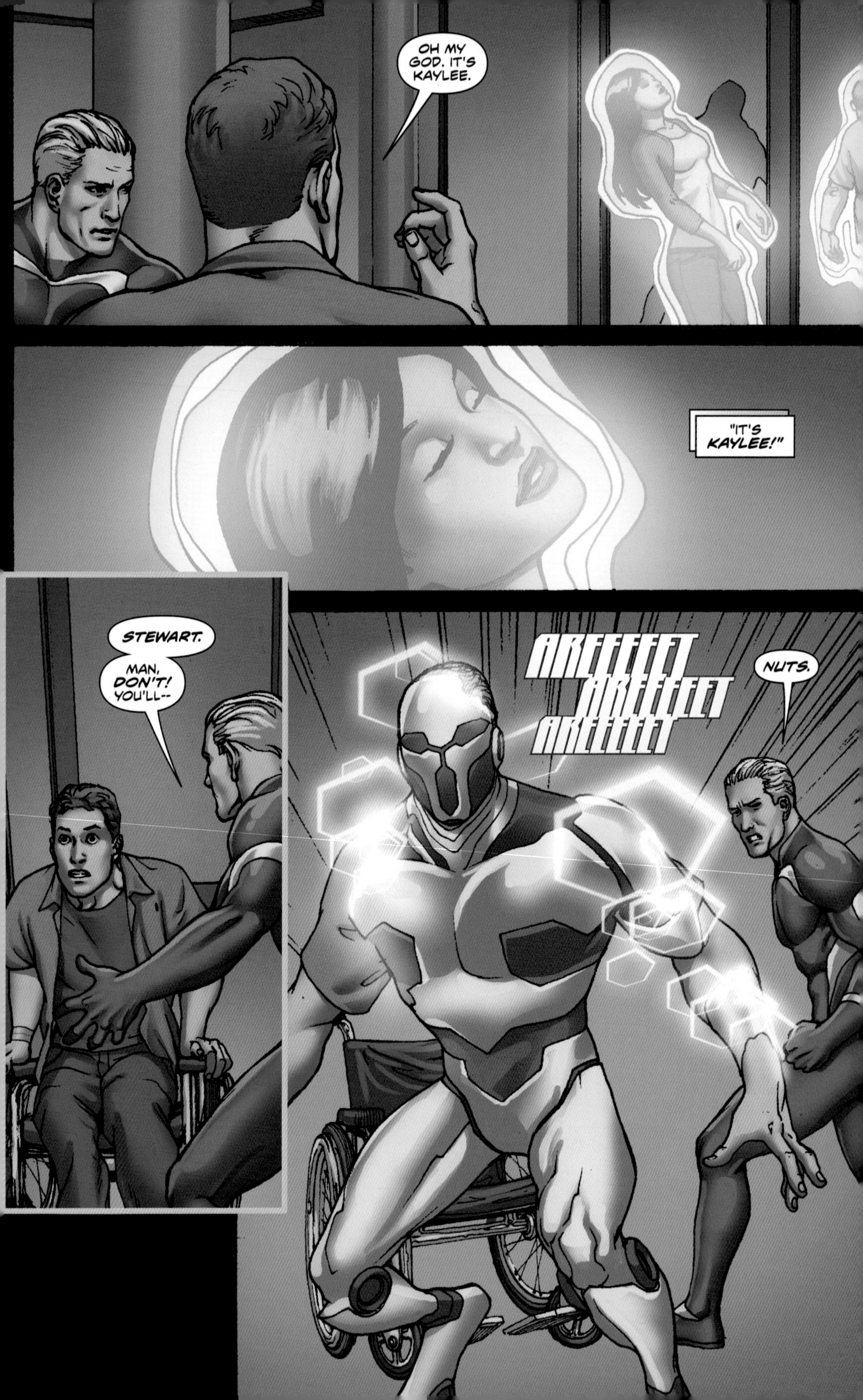

OH MY GOD. IT'S KAYLEE.
"IT'S KAYLEE!"
STEWART.
MAN, DON'T! YOU'LL--
AREEEEET AREEEEET AREEEEET
NUTS.

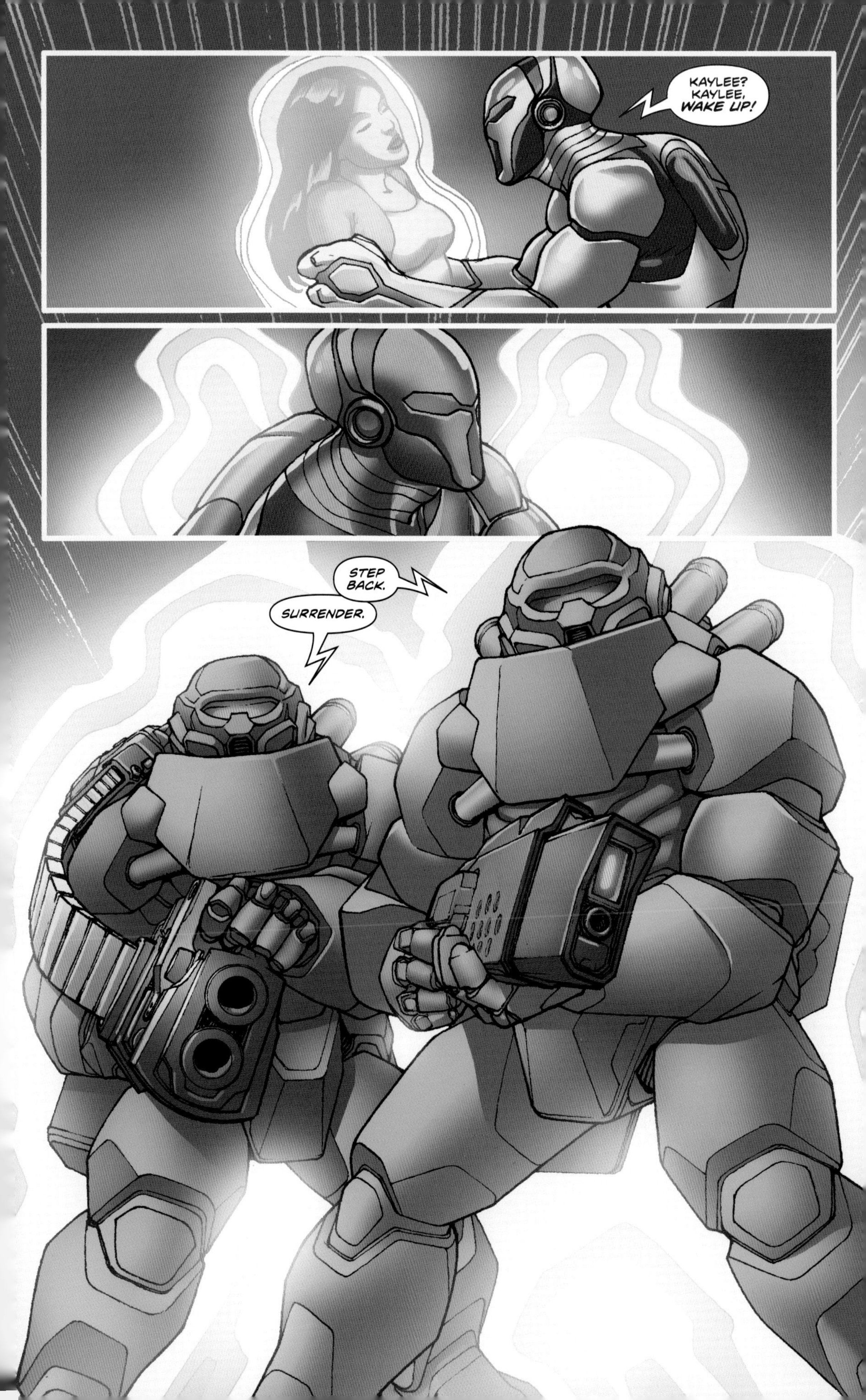
KAYLEE? KAYLEE, WAKE UP!
STEP BACK.
SURRENDER.

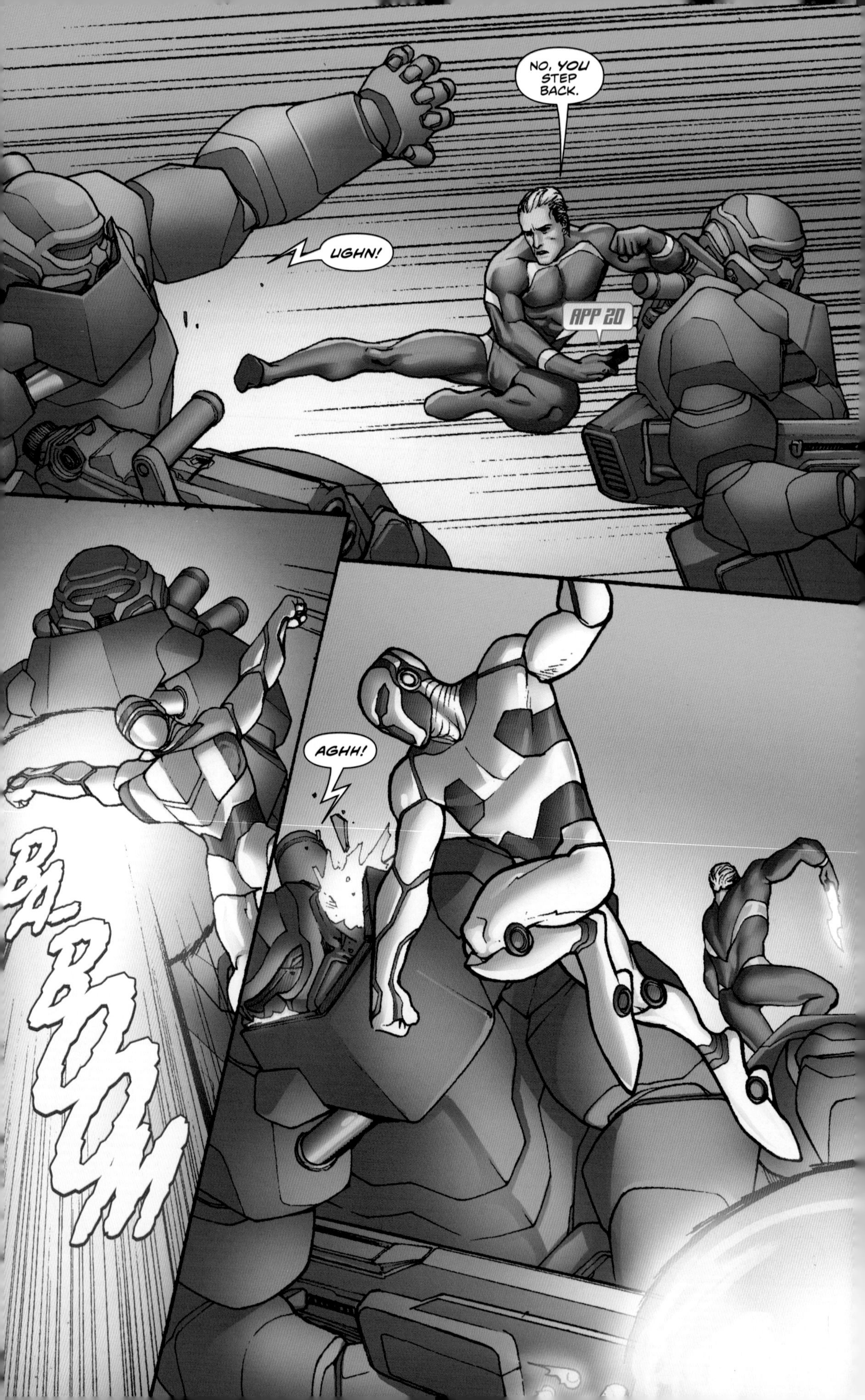
NO, YOU STEP BACK.
UGHN!
APP 20
AGHH!
BA-BOOM

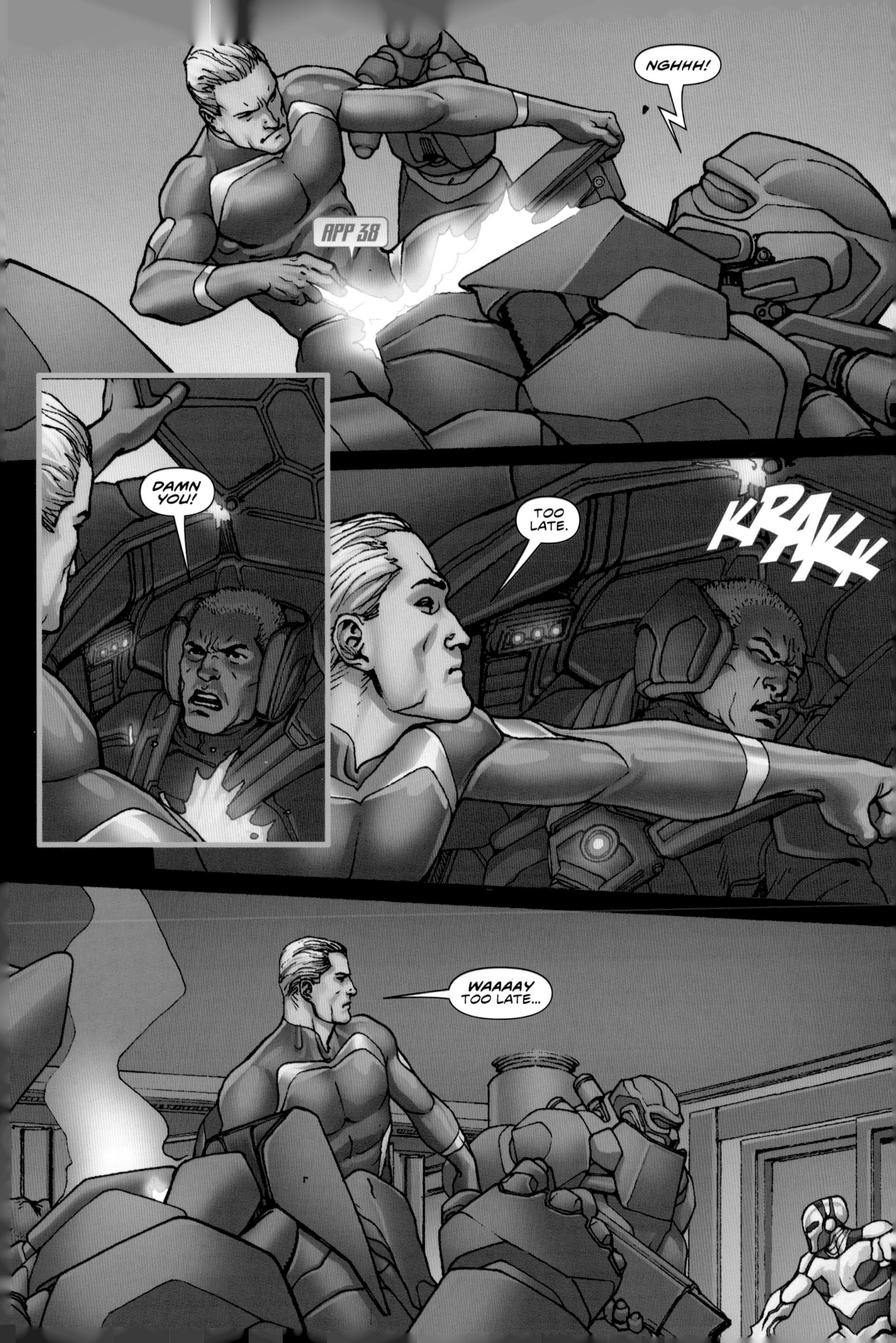
NGHHH!
APP 38
DAMN YOU!
TOO LATE.
KRAKK
WAAAAY TOO LATE...

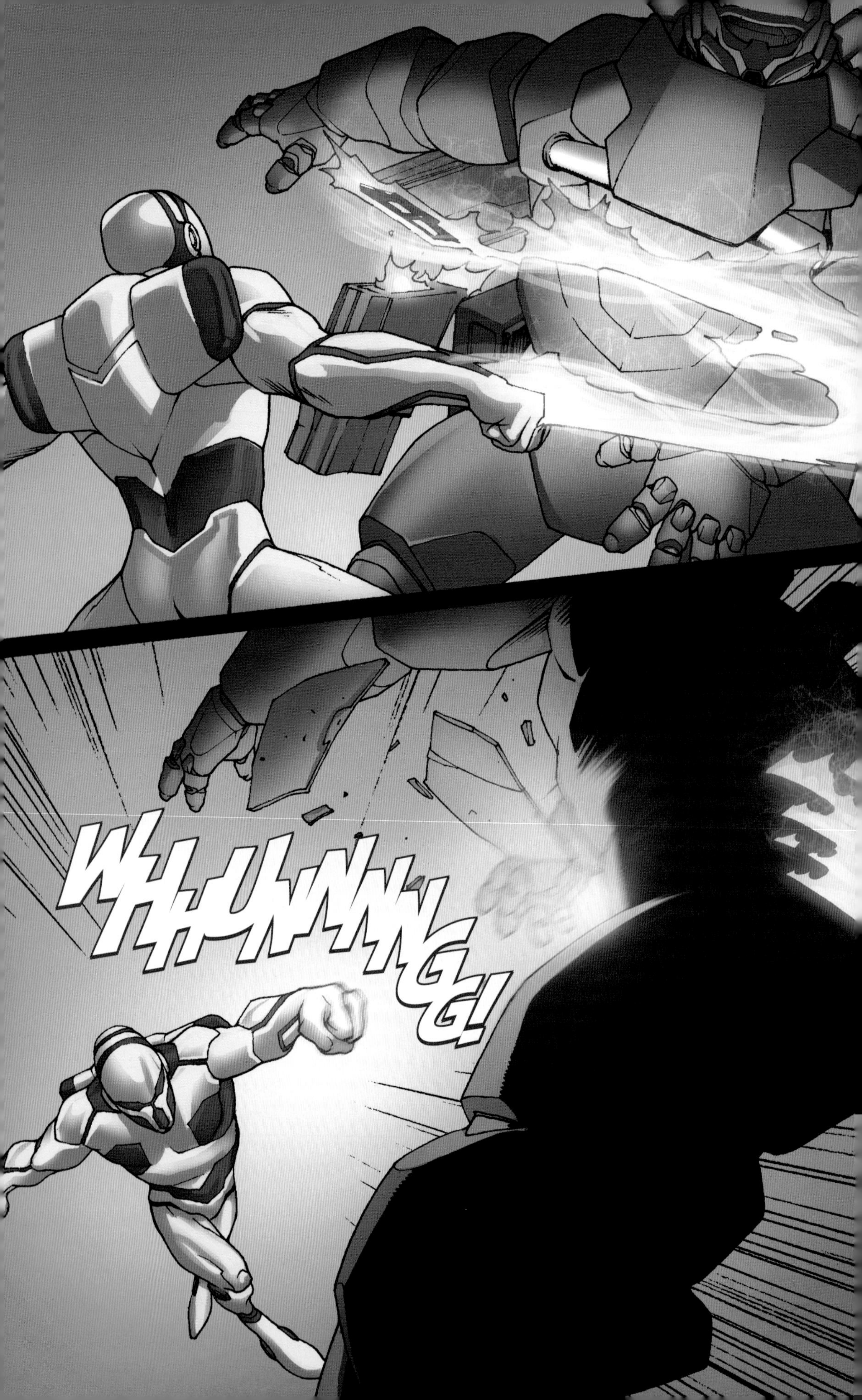
WHHUNNNG!

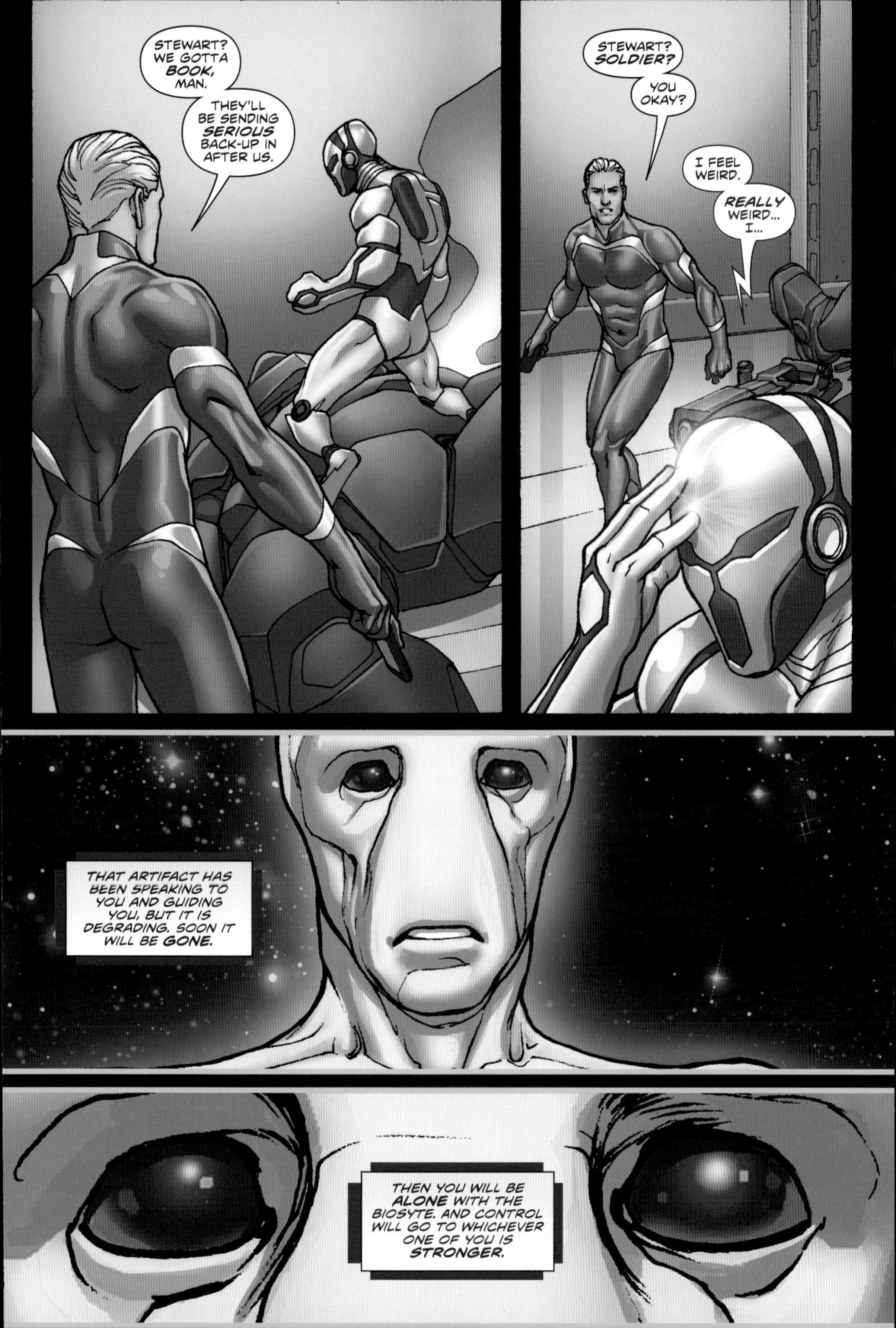
STEWART? WE GOTTA BOOK, MAN.
THEY'LL BE SENDING SERIOUS BACK-UP IN AFTER US.
STEWART? SOLDIER?
YOU OKAY?
I FEEL WEIRD.
REALLY WEIRD... I...
THAT ARTIFACT HAS BEEN SPEAKING TO YOU AND GUIDING YOU, BUT IT IS DEGRADING. SOON IT WILL BE GONE.
THEN YOU WILL BE ALONE WITH THE BIOSYTE. AND CONTROL WILL GO TO WHICHEVER ONE OF YOU IS STRONGER.

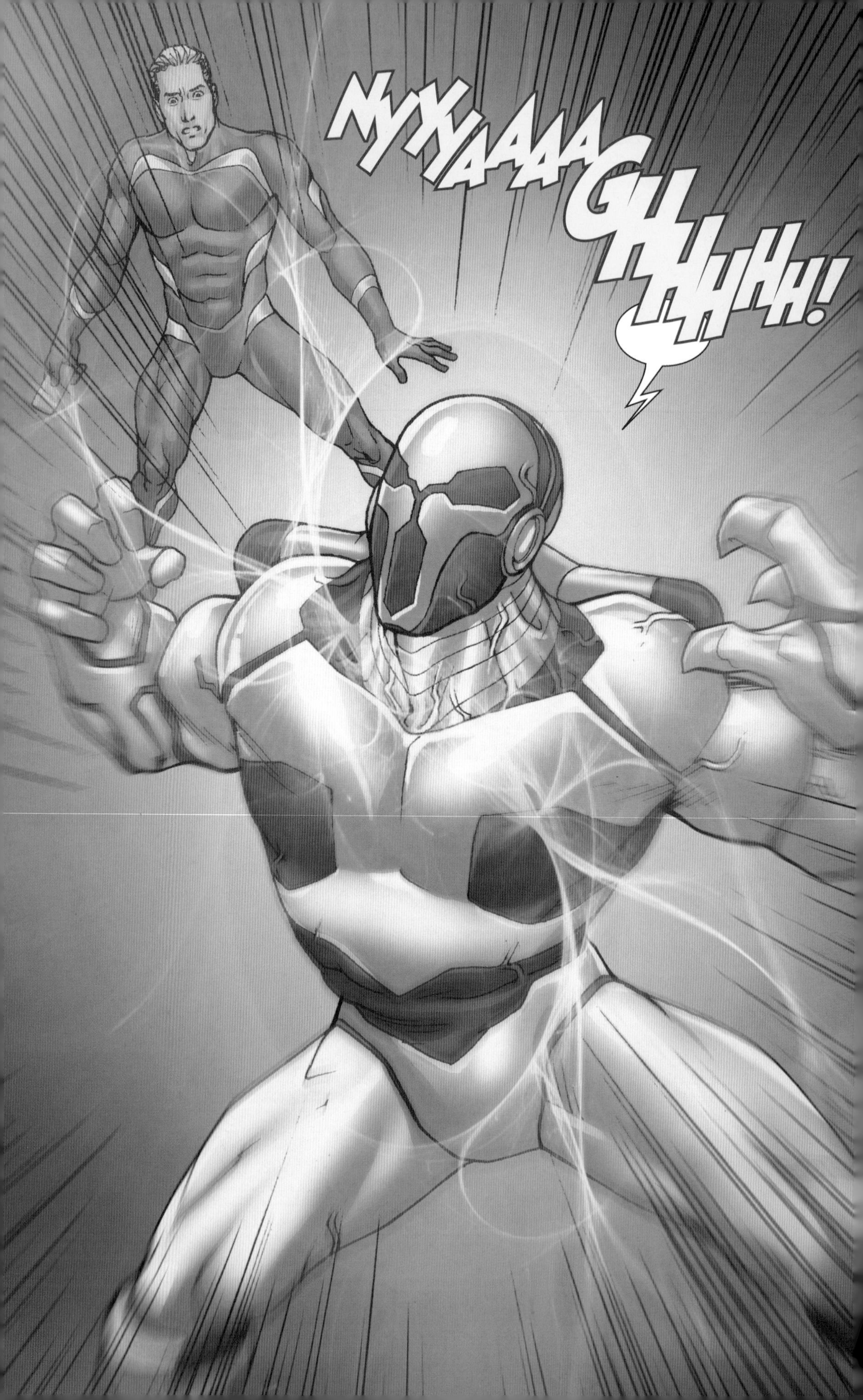
NYYAAAAGHHHHH!

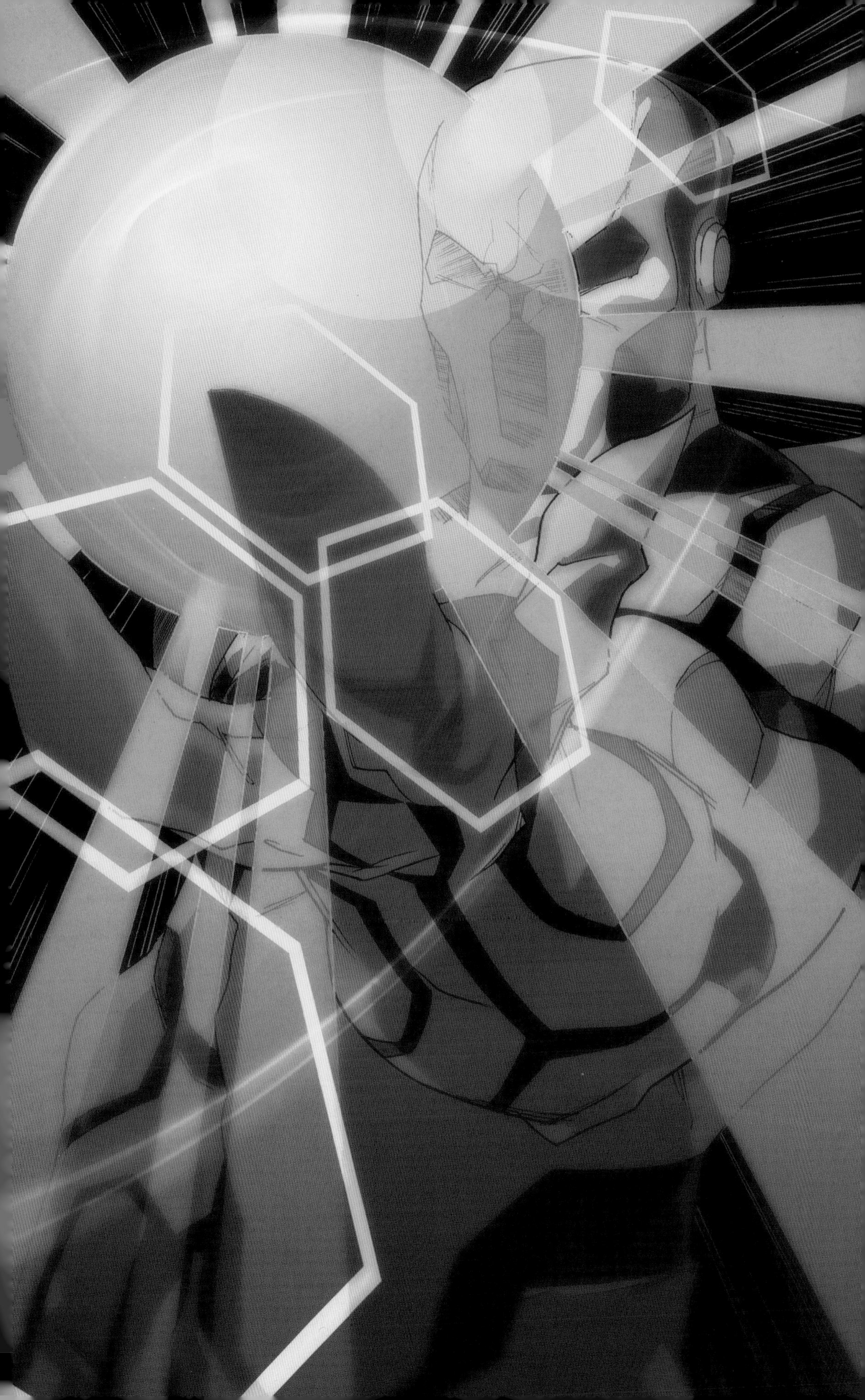

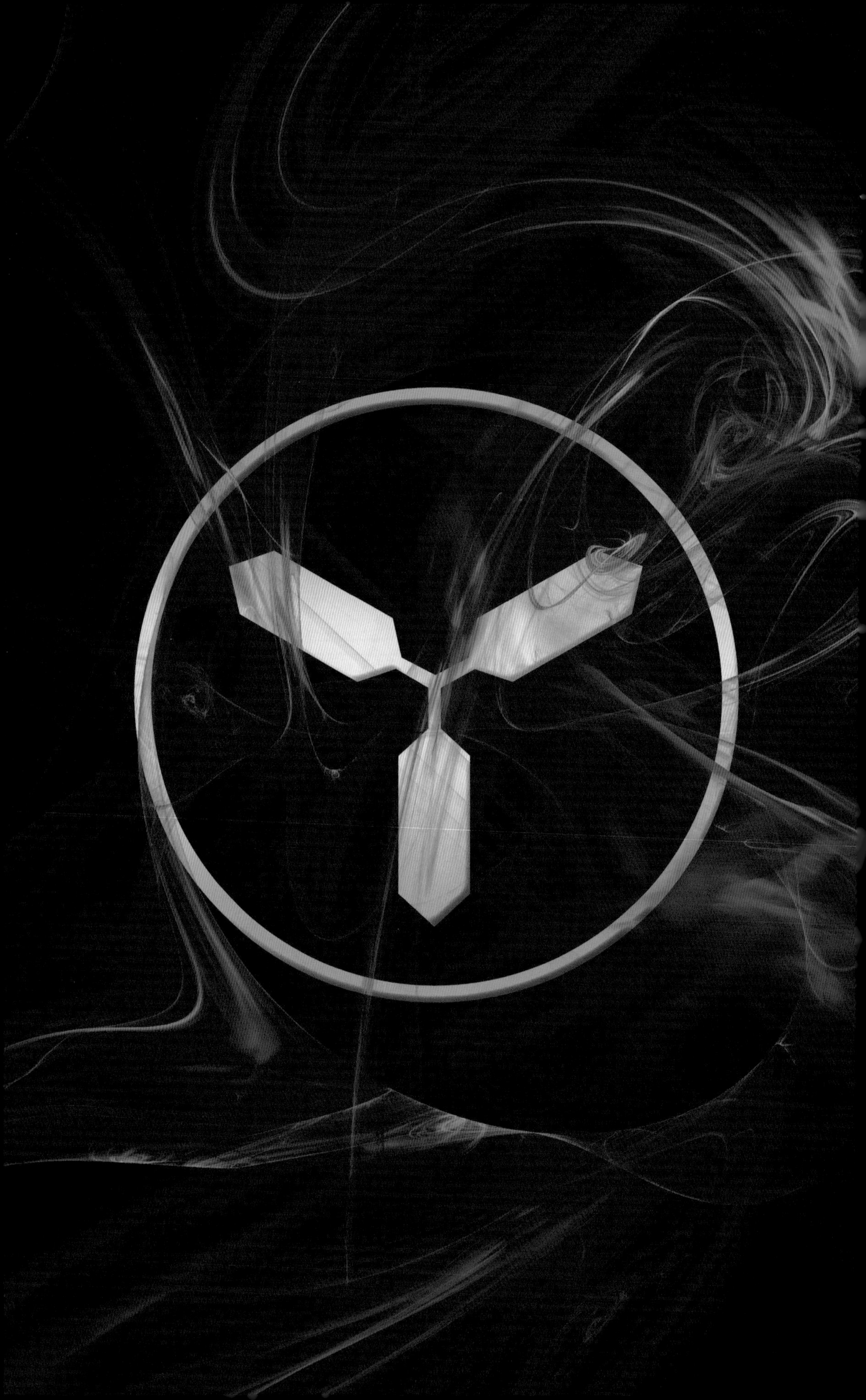

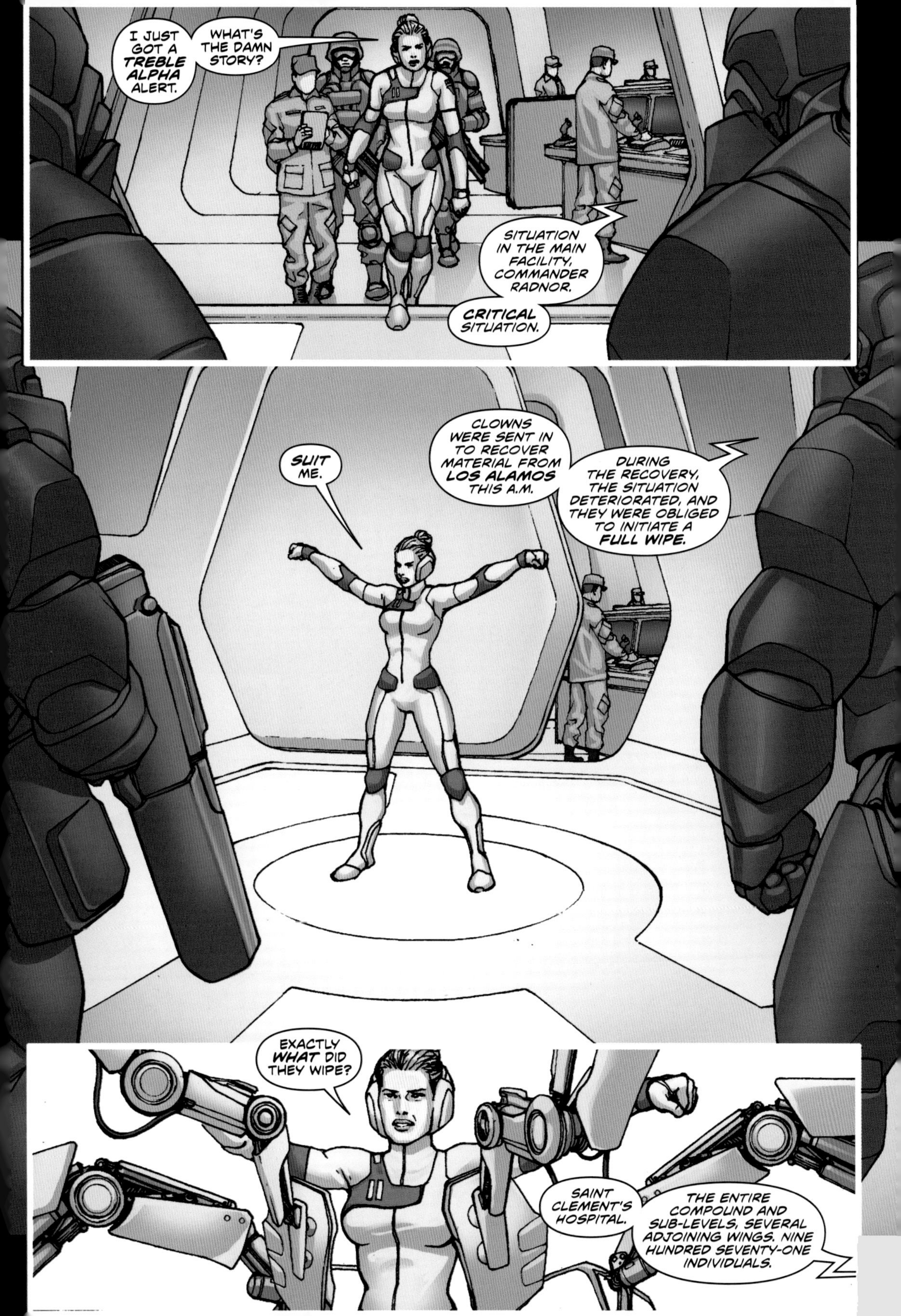
I JUST GOT A TREBLE ALPHA ALERT.
WHAT'S THE DAMN STORY?
SITUATION IN THE MAIN FACILITY, COMMANDER RADNOR.
CRITICAL SITUATION.
SUIT ME.
CLOWNS WERE SENT IN TO RECOVER MATERIAL FROM LOS ALAMOS THIS A.M.
DURING THE RECOVERY, THE SITUATION DETERIORATED, AND THEY WERE OBLIGED TO INITIATE A FULL WIPE.
EXACTLY WHAT DID THEY WIPE?
SAINT CLEMENT'S HOSPITAL.
THE ENTIRE COMPOUND AND SUB-LEVELS, SEVERAL ADJOINING WINGS. NINE HUNDRED SEVENTY-ONE INDIVIDUALS.

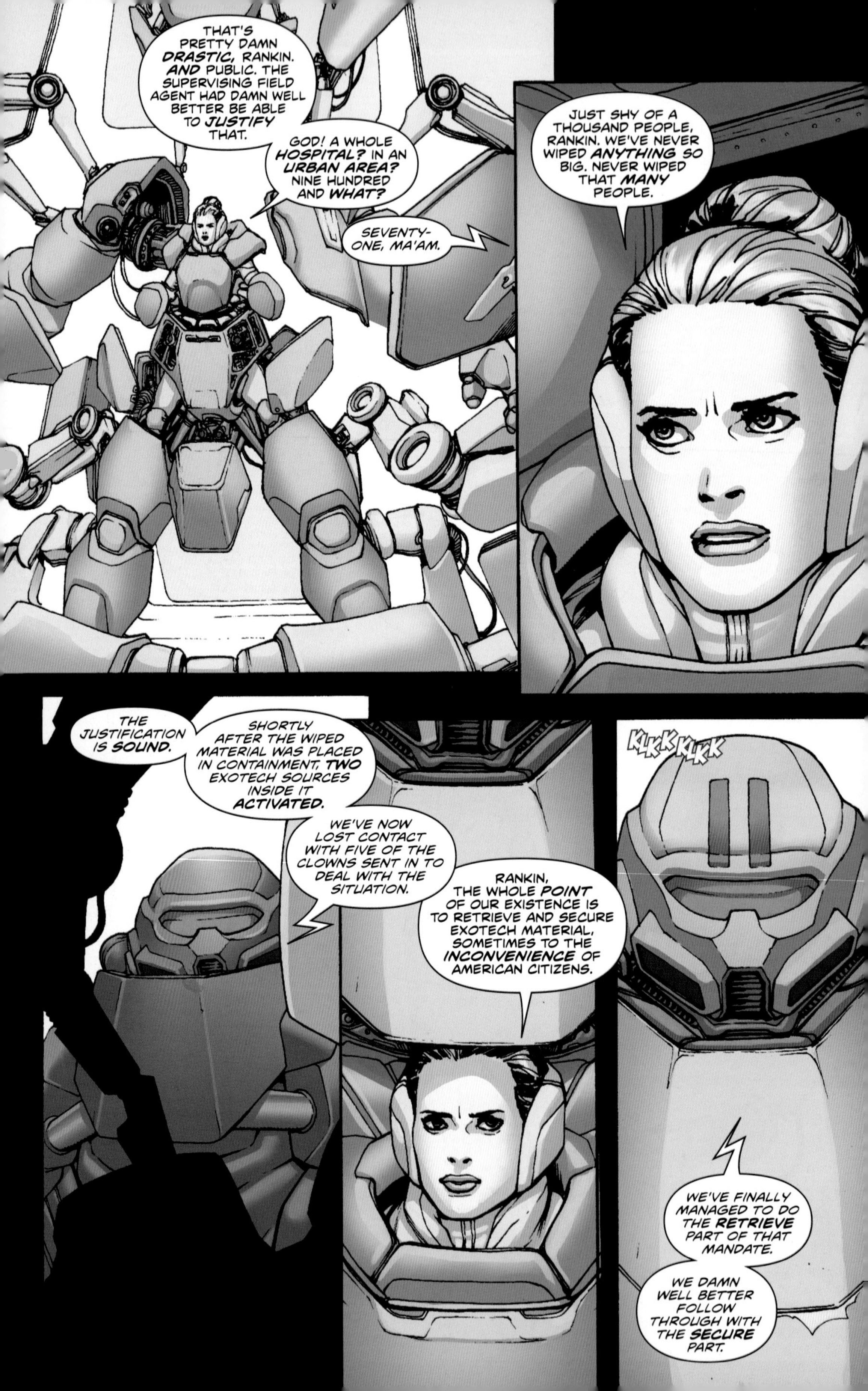
THAT'S PRETTY DAMN DRASTIC, RANKIN. AND PUBLIC. THE SUPERVISING FIELD AGENT HAD DAMN WELL BETTER BE ABLE TO JUSTIFY THAT.
GOD! A WHOLE HOSPITAL? IN AN URBAN AREA? NINE HUNDRED AND WHAT?
SEVENTY-ONE, MA'AM.
JUST SHY OF A THOUSAND PEOPLE, RANKIN. WE'VE NEVER WIPED ANYTHING SO BIG. NEVER WIPED THAT MANY PEOPLE.
THE JUSTIFICATION IS SOUND.
SHORTLY AFTER THE WIPED MATERIAL WAS PLACED IN CONTAINMENT, TWO EXOTECH SOURCES INSIDE IT ACTIVATED.
WE'VE NOW LOST CONTACT WITH FIVE OF THE CLOWNS SENT IN TO DEAL WITH THE SITUATION.
RANKIN, THE WHOLE POINT OF OUR EXISTENCE IS TO RETRIEVE AND SECURE EXOTECH MATERIAL, SOMETIMES TO THE INCONVENIENCE OF AMERICAN CITIZENS.
KLIKK KLIKK
WE'VE FINALLY MANAGED TO DO THE RETRIEVE PART OF THAT MANDATE.
WE DAMN WELL BETTER FOLLOW THROUGH WITH THE SECURE PART.

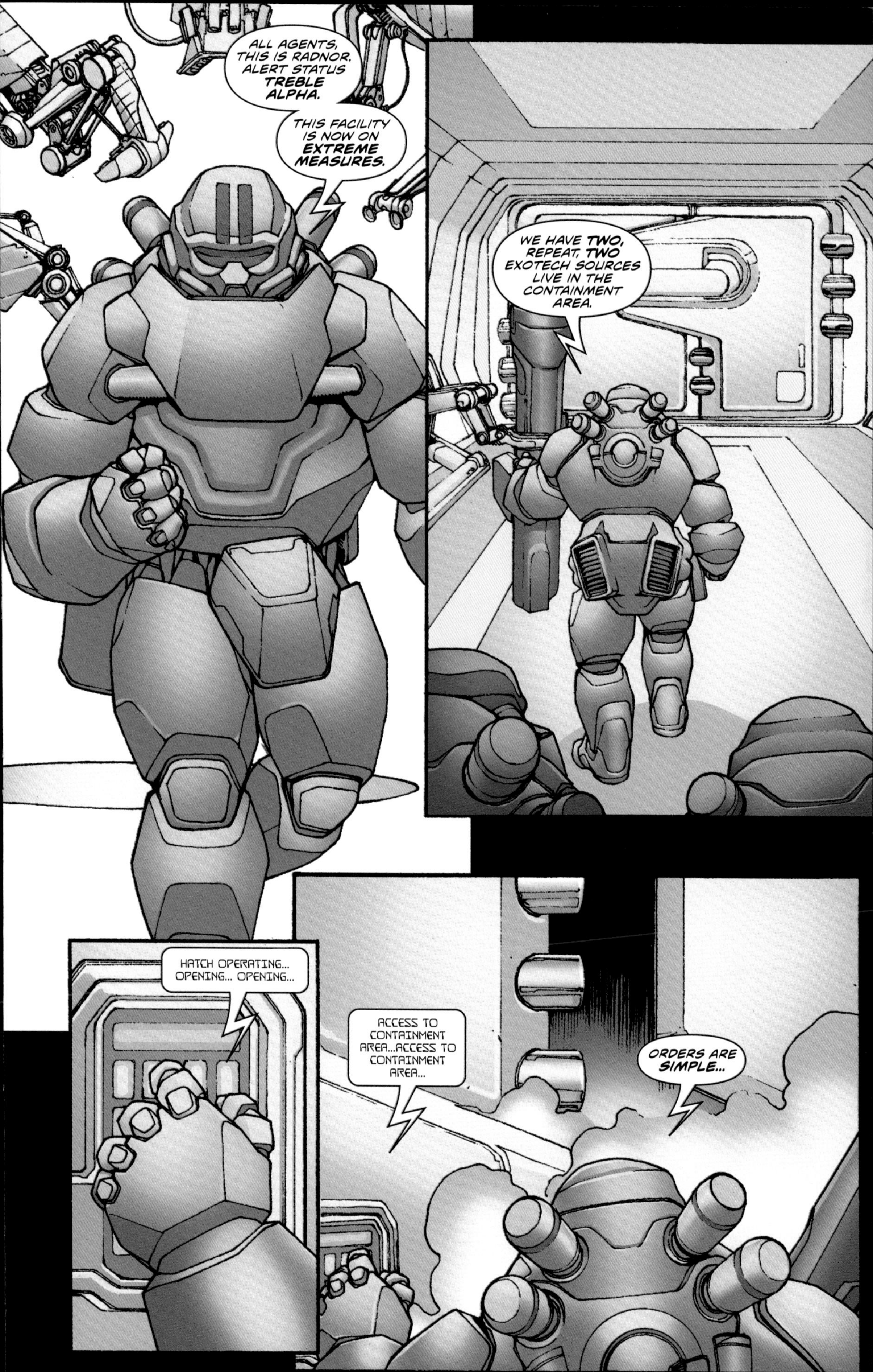
ALL AGENTS, THIS IS RADNOR. ALERT STATUS TREBLE ALPHA.
THIS FACILITY IS NOW ON EXTREME MEASURES.
WE HAVE TWO, REPEAT, TWO EXOTECH SOURCES LIVE IN THE CONTAINMENT AREA.
HATCH OPERATING... OPENING... OPENING...
ACCESS TO CONTAINMENT AREA...ACCESS TO CONTAINMENT AREA...
ORDERS ARE SIMPLE...

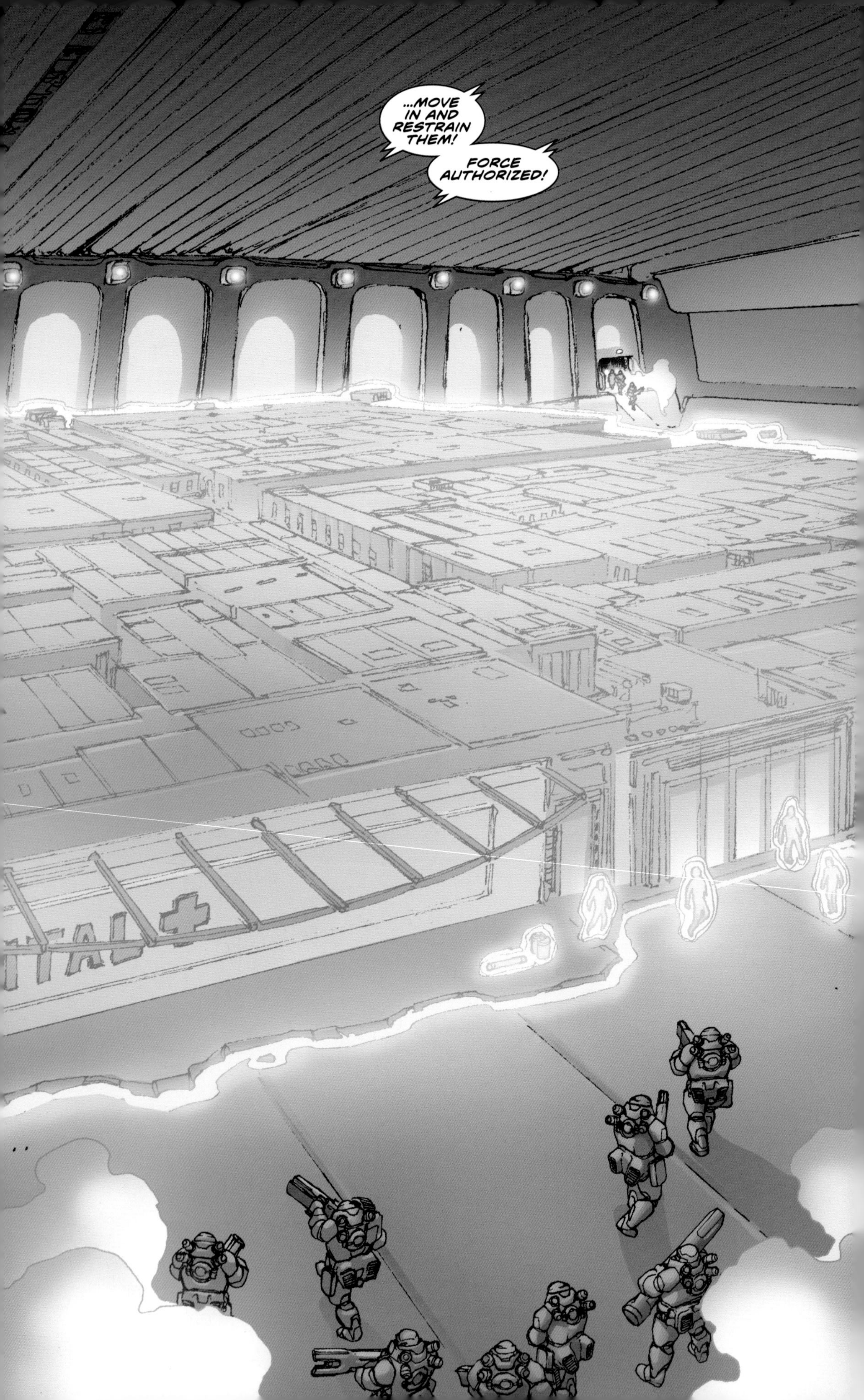

...MOVE IN AND RESTRAIN THEM!
FORCE AUTHORIZED!

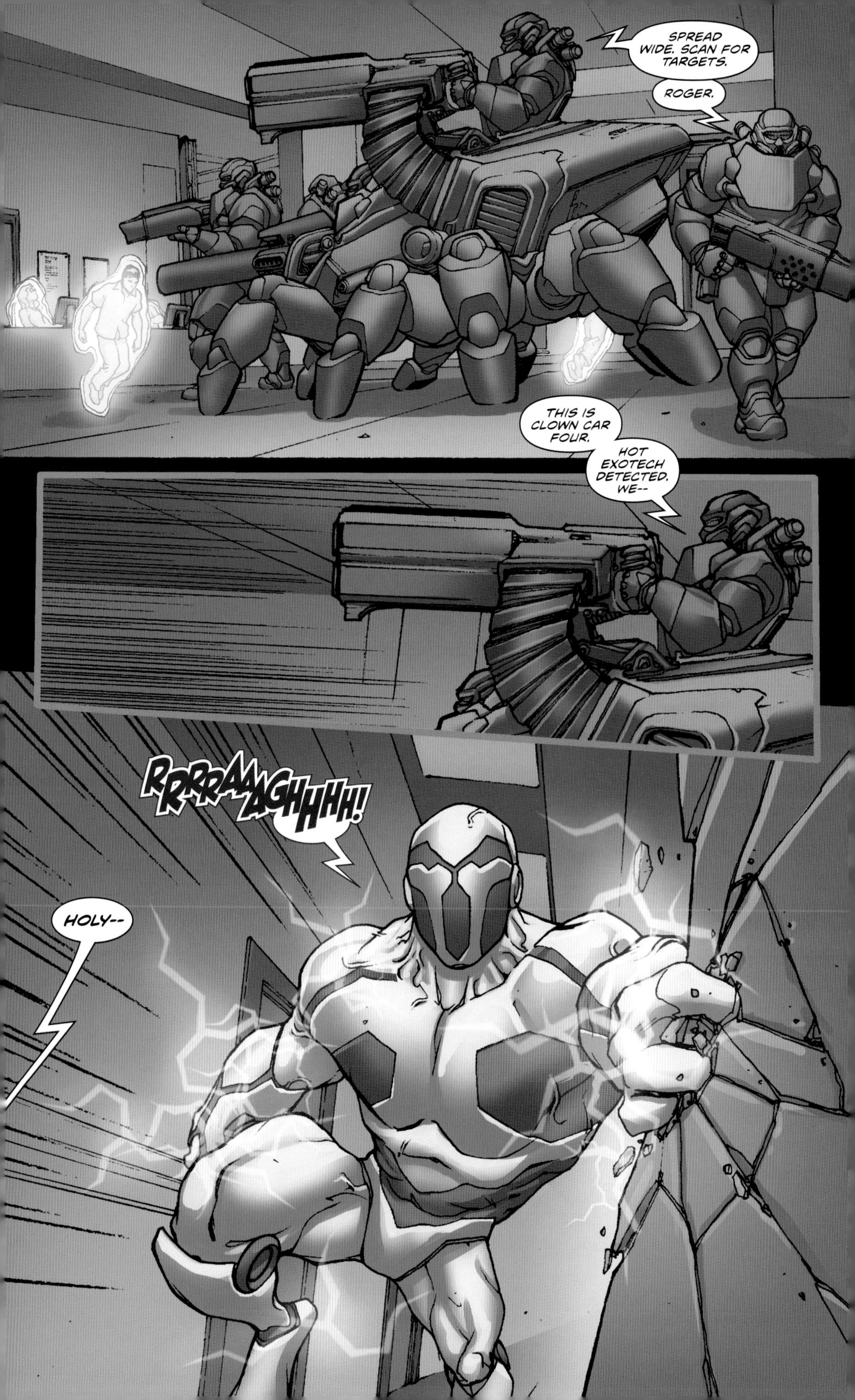
SPREAD WIDE. SCAN FOR TARGETS.
ROGER.
THIS IS CLOWN CAR FOUR.
HOT EXOTECH DETECTED. WE--
RRRRAAAGHHHH!
HOLY--

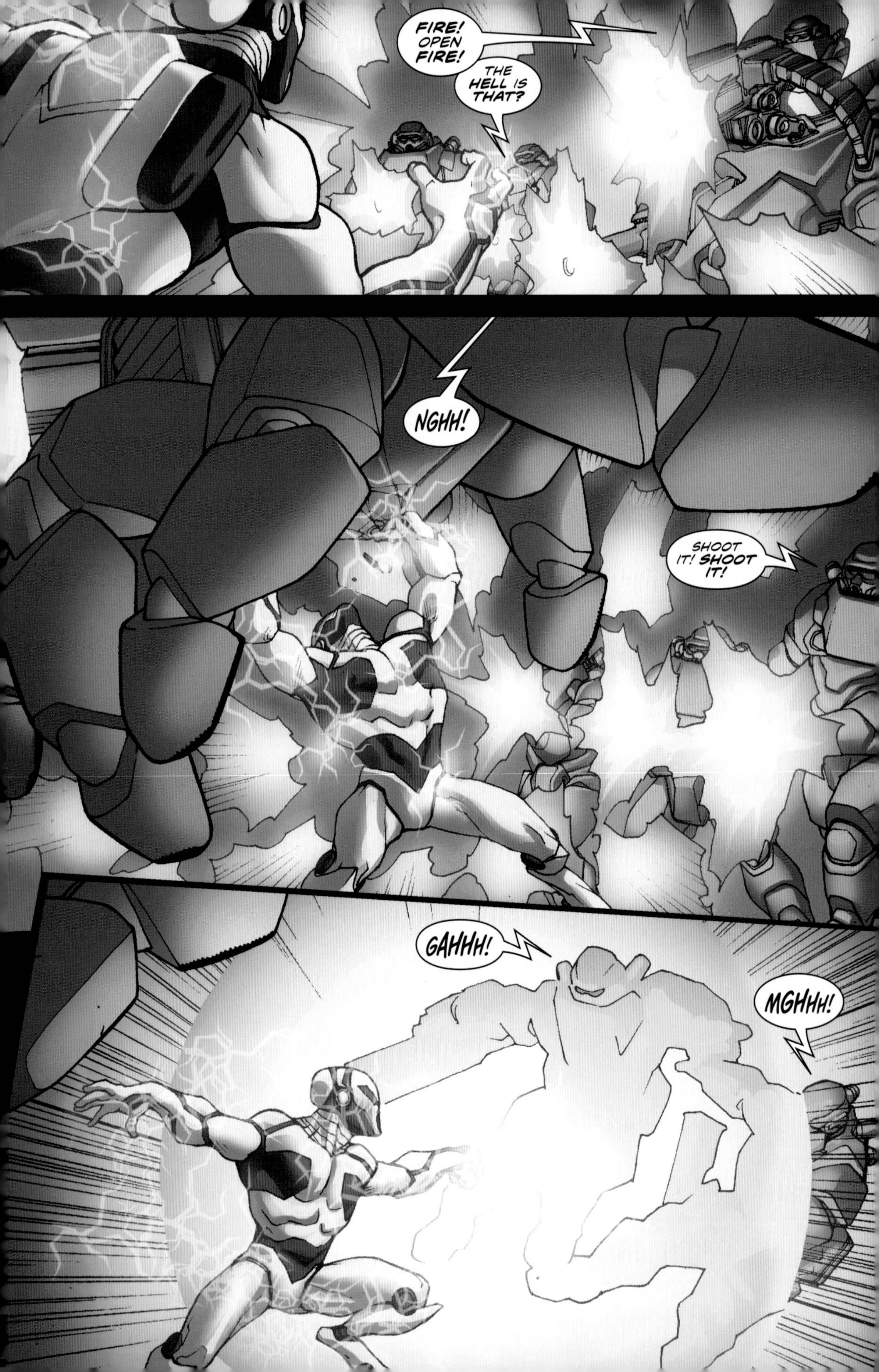
FIRE! OPEN FIRE!
THE HELL IS THAT?
NGHH!
SHOOT IT! SHOOT IT!
GAHHH!
MGHHH!

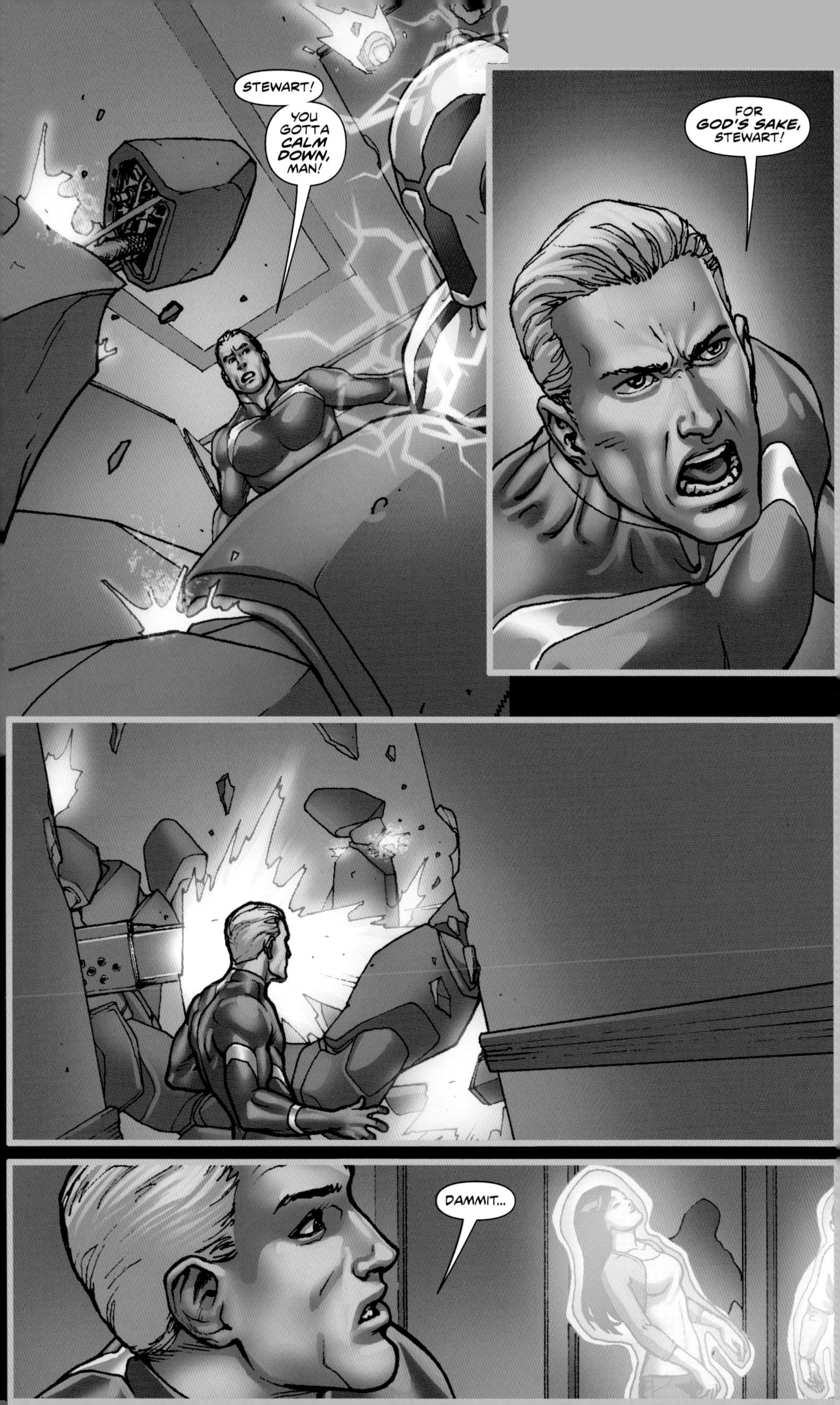
STEWART!
YOU GOTTA CALM DOWN, MAN!
FOR GOD'S SAKE, STEWART!
DAMMIT...

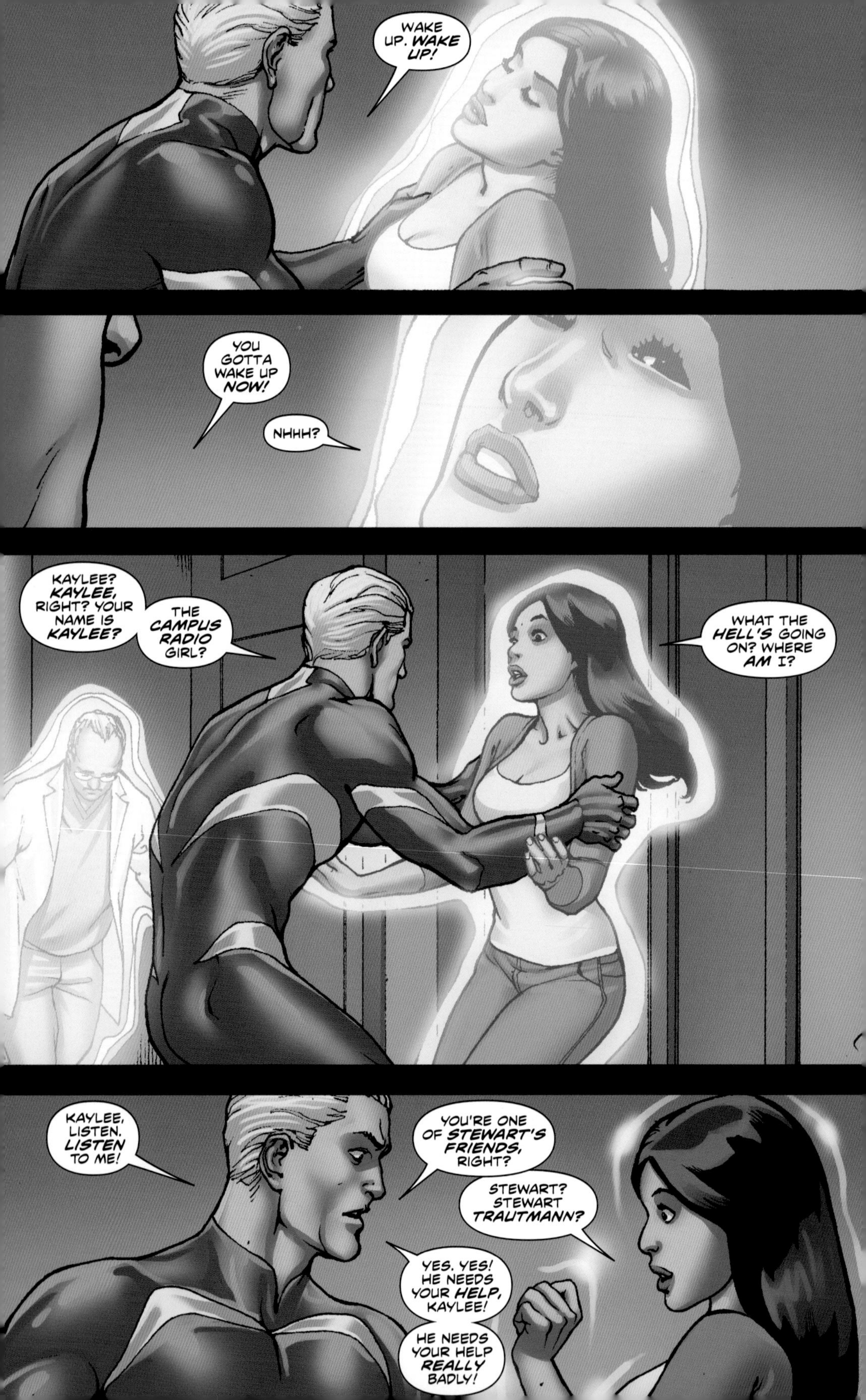
WAKE UP. WAKE UP!
YOU GOTTA WAKE UP NOW!
NHHH?
KAYLEE? KAYLEE, RIGHT? YOUR NAME IS KAYLEE?
THE CAMPUS RADIO GIRL?
WHAT THE HELL'S GOING ON? WHERE AM I?
KAYLEE, LISTEN. LISTEN TO ME!
YOU'RE ONE OF STEWART'S FRIENDS, RIGHT?
STEWART? STEWART TRAUTMANN?
YES. YES! HE NEEDS YOUR HELP, KAYLEE!
HE NEEDS YOUR HELP REALLY BADLY!

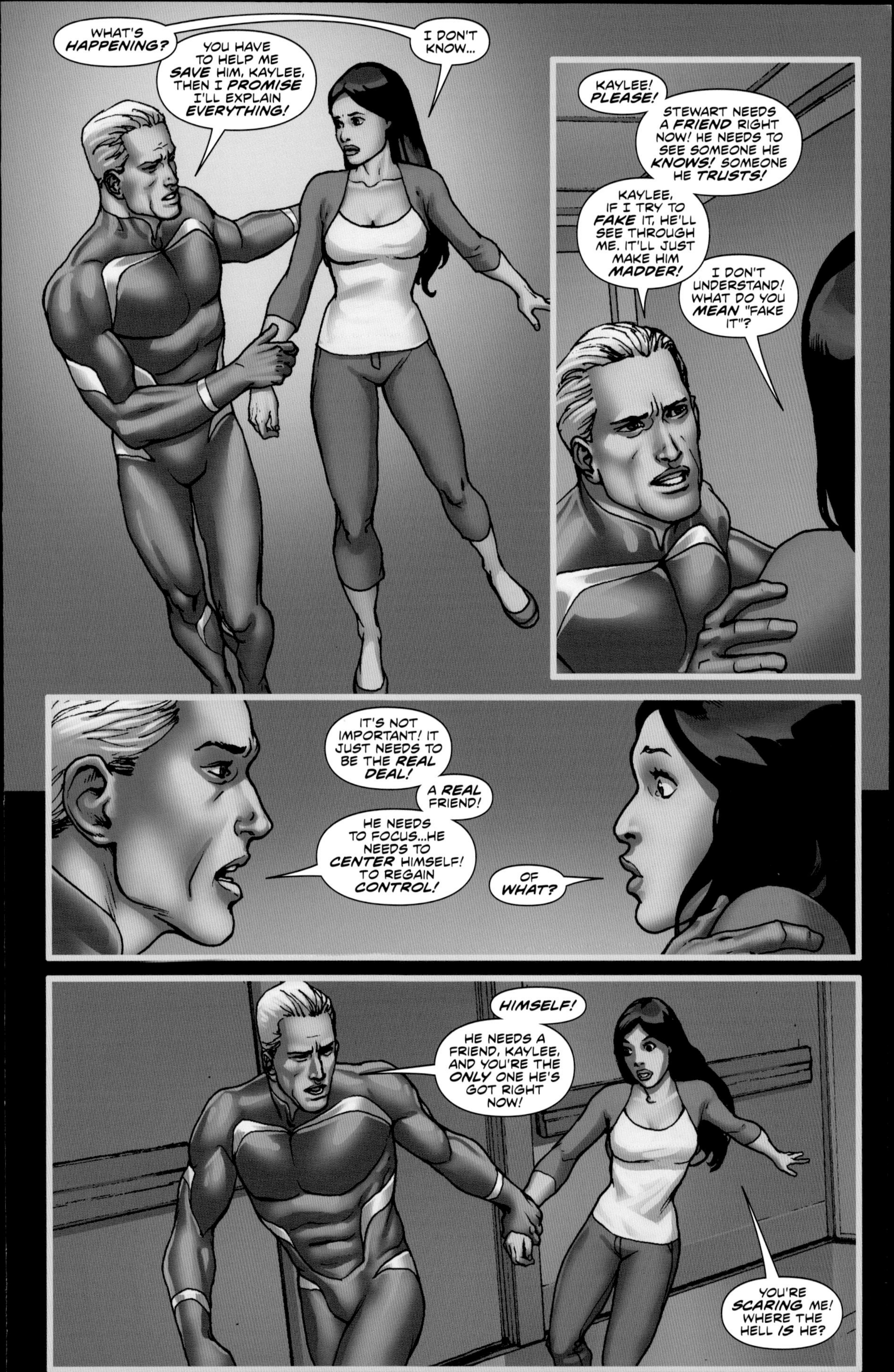
WHAT'S HAPPENING?
YOU HAVE TO HELP ME SAVE HIM, KAYLEE, THEN I PROMISE I'LL EXPLAIN EVERYTHING!
I DON'T KNOW...
KAYLEE! PLEASE!
STEWART NEEDS A FRIEND RIGHT NOW! HE NEEDS TO SEE SOMEONE HE KNOWS! SOMEONE HE TRUSTS!
KAYLEE, IF I TRY TO FAKE IT, HE'LL SEE THROUGH ME. IT'LL JUST MAKE HIM MADDER!
I DON'T UNDERSTAND! WHAT DO YOU MEAN "FAKE IT"?
IT'S NOT IMPORTANT! IT JUST NEEDS TO BE THE REAL DEAL!
A REAL FRIEND!
HE NEEDS TO FOCUS...HE NEEDS TO CENTER HIMSELF! TO REGAIN CONTROL!
OF WHAT?
HIMSELF!
HE NEEDS A FRIEND, KAYLEE, AND YOU'RE THE ONLY ONE HE'S GOT RIGHT NOW!
YOU'RE SCARING ME! WHERE THE HELL IS HE?

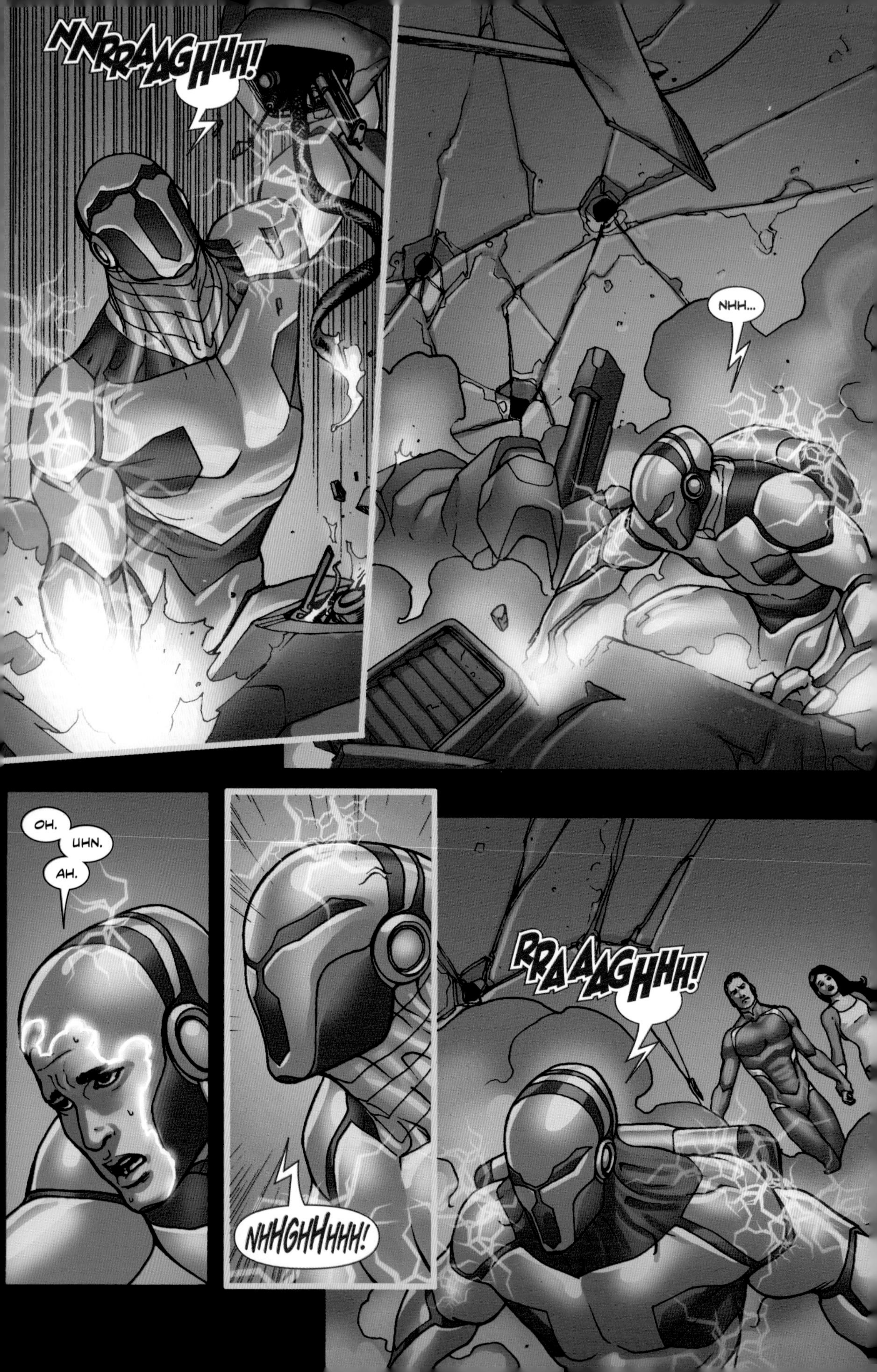
NNRRAAGHHH!
NHH...
OH.
UHN.
AH.
NHHGHHHHH!
RRAAAGHHH!

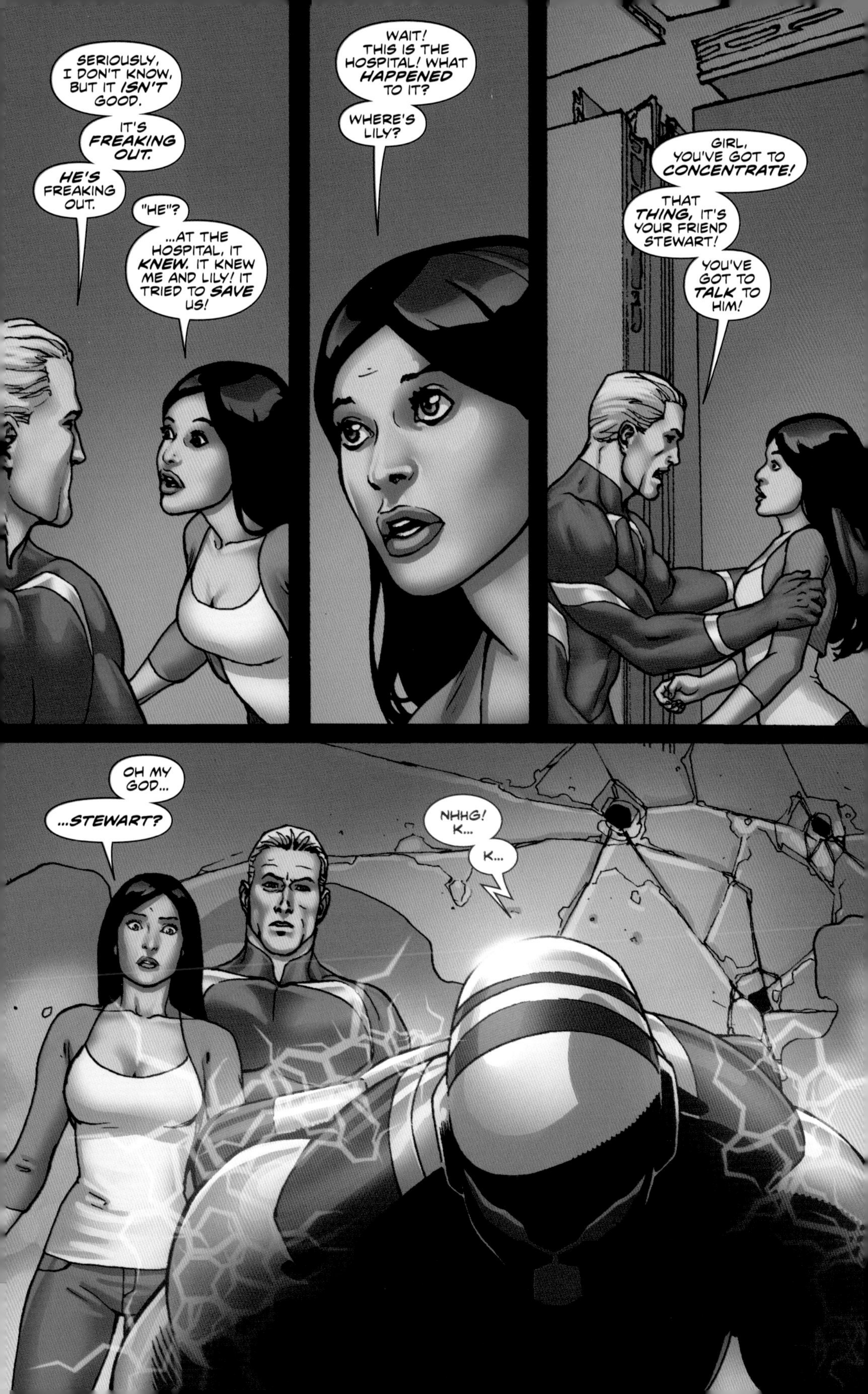
SERIOUSLY, I DON'T KNOW, BUT IT *ISN'T* GOOD.
IT'S *FREAKING OUT.*
*HE'S* FREAKING OUT.
"HE"?
...AT THE HOSPITAL, IT *KNEW.* IT KNEW ME AND LILY! IT TRIED TO *SAVE* US!
WAIT! THIS IS THE HOSPITAL! WHAT *HAPPENED* TO IT?
WHERE'S LILY?
GIRL, YOU'VE GOT TO *CONCENTRATE!*
THAT *THING,* IT'S YOUR FRIEND STEWART!
YOU'VE GOT TO *TALK* TO HIM!
OH MY GOD...
...*STEWART?*
NHHG! K...
K...

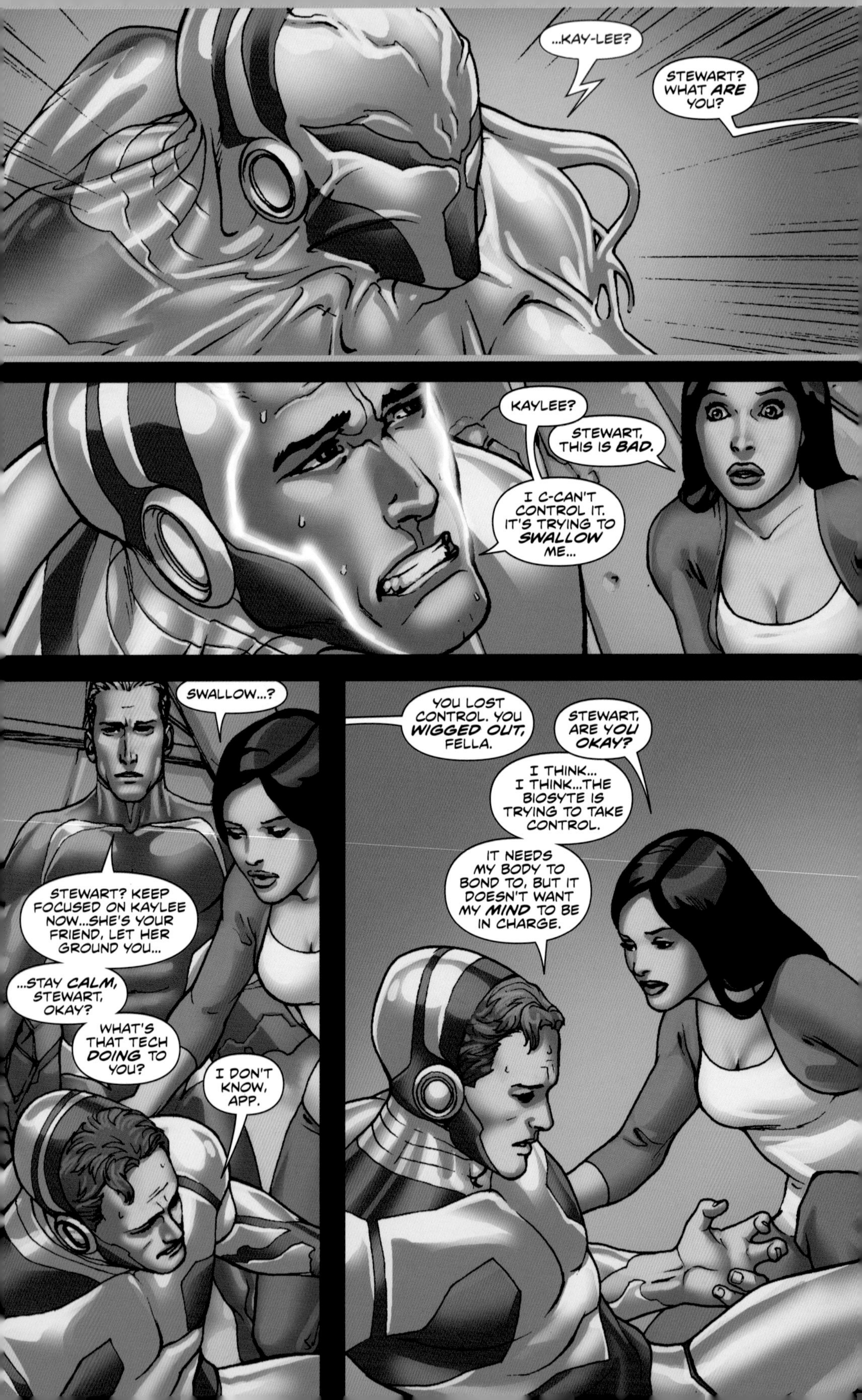

...KAY-LEE?
STEWART? WHAT ARE YOU?
KAYLEE?
STEWART, THIS IS BAD.
I C-CAN'T CONTROL IT. IT'S TRYING TO SWALLOW ME...
SWALLOW...?
STEWART? KEEP FOCUSED ON KAYLEE NOW...SHE'S YOUR FRIEND, LET HER GROUND YOU...
...STAY CALM, STEWART, OKAY?
WHAT'S THAT TECH DOING TO YOU?
I DON'T KNOW, APP.
YOU LOST CONTROL. YOU WIGGED OUT, FELLA.
STEWART, ARE YOU OKAY?
I THINK... I THINK...THE BIOSYTE IS TRYING TO TAKE CONTROL.
IT NEEDS MY BODY TO BOND TO, BUT IT DOESN'T WANT MY MIND TO BE IN CHARGE.

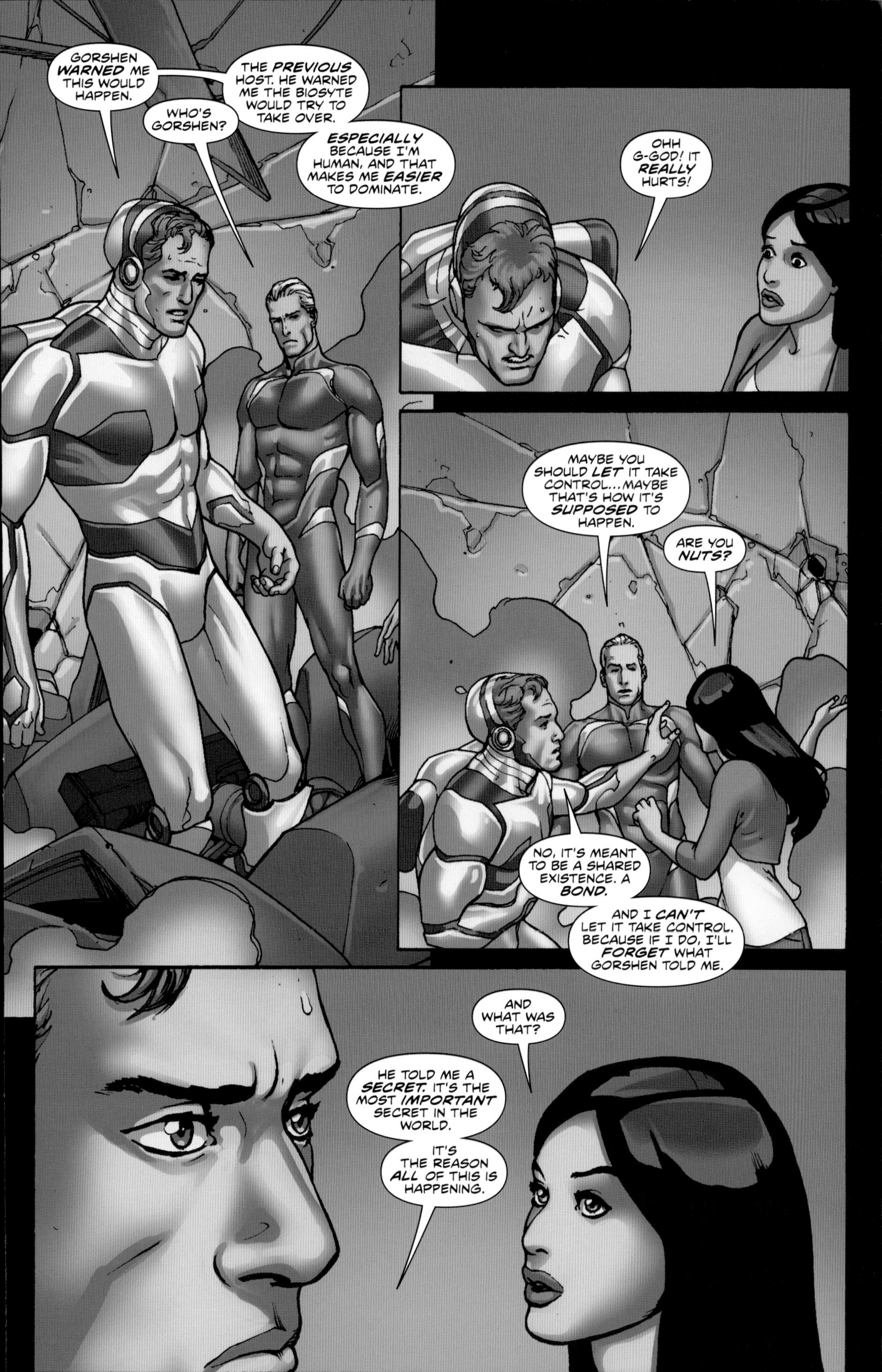
GORSHEN WARNED ME THIS WOULD HAPPEN.
WHO'S GORSHEN?
THE PREVIOUS HOST. HE WARNED ME THE BIOSYTE WOULD TRY TO TAKE OVER.
ESPECIALLY BECAUSE I'M HUMAN, AND THAT MAKES ME EASIER TO DOMINATE.
OHH G-GOD! IT REALLY HURTS!
MAYBE YOU SHOULD LET IT TAKE CONTROL... MAYBE THAT'S HOW IT'S SUPPOSED TO HAPPEN.
ARE YOU NUTS?
NO, IT'S MEANT TO BE A SHARED EXISTENCE. A BOND.
AND I CAN'T LET IT TAKE CONTROL. BECAUSE IF I DO, I'LL FORGET WHAT GORSHEN TOLD ME.
AND WHAT WAS THAT?
HE TOLD ME A SECRET. IT'S THE MOST IMPORTANT SECRET IN THE WORLD.
IT'S THE REASON ALL OF THIS IS HAPPENING.

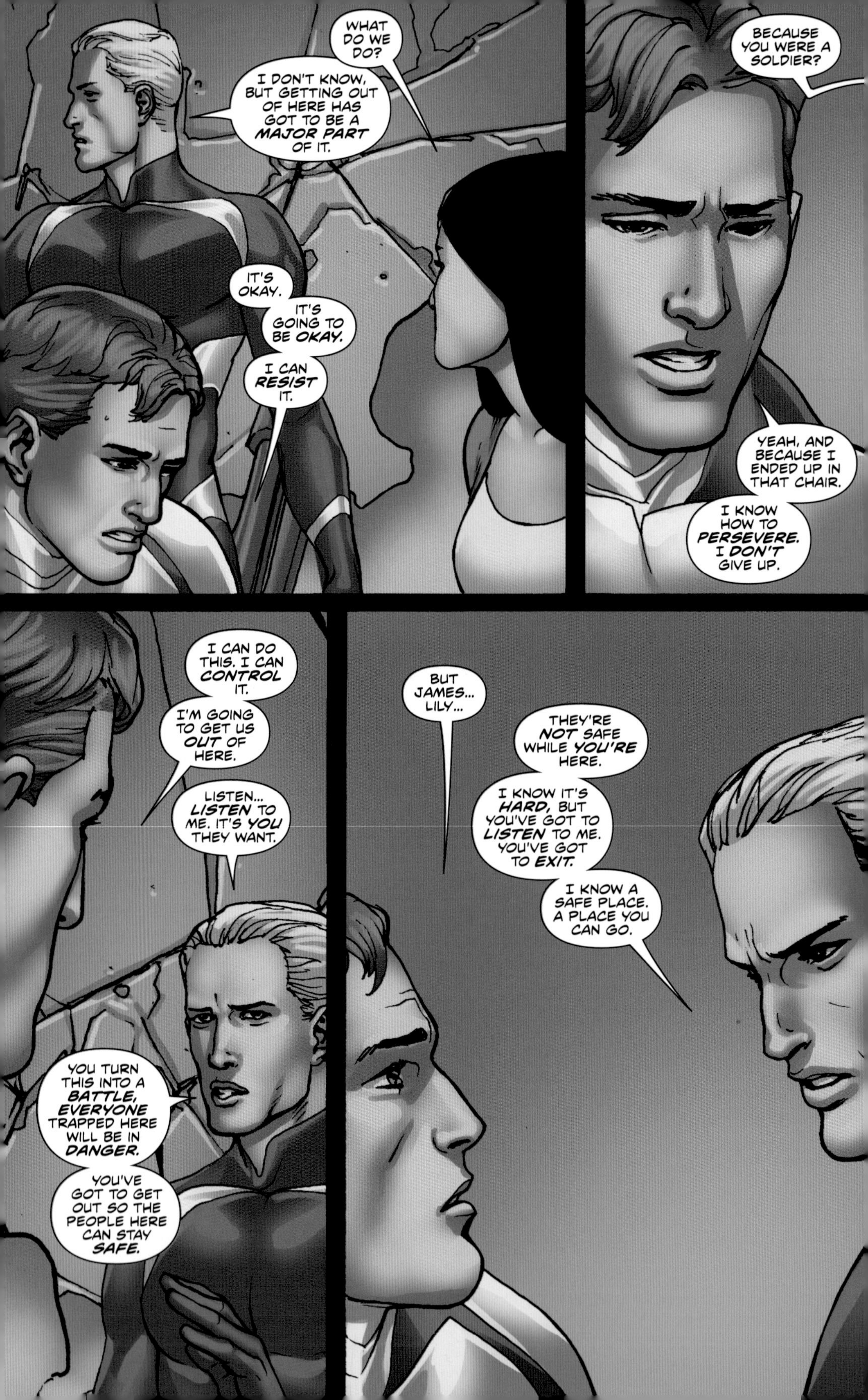
WHAT DO WE DO?
I DON'T KNOW, BUT GETTING OUT OF HERE HAS GOT TO BE A MAJOR PART OF IT.
IT'S OKAY.
IT'S GOING TO BE OKAY.
I CAN RESIST IT.
BECAUSE YOU WERE A SOLDIER?
YEAH, AND BECAUSE I ENDED UP IN THAT CHAIR.
I KNOW HOW TO PERSEVERE. I DON'T GIVE UP.
I CAN DO THIS. I CAN CONTROL IT.
I'M GOING TO GET US OUT OF HERE.
LISTEN... LISTEN TO ME. IT'S YOU THEY WANT.
YOU TURN THIS INTO A BATTLE, EVERYONE TRAPPED HERE WILL BE IN DANGER.
YOU'VE GOT TO GET OUT SO THE PEOPLE HERE CAN STAY SAFE.
BUT JAMES... LILY...
THEY'RE NOT SAFE WHILE YOU'RE HERE.
I KNOW IT'S HARD, BUT YOU'VE GOT TO LISTEN TO ME. YOU'VE GOT TO EXIT.
I KNOW A SAFE PLACE. A PLACE YOU CAN GO.

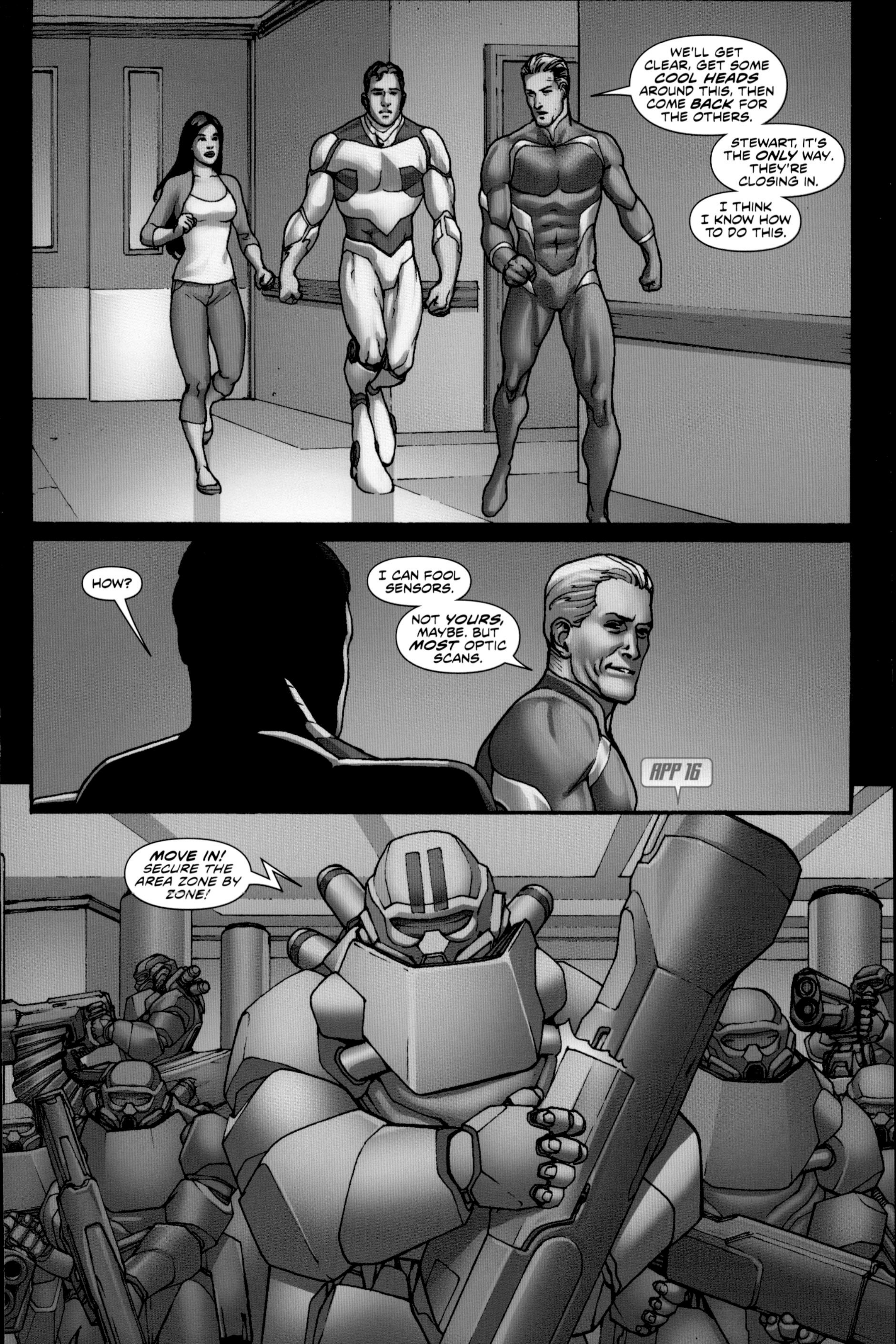
WE'LL GET CLEAR, GET SOME COOL HEADS AROUND THIS, THEN COME BACK FOR THE OTHERS.
STEWART, IT'S THE ONLY WAY. THEY'RE CLOSING IN.
I THINK I KNOW HOW TO DO THIS.
HOW?
I CAN FOOL SENSORS.
NOT YOURS, MAYBE. BUT MOST OPTIC SCANS.
APP 16
MOVE IN! SECURE THE AREA ZONE BY ZONE!

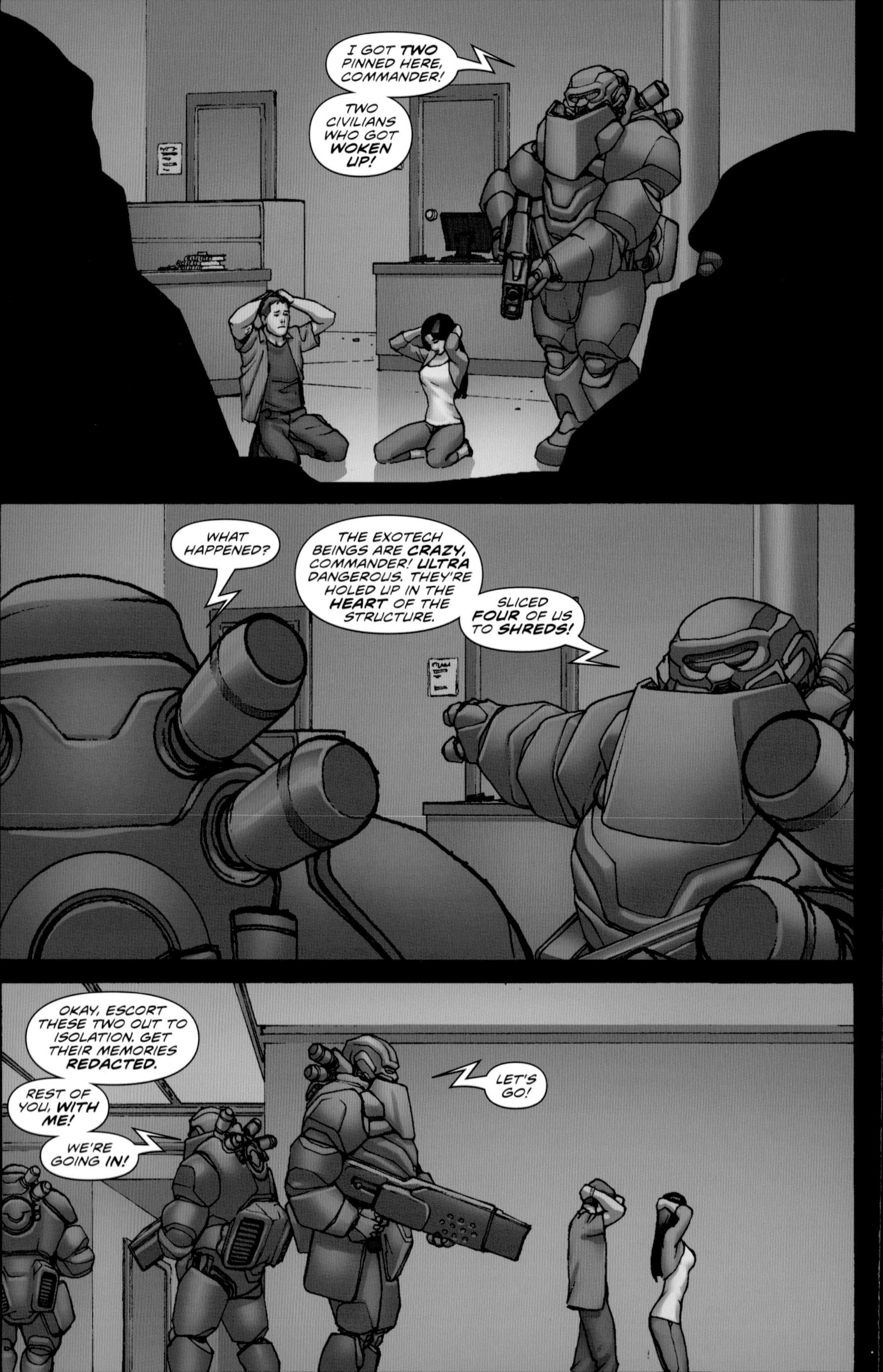
I GOT TWO PINNED HERE, COMMANDER!
TWO CIVILIANS WHO GOT WOKEN UP!
WHAT HAPPENED?
THE EXOTECH BEINGS ARE CRAZY, COMMANDER! ULTRA DANGEROUS. THEY'RE HOLED UP IN THE HEART OF THE STRUCTURE.
SLICED FOUR OF US TO SHREDS!
OKAY, ESCORT THESE TWO OUT TO ISOLATION. GET THEIR MEMORIES REDACTED.
REST OF YOU, WITH ME!
WE'RE GOING IN!
LET'S GO!

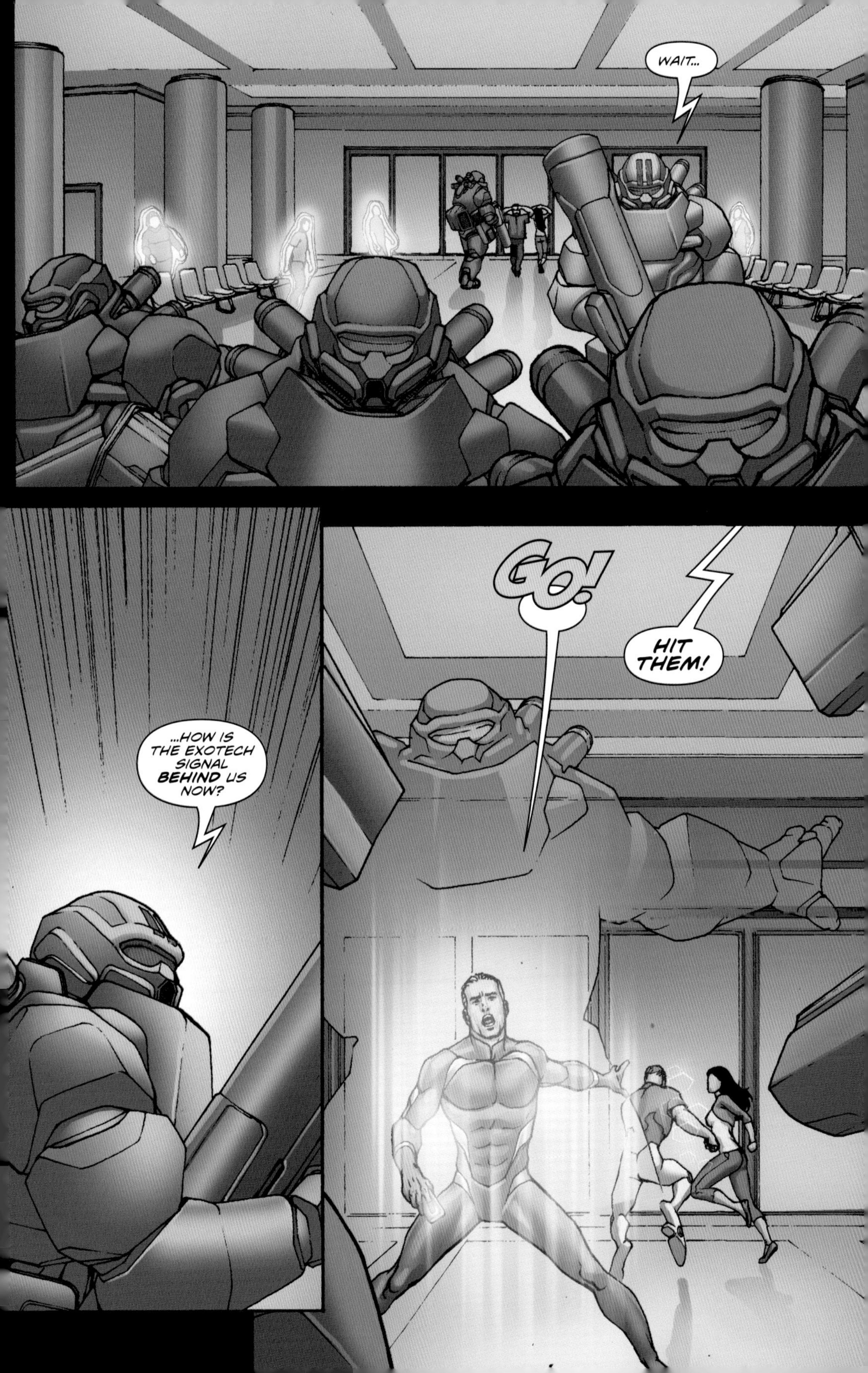
WAIT...
...HOW IS THE EXOTECH SIGNAL **BEHIND** US NOW?
GO!
HIT THEM!

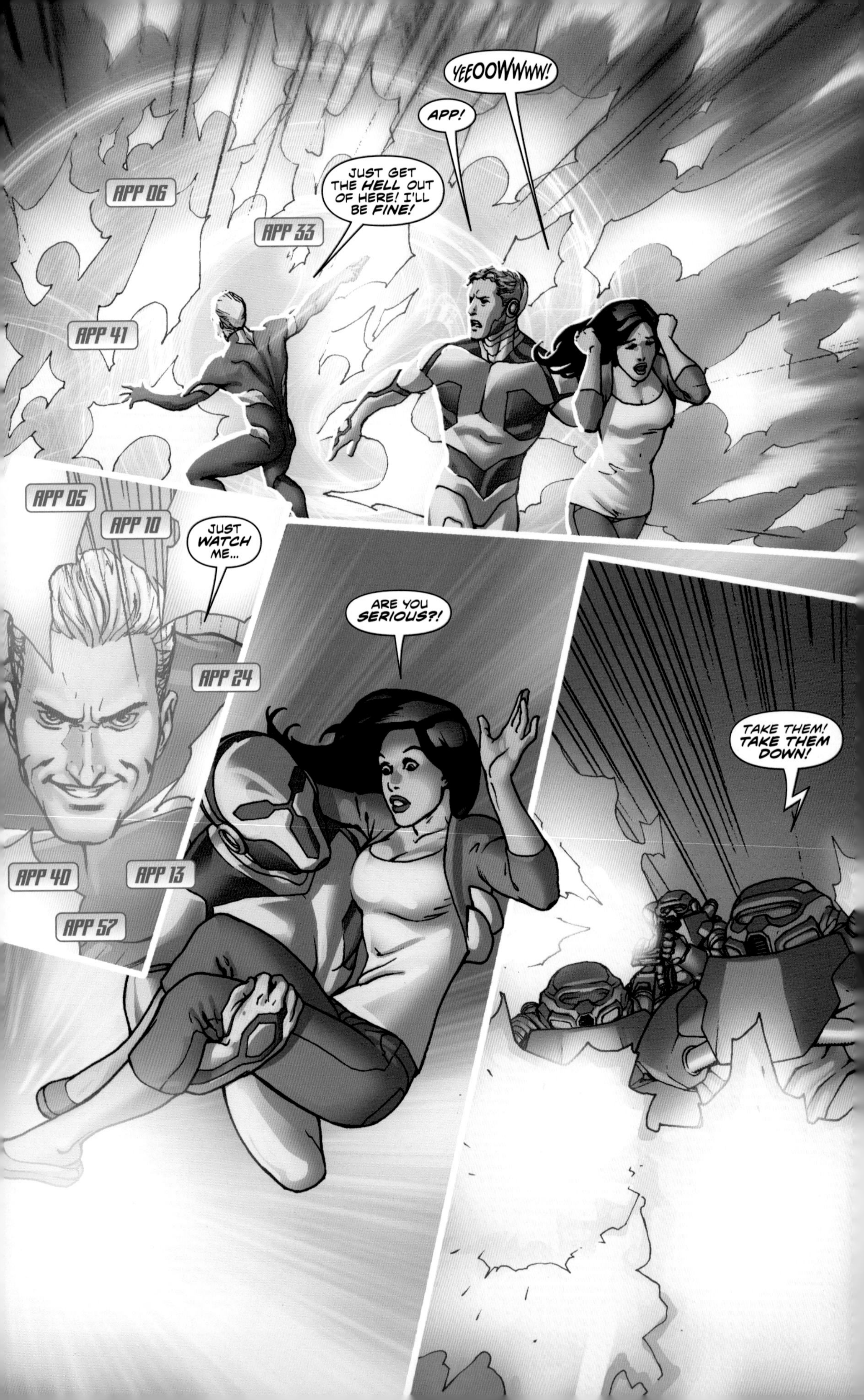
YEEOOWWWW!
APP!
JUST GET THE HELL OUT OF HERE! I'LL BE FINE!
APP 06
APP 33
APP 41
APP 05
APP 10
JUST WATCH ME...
APP 24
APP 40
APP 13
APP 57
ARE YOU SERIOUS?!
TAKE THEM! TAKE THEM DOWN!

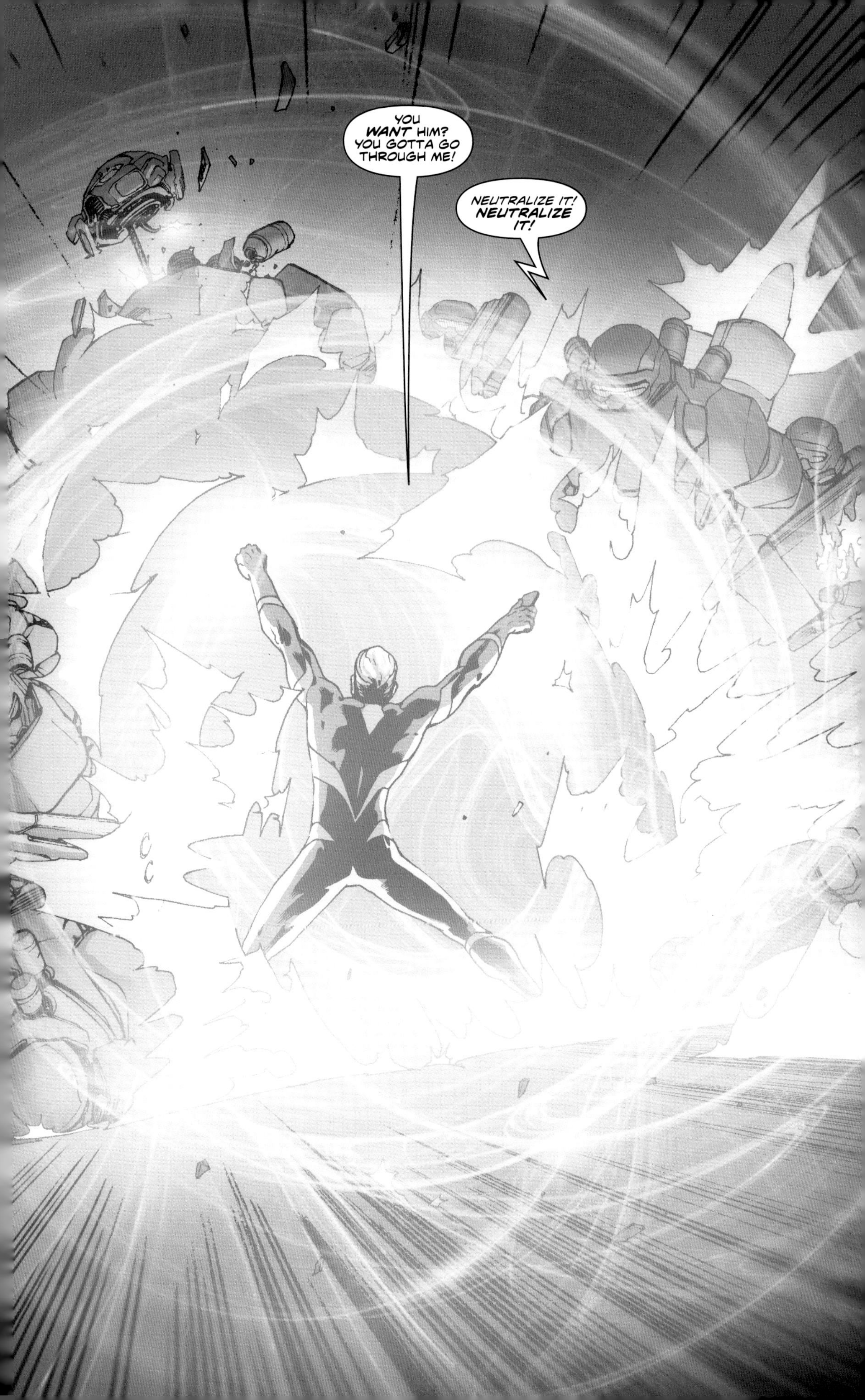
YOU WANT HIM? YOU GOTTA GO THROUGH ME!
NEUTRALIZE IT! NEUTRALIZE IT!

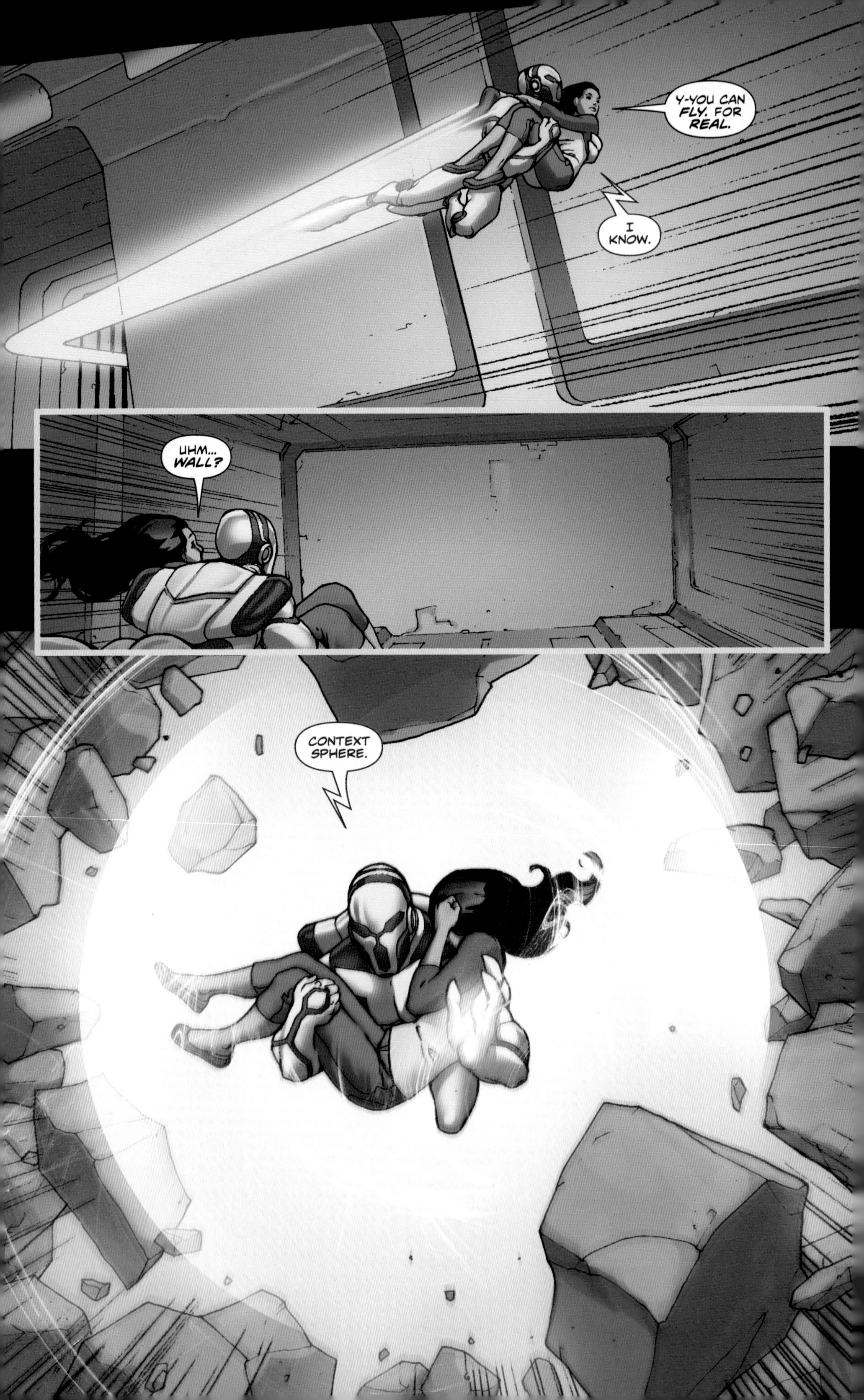
Y-YOU CAN *FLY*. FOR *REAL*.
I KNOW.
UHM... *WALL?*
CONTEXT SPHERE.

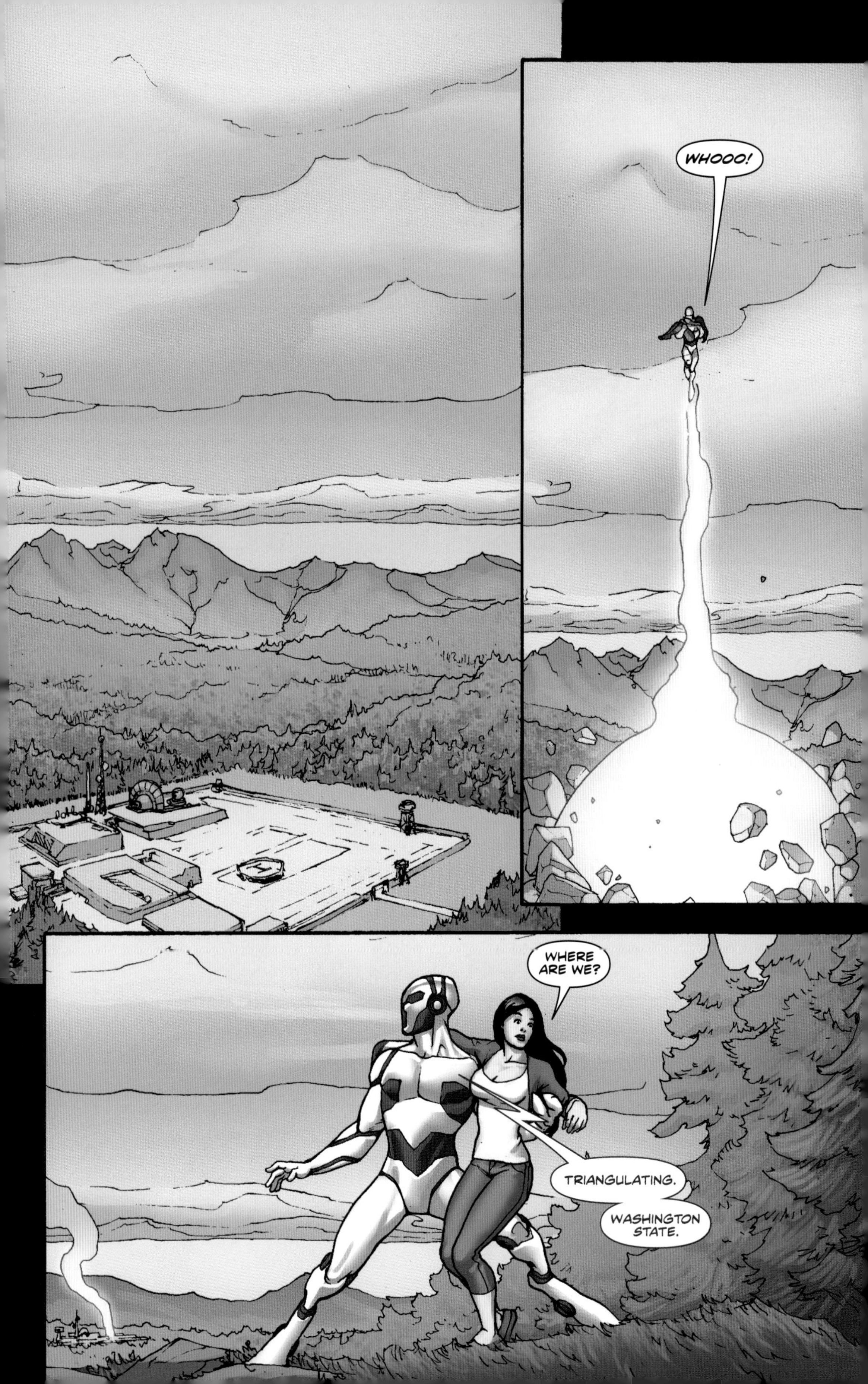
WHOOO!
WHERE ARE WE?
TRIANGULATING.
WASHINGTON STATE.

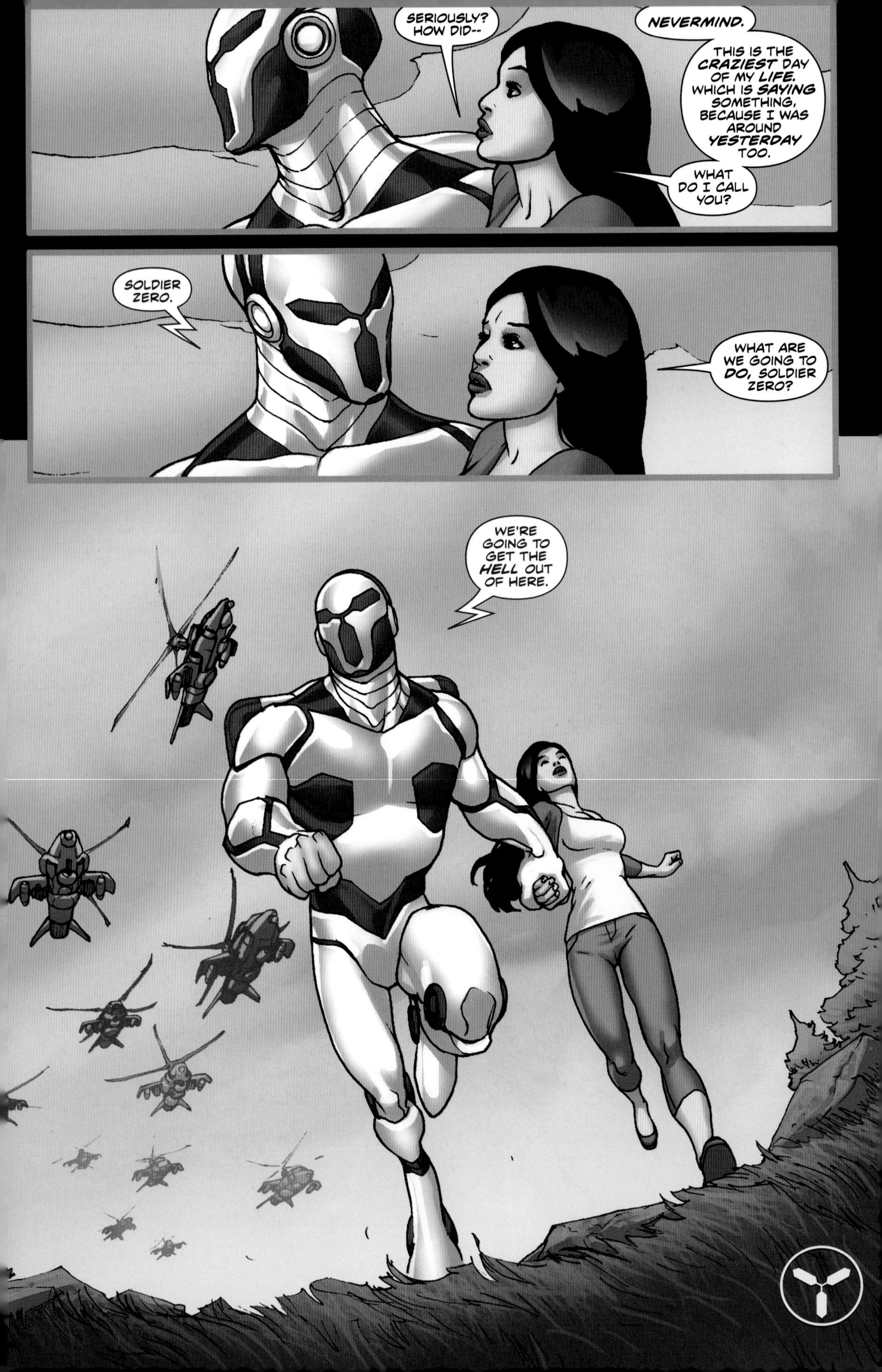
SERIOUSLY? HOW DID--
NEVERMIND.
THIS IS THE CRAZIEST DAY OF MY LIFE. WHICH IS SAYING SOMETHING, BECAUSE I WAS AROUND YESTERDAY TOO.
WHAT DO I CALL YOU?
SOLDIER ZERO.
WHAT ARE WE GOING TO DO, SOLDIER ZERO?
WE'RE GOING TO GET THE HELL OUT OF HERE.

# COMING SOON

 THE INHERITORS

STAN LEE

# SOLDIER ZERO

DAN ABNETT

ANDY LANNING

JAVIER PINA

RAMON BACHS

# VOLUME THREE

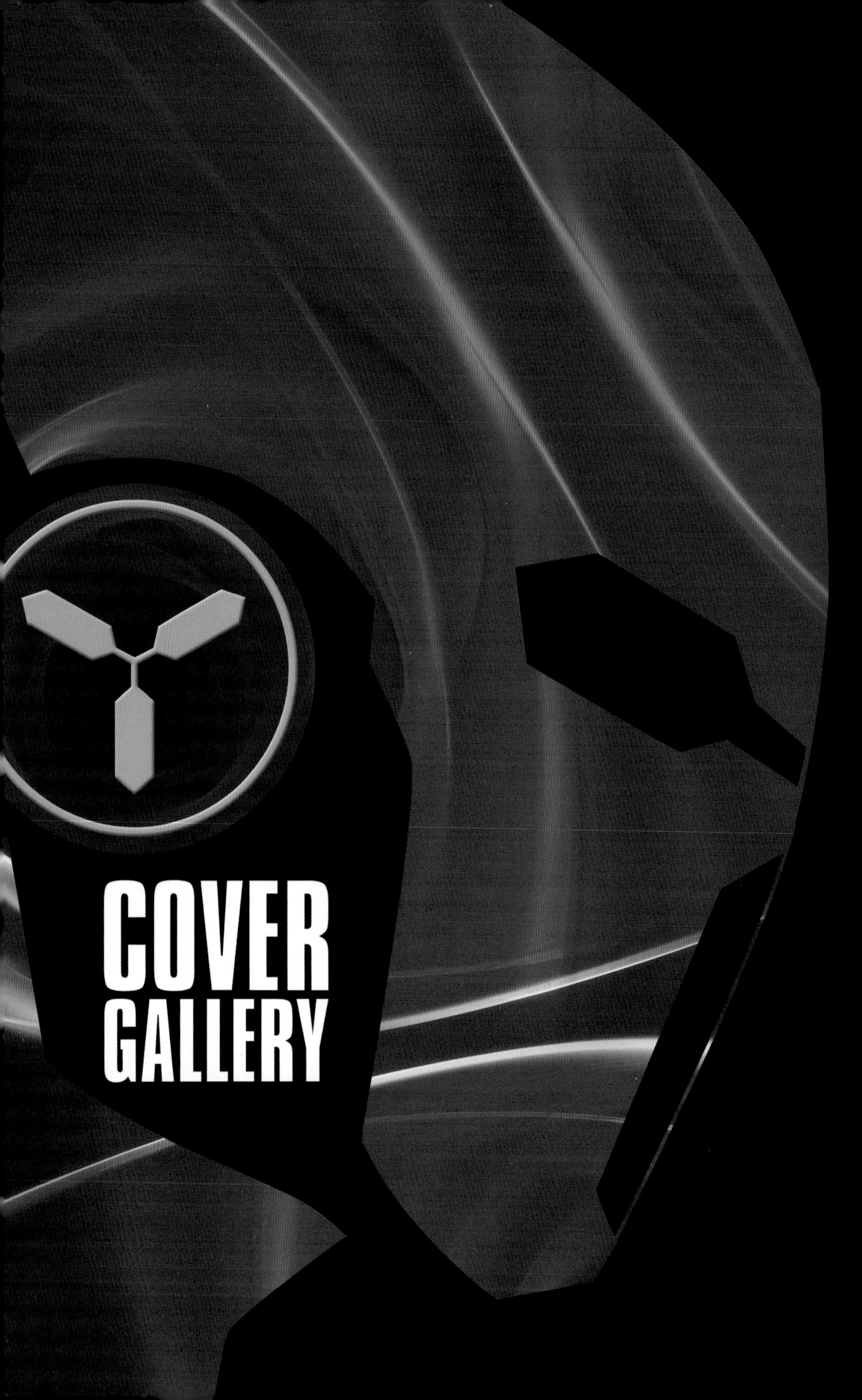
COVER
GALLERY

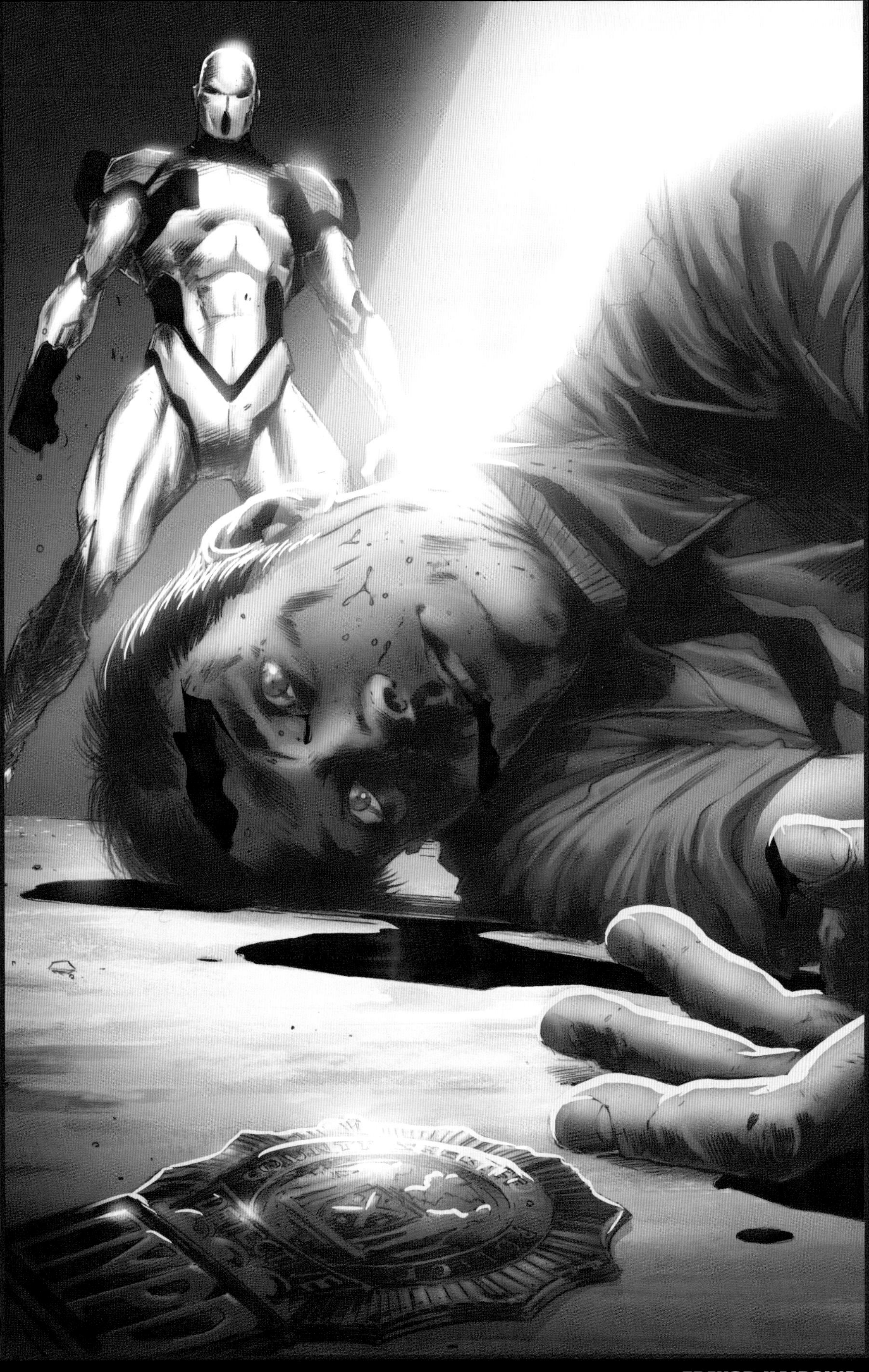

ISSUE FIVE: **TREVOR HAIRSINE**

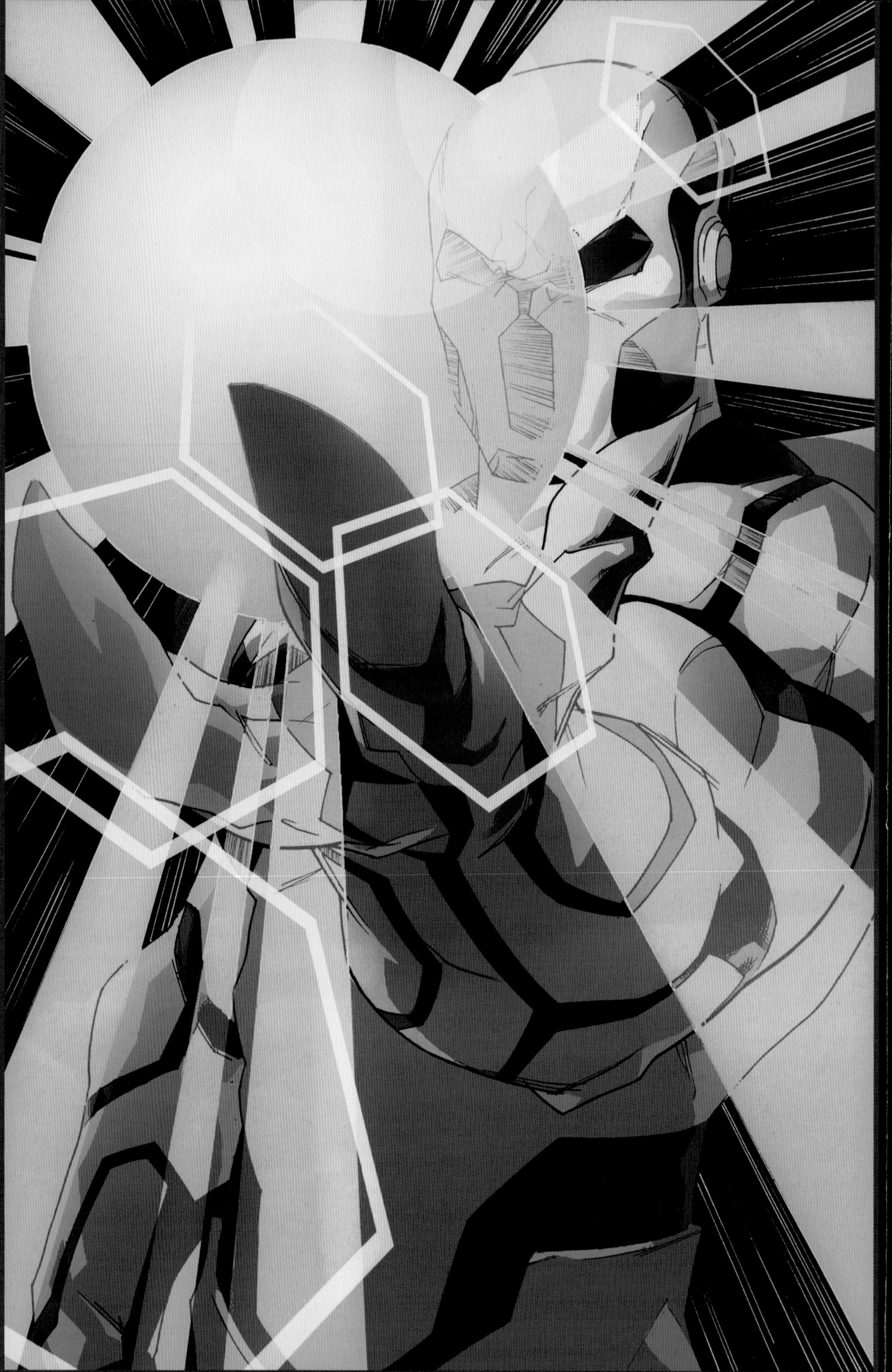

ISSUE FIVE: KALMAN ANDRASOFSZKY

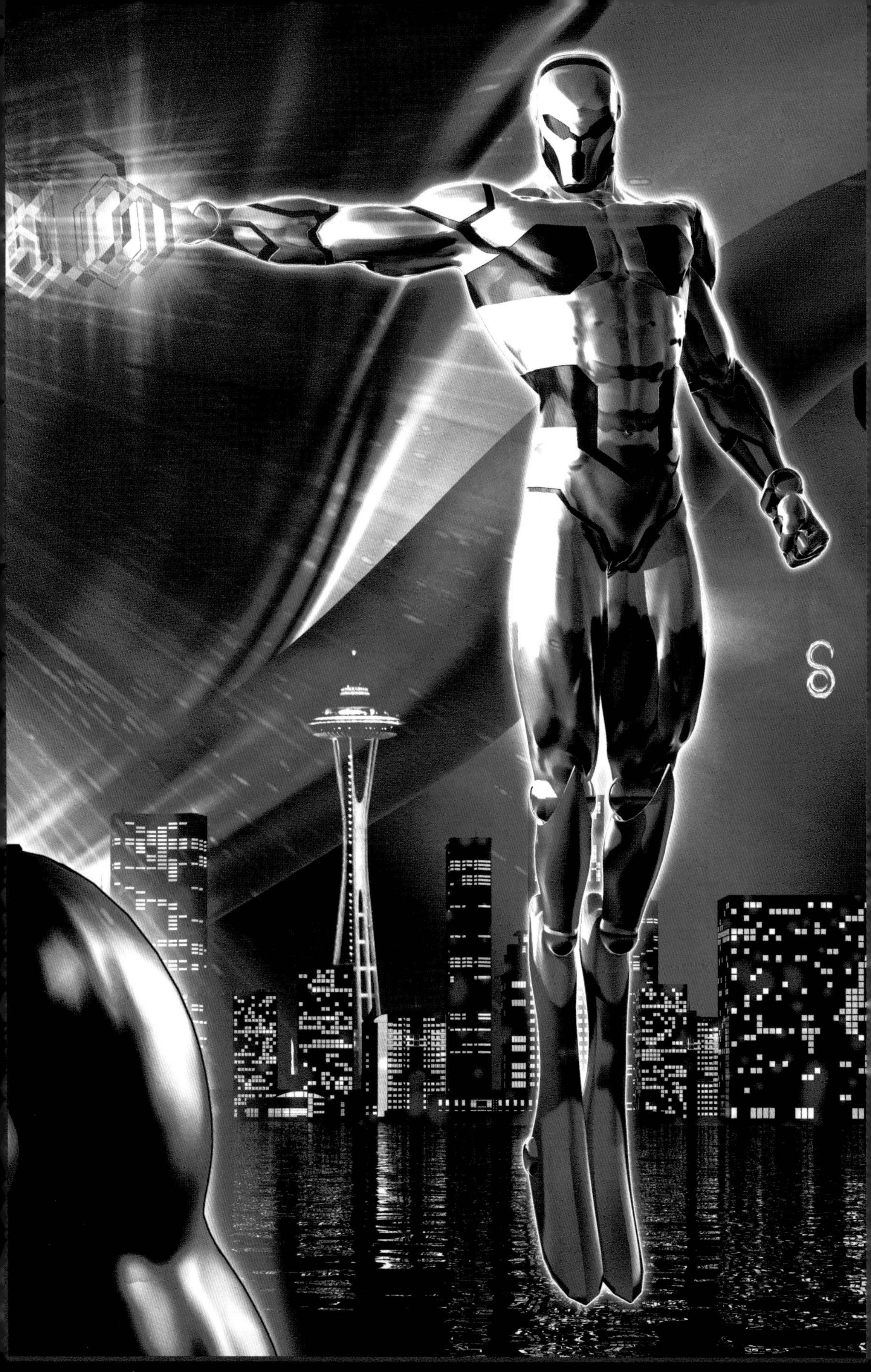

ISSUE FIVE ECCC EXCLUSIVE COVER: SCOTT CLARK

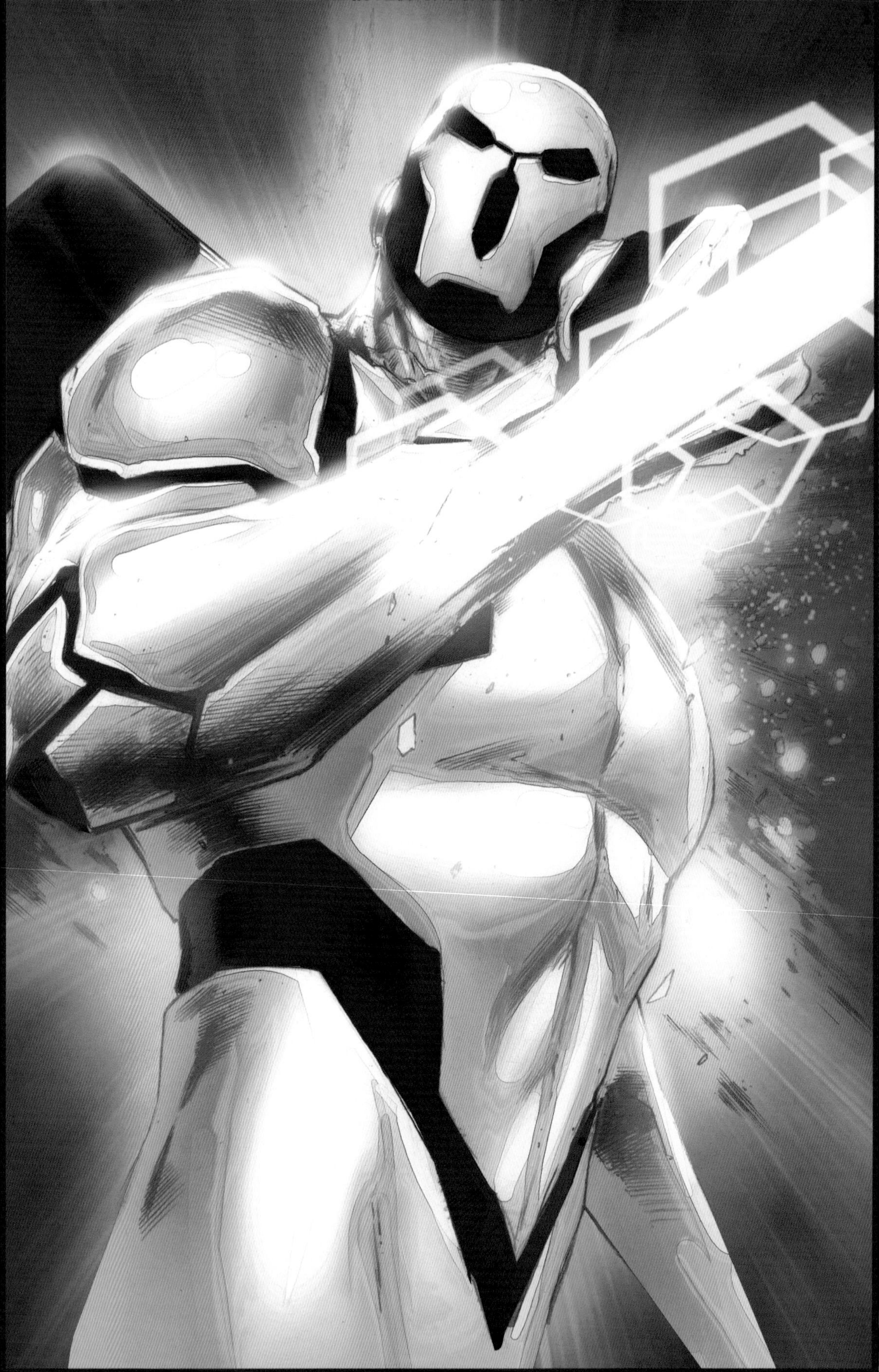

ISSUE SIX: TREVOR HAIRSINE
WITH ARCHIE VAN BUREN

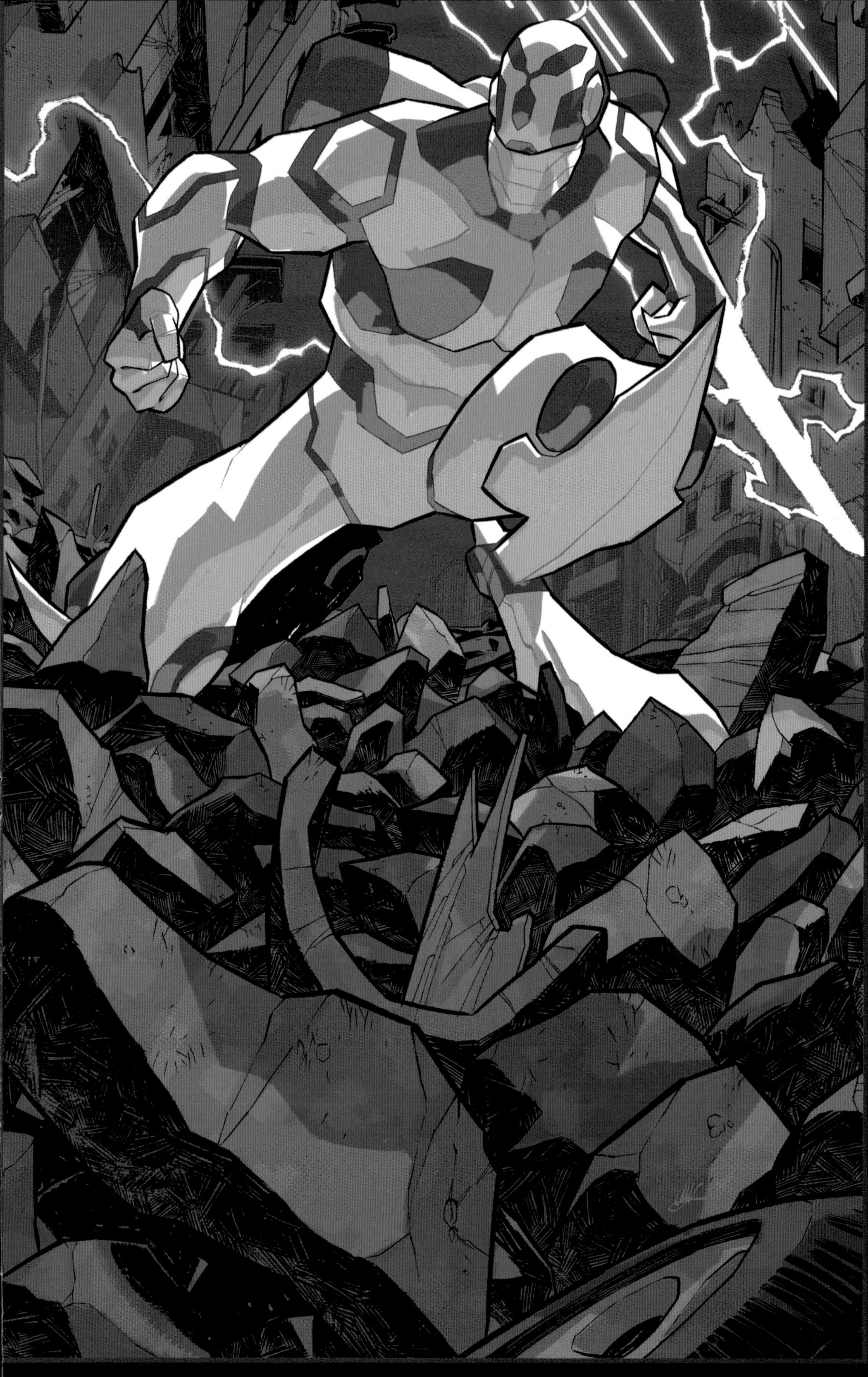

ISSUE SIX: MATTEO SCALERA

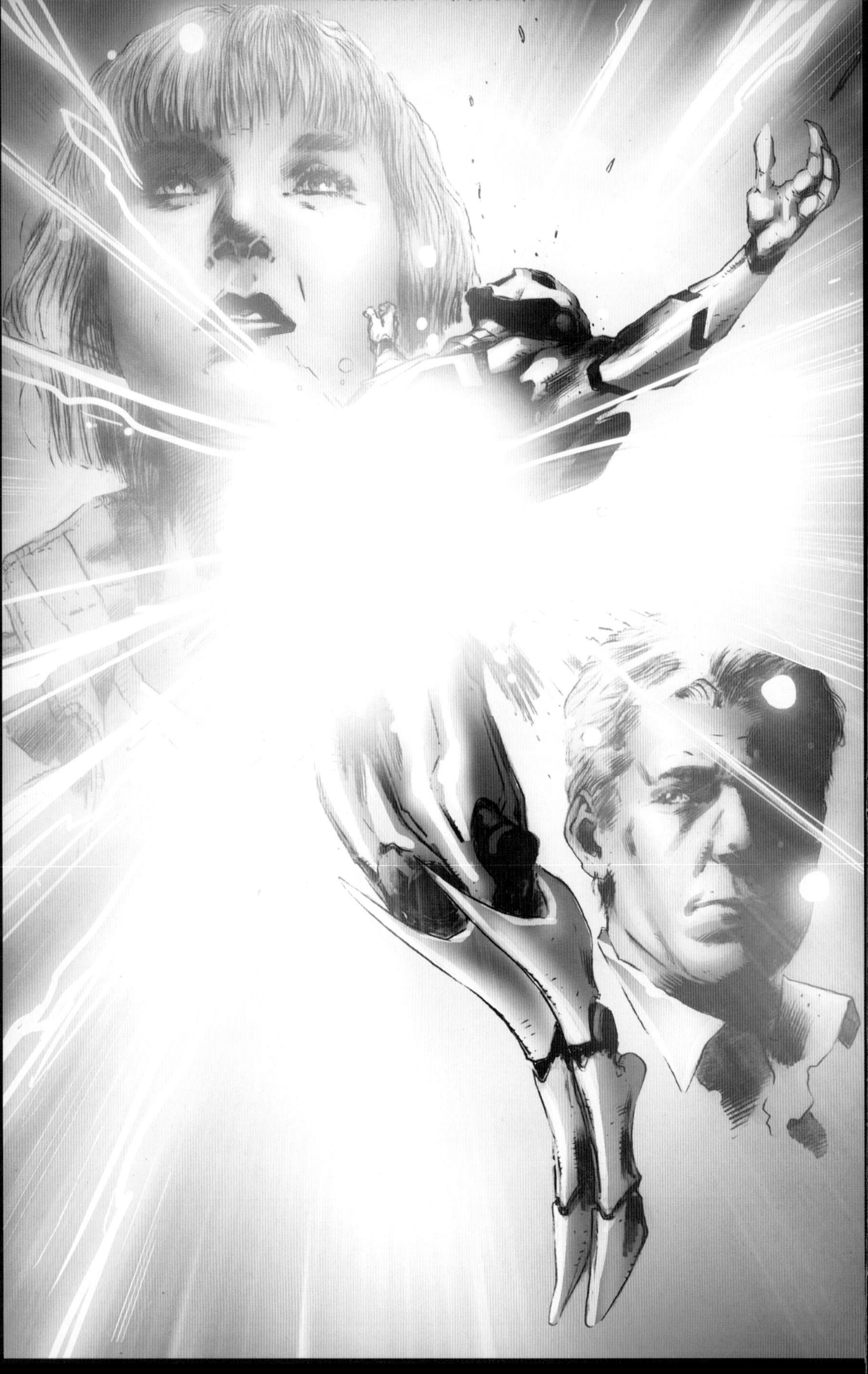

ISSUE SEVEN: TREVOR HAIRSINE

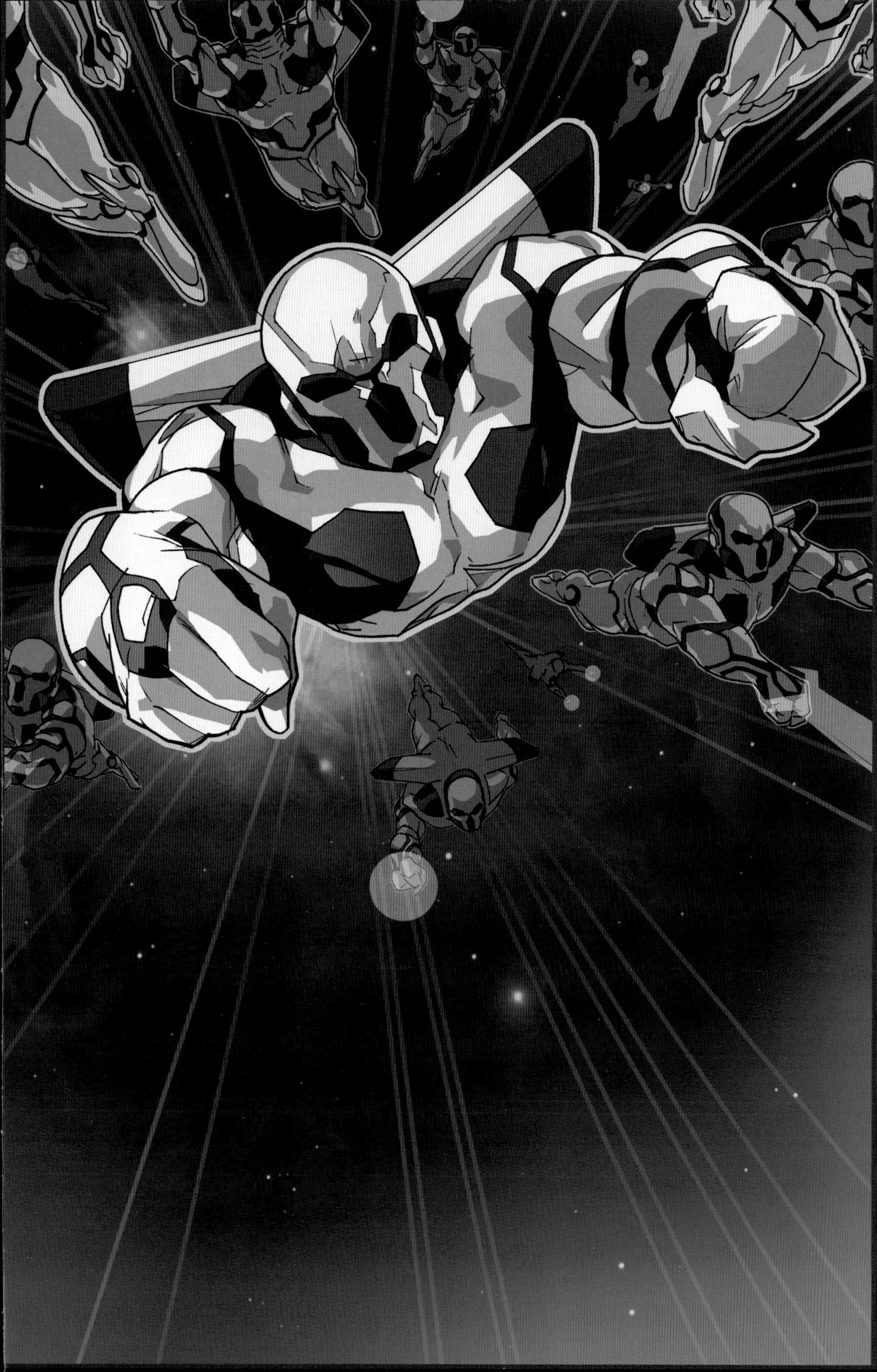

ISSUE SEVEN: KALMAN ANDRASOFSZKY

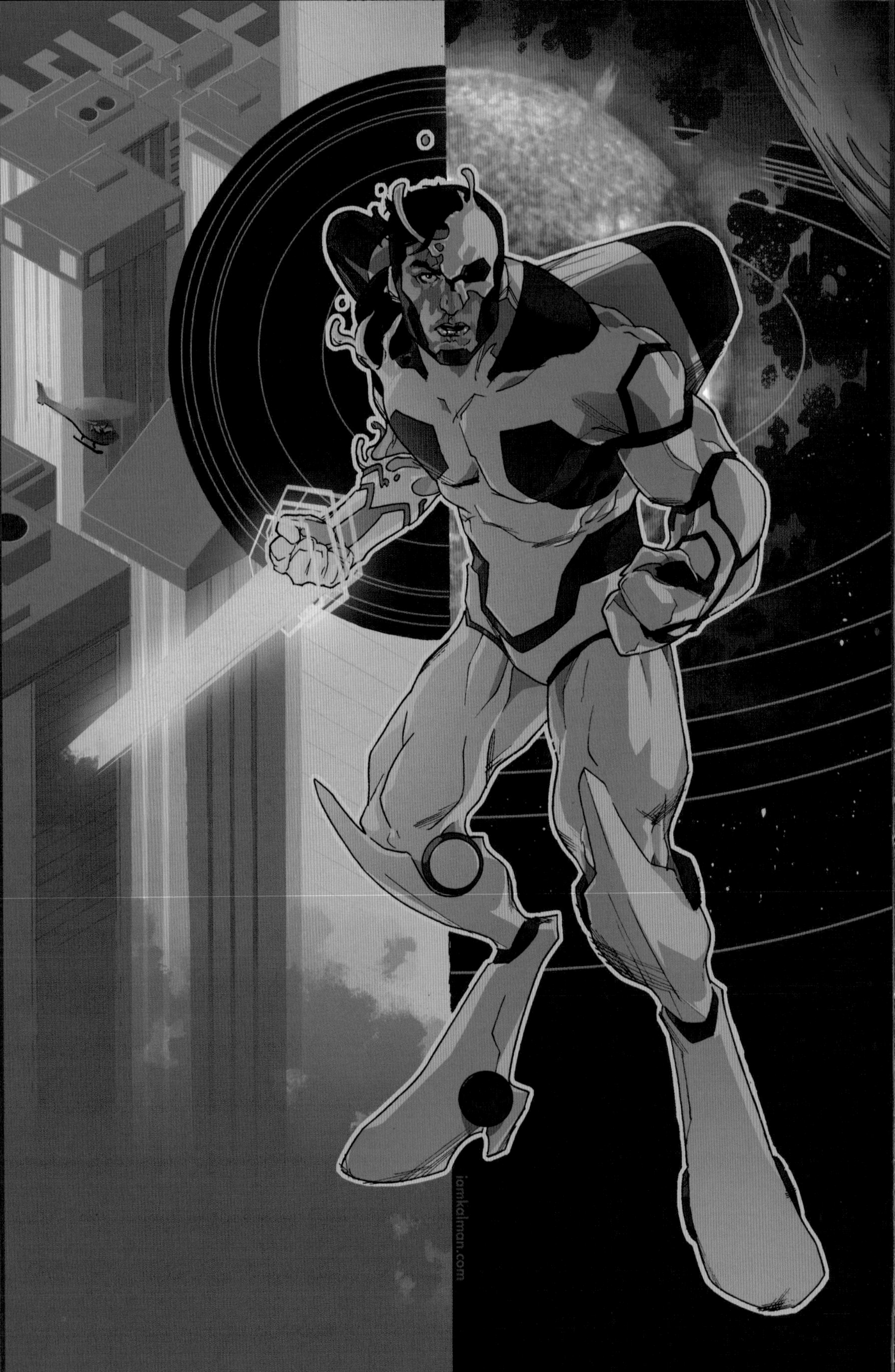
iamkalman.com

ISSUE EIGHT: KALMAN ANDRASOFSZKY

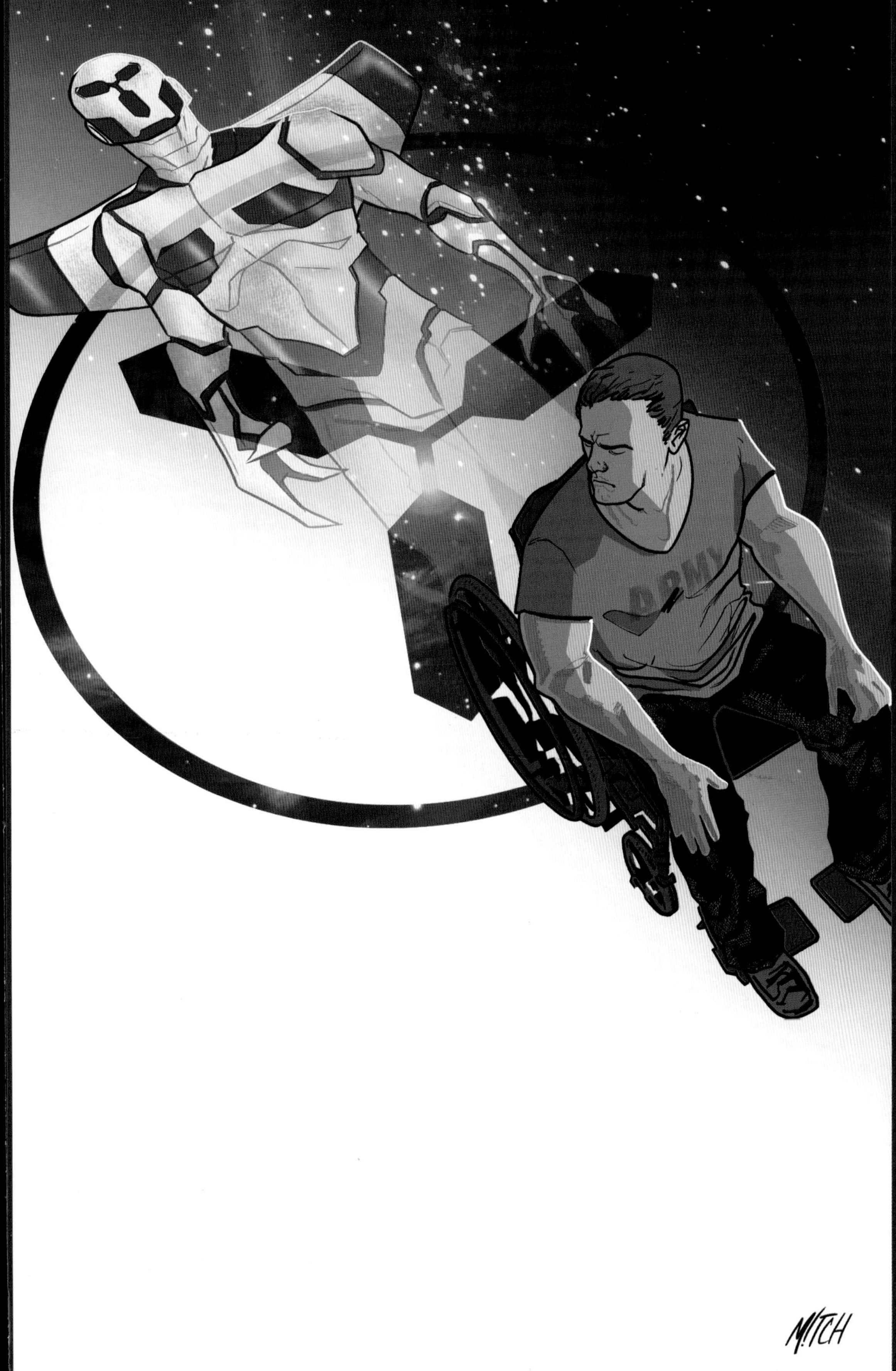
ARMY
MITCH

ISSUE EIGHT: MITCH GERADS

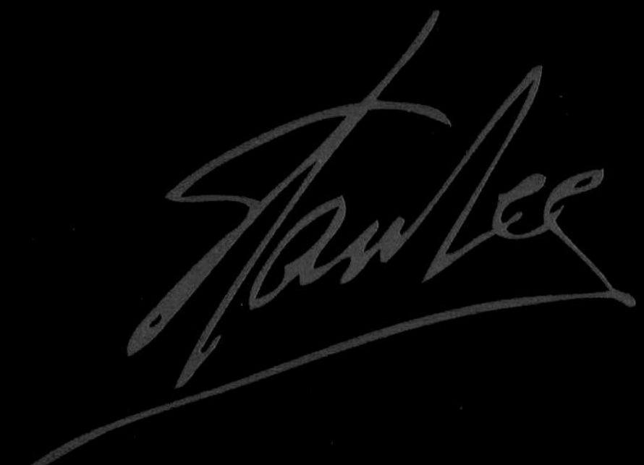